LANGUAGE, SOCIETY, AND
BIBLE TRANSLATION

*With special reference to the style and
structure of segments of direct speech
in the Scriptures*

Ernst R. Wendland

Bible Society of South Africa

LANGUAGE, SOCIETY, AND
BIBLE TRANSLATION

Ernst R. Wendland

First edition 1985

© BIBLE SOCIETY OF SOUTH AFRICA 1985

Published by the Bible Society of South Africa,
P.O. Box 6215, Roggebaai, Cape Town 8012

*The Scripture quotations in this publication are from
the Revised Standard Version of the Bible copyrighted
1946, 1952 © 1971, 1973 by the Division of Christian
Education of the National Council of the Churches of
Christ in the U.S.A. and are used by permission.*

Printed by National Book Printers,
Goodwood, Cape
BSSA–1½M–1985

ISBN 0 7982 0659 4

ACKNOWLEDGEMENTS

I would like to express my deep appreciation to Prof. J. P. Louw for inviting me to participate in the seminar series of the Insti= tute for Interlingual Communication and for his hearty encourage= ment of my efforts. A debt of gratitude is due Dr. Eugene A. Nida for stimulating this study in the first place and for his many helpful comments on the original manuscript which greatly improved the final result. He is not responsible, of course, for any errors or awkwardness that may still remain in the text. I also wish to thank my colleague, Rev. Salimo Hachibamba, for giving me a valuable insight into the Tonga world view and system of beliefs, and Rev. Gerrit van der Merwe and the Bible Society of South Africa for sponsoring my participation in these annual seminars and, indeed, for supporting the publication of this monograph.

Ernst R. Wendland
Lusaka, Zambia
January, 1985

CONTENTS

CHAPTER 1

Direct Speech in the Bible

In all forms of verbal communication, language and society are very closely interrelated. Language influences society both semantically by making certain concepts, conceptual categories (e.g. similarities and contrasts), groupings, and arrangements more apparent and manipulatable than others and also formally by making certain ways of conveying meaning more accessible to its users than others. Society, in turn, influences language on all levels of linguistic structure and with respect to many different aspects of the meaning that is communicated. The purpose of this study is to examine some of the more important of these diverse interrelationships as they concern the transmission of God's word from one socio-cultural and linguistic environment to another. The focus of our attention will be upon the various contextual factors which need to be considered in order to ensure that the meaning of the original divine message is recreated with the same impact and with the least possible distortion in its new human setting.

Bible translation is a particular instance of language use in a given speech community. It therefore stands to profit from the insights to be derived from the field of sociolinguistics, a discipline that is devoted to the study of how language operates in society. In this book we will explore several aspects of sociolinguistic analysis which are of special relevance to the translation of Scripture, especially those portions that are realized as direct discourse. In this chapter we begin with a short introductory survey which outlines the relative significance of the primary focus of attention in our investigation, namely, direct speech as found in the Old and New Testaments.

This study of the relation between sociolinguistics and Bible translation focuses upon the dialogue portions of Scripture for several reasons. First of all, direct discourse is a primary, or complete, mode of communication (as opposed to a secondary, or derived, mode such as writing) in the sense that in oral, face-to-face verbal interaction one experiences the full range of feed=

back, noise as well as paralinguistic and extralinguistic messages
(Nida, 1981, pp. 39-40). This is due to the fact that all of the
major components of communication events are explicitly manifested
within a specific sociocultural setting. Hence the application of
sociolinguistic principles in a formal analysis is easier to make,
and the insights to be derived are more readily apparent. To be
sure, in the study of Scripture we are dealing with literature,
and therefore the conversations recorded there are also incom=
plete, or representative, in different ways and to varying
degrees. But it is this very characteristic of selectivity which
gives rise to some interesting problems for translators -- pro=
blems which sociolinguistic theory can help to clarify and indeed
to resolve through a systematic exposition of the operation of
verbal texts in actual contexts of communication.

A second and more important reason for basing this investigation
upon direct speech is its importance in the Bible, both in terms
of quantity and quality. The Scriptures abound in dialogue, in
the narrative portions as one would expect, and also in the non-
narrative sections, whether poetic, prophetic, or epistolary in
nature. One continually senses in the text, the Hebrew Testament
in particular, a constant pressure to break into direct discourse,
and this tension is quite regularly satisfied, even in the most
unexpected places. Furthermore, the occurrence of dialogue is not
a haphazard affair, the result of mere stylistic caprice. Rather,
its appearance always coincides with some type of emphasis: direct
discourse either highlights the interpersonal relationships
between participants and the dramatic situation they are in, or
its stresses some aspect of the topic at hand. The latter would
apply then to non-narrative as well as to narrative discourse.

Hebrew narrative shows a definite preference for dialogue. Many
stories are composed almost entirely of direct speech, with narra=
tive appearing only to effect transitions (e.g. beginning, ending,
motion to and from), as a summarizing or explanatory device (often
a reiteration of what was already said in direct speech), or to
render information of secondary importance to the story line (e.g.
expository and descriptive material) or actions which could not be

adequately represented in dialogue. Notice, for example, the use
of direct discourse in the following passage:

(a) All his sons and all his daughters rose up to <u>comfort</u>
him;

(b) but he <u>refused to be comforted</u>, and said,

(c) "<u>No</u>, I shall go down to Sheol to my son, <u>mourning</u>."

(d) Thus his father <u>wept</u> for him.

(Gn 37:35 -- All quotations are from the RSV, except where
indicated otherwise. Underlining indicates points of special
emphasis, importance or relevance in the discussion at hand.)

Everything in this passage points the reader either foreward
(cataphorically -- b) or backward (anaphorically -- d) to Jacob's
expression of sorrow (c), which vividly reveals the intensity of
his despair over the loss of his beloved son Joseph. The hypocri=
tical attempts of his sons to console him (a) are not worthy to be
dignified by means of direct speech.

Another significant feature of biblical quotation is evident here,
and that is its capacity to reveal character. This passage (i.e.
(c)) gives us a glimpse of the stubbornness, or better, single-
mindedness, coupled with a singular depth of feeling which
typified the personality of Jacob in his mature years. In effect,
the participants of narrative are personalized and developed more
by what they say (and do) than by author description or commen=
tary. Interpreting the full significance of such character inter=
action thus requires a sociolinguistic perspective, for instance,
to grasp the import of the word "Sheol" in this situation, i.e.
not simply the grave, but in Hebrew thought a remote joyless
region "down" beneath the ground where the departed spirits dwell.

The Old Testament narrators generally avoid indirect speech,
except for the reasons mentioned above, and this often results in
the use of direct speech in contexts where we would not normally
employ it (or even expect it -- hence the relevance for transla=
tion). This can result in embeddings which sound rather awkward
in other languages, e.g.

"...And God caused me to wander from my father's house,
and I said to her, 'This is the kindness you must do to
me, at every place to which we come, say to me, "He is
<u>my brother</u>."'" (Gn 20:13)

This preference for the direct mode pertains not only to speech, but also to the thoughts of an individual. Character cognition, then, is usually presented in the form of direct speech, e.g.

> So Sarah <u>laughed to herself, saying</u>, "After I have grown old, and <u>my husband is old</u>, shall I have pleasure?" (Gn 18:12)

This naturally invites an immediate response on the part of Yahweh (Gn 18:13-14). Thus, the crucial social and spiritual relation= ships between man and his fellowman or between God and man are always foregrounded in Hebrew narrative by means of direct speech.

This affinity for direct discourse in narrative carries over into the non-narrative sections of the Old Testament. The Psalms, for example, are normally represented as speech addressed either directly to God or to someone (thing) else about God -- his ac= tions and attributes. At times this is even heightened by the quotation formula, which is a reliable marker of the onset of direct speech in the Bible, e.g.

> "O my God," <u>I say</u>, "take me not hence in the midst of my days..." (Ps 102:24)

These songs are not composed as pure monologue either, for it is not unusual to find one which features the words of God rather than, or in addition to, those of the Psalmist, e.g.

> (God) calls to the heavens above..."Gather to me my fruitful ones..." (Ps 50:5)

Quotations are also utilized, especially to epitomize the evil intentions of the wicked, e.g.

> The kings of the earth set themselves...saying, "Let us burst their bonds asunder..." (Ps 2:2-3)

Psalms 2 is unique in that it manifests at least five distinct speech pairs, all within the space of eleven verses.

Dialogue acts as a structuring principle as well as a vehicle for presenting the argument of Job and the Song of Songs. It also plays a significant role in the Proverbs both on a macrolevel (i.e. where the words of wisdom of a given section are introduced through an address to a specific individual, e.g. "My son" (2:1) or "O sons" (4:1)) and as a means of highlighting antithetic atti= tudes and activities, e.g.

> Do not say, "I will repay evil." (Pr 20:22)

Similarly, Ecclesiastes may be viewed as an extended set of in= structions and advice addressed to a youth (Ec 11:9, 12:12), with the Preacher at times quoting himself, e.g.

> "I said to myself, 'Come now, I will make a test of pleasure...'" (Ec 2:1)

Prophetic literature, of course, derives its authority and impact from the fact that it is composed primarily of the direct dis= course of Yahweh, speaking either in person or through the mouth of his chosen prophet. This fact is stressed repeatedly by means of the recurrent phrase, "Thus says the LORD..." and its variants. The two "sources" are not always clearly distinguished since the prophet at least, if not his people, regarded himself as being the spokesman of God. But this lack of demarcation can cause some difficulty for translators who may be forced to specify and clarify (through the use of quote introducers, vocatives, pronomi= nal shifts, etc.) what the original left implicit or ambiguous, e.g.

> They shall go after the LORD,
> he will roar like a lion;
> ...and I will return them to their houses,
> says the LORD. (Ho 11.10-11)

Most modern versions shift all references in the above passage to the first person (e.g. GNB: "My people will follow me...") because that interpretation is favored by the larger discourse context, i.e. the oracle spanning chapter 11 records the speech of Yahweh everywhere else.

As in narration, so also the prophets like to dramatize a contrast in attitude or to spotlight a particular opinion (whether good or bad) by means of direct speech, e.g.

> For now they will say: "We have no king, for we fear not
> the LORD..." (Ho 10:3)

Conversational interaction increases in incidence when prophetic poetry merges into prose, whether for narrative purposes (e.g. Jeremiah 36) or as a pedagogical device, e.g.

> And the LORD said to me, "Amos, what do you see?"
> And I said, "A plumb line."
> Then the LORD said, "Behold, I am setting a plumb line..." (Am 7:7)

This raises the issue of the formal difference between prose and poetry in the Old Testament. Such a distinction, while useful perhaps in generalisations (e.g. Genesis is prose, Isaiah is poetry), is difficult to maintain on the microlevel of analysis. Instead of being viewed as opposite points on a scale, the reality of usage suggests a continuum of almost indistinguishable grada= tions based on the incidence of typically poetic versus prosaic linguistic features (cf. Kugel, 1981). For ease of classification then, one might posit four categories: pure (narrative) prose, poetic prose (oratory), prose-like poetry (e.g. didactic, admoni= tory), and pure (lyric, affective) poetry. It is interesting to note that in both of the medial types dialogue is prominent as a rhetorical feature. Prose-like poetry would occupy large sections of the so-called "prophetic" books, while poetic prose is featured in many of the conversations of narrative, Genesis in particular, especially the speech of Yahweh, e.g.

> And the LORD said to her,
>> "Two nations are in your womb,
>> And two peoples, born of you --
>>> shall be divided;
>> the one shall be stronger than the other,
>> the elder shall serve the younger." (Gn 25:23)

The poetic qualities of this prediction are obvious, i.e. semantic parallelism followed by a reversal, with the boundary or turning point marked by a thematic peak ("shall be divided"). Thus direct speech serves to bridge the gap between prose and poetry in the Old Testament.

The situation in the New Testament does not differ much from that outlined above, perhaps due to literary and linguistic influence from the Hebrew Scriptures and its translation into Greek (the Septuagint). Dialogue is a dominant characteristic of the Gospels and Acts, and it also appears prominently in the book of Revela=

tion where it acts as a structuring device and also to foreground
the major themes of the book. Its general function is nearly the
same, that is, to draw attention to those portions of the account
which need emphasizing, whether from a topical, didactic, exposi=
tory, hortatory or theological perspective. The Gospels naturally
focus upon the sayings of Christ, with entire chapters being
encoded as direct discourse (e.g. Matthew 5-7, John 14-16). The
preeminence of recorded as opposed to reported speech is manifest=
ed in passages such as these:

> Jesus said to them,
>
> "...Which is easier, to say to the paralytic,
>
> (A) 'Your sins are forgiven'
>
> or to say,
>
> (B) 'Rise, take up your pallet and walk'?
>
> But that you might know
>
> (A') that the Son of Man has authority on earth to forgive
> sins" -- he said to the paralytic --
>
> "I say to you,
>
> (B') rise, take up your pallet and go home." (Mk 2:8-11)

The rhetorical structuring of this passage, "poetic prose", which
is typical of the discourses of Christ, especially in John, adds
another dimension to the analysis of these words as speech acts in
their context of occurrence. Observe that the sudden shift in
addressee at the end is not unmotivated. It rather completes the
declaration which Christ began at the close of verse five -- be=
fore he was "interrupted" by the thoughts (in direct discourse!)
of the scribes. He then proceeds to deal with their spiritual
problem first before returning to fulfil his ministry to the pa=
ralytic (this is a narrative ring construction, i.e. A - B - A').
The topic of the entire discourse, namely, the forgiveness of
sins, is introduced in that initial segment of direct speech in
verse five, a rhetorical device which is quite common also in
Hebrew narrative (cf. Alter, 1981, p. 74).

Each of the New Testament epistles is composed in the form of a
direct address, written from a pastor (apostle) to his congrega=
tion(s), members or co-workers. A great deal of exegetical energy
is expended in the attempt to specify the extralinguistic context

in which these letters were realized -- who, when, where, why,
how, etc. (in addition to the "what" of the text) -- for this has
an important bearing on the interpretation of the discourse itself
as a whole (e.g. Galatians) as well as individual portions of it
(e.g. 1 Corinthians chapter 7). This contextualization process
can benefit much from the insights to be gained from a sociolin=
guistic approach. This is true with respect to the form as well,
particularly in letters such as Galatians and James, which feature
a diatribe style of composition. Here the positions (whether real
or hypothetical) of detractors and opponents are woven into the
argument, often via direct speech, for the purpose of contrastive
emphasis and/or illustration, e.g.

> What does it profit, my brethren, if...one of you says
> to them, "Go in peace, be warmed and filled,"...
>
> But someone will say, "You have faith and I have works."
> Show me your faith apart from your works... (Js 2:16,
> 18)

In such instances it is important to clearly distinguish the words
of the writer from those whom he is reproving in his letter e.g.
"Someone will say...Someone else will say..." (1 Co 6:12-13, GNB).

Other examples of embedded direct discourse in the epistles per=
form the function of foregrounding, for reasons similar to those
mentioned above, e.g.

> ...scoffers will come...saying,
> "Where is the promise of his coming? For ever since the
> fathers fell asleep, all things have continued as they
> were from the beginning of creation." (2 Pt 3:3-4)

This quotation serves to highlight the two anti-Scriptural
teachings which Peter then proceeds to refute (in reverse order),
namely, that all things have continued unchanged since creation
(3:5-7) and that God does not keep his promises (3:8-10). This is
another example (i.e. topicalization) of the larger discourse
function of direct speech in the Bible.

A rather different purpose is carried out by the interjective
comments, or asides, which we find particularly in the epistles of

Paul. These digressions, which are quite varied in nature, func=
tion as segments of direct speech that are embedded into the
exposition, exhortation or admonition, both to personalize the
epistle (as if he were actually speaking directly to his audience)
and also to punctuate the discussion in various ways. These range:

from highly emotional exclamations, e.g.

But whatever anyone does to boast of -- I am speaking as
a fool -- I also dare to boast of that. (2 Co 11:21)

to a stinging rebuke, e.g.

O foolish Galatians! Who has bewitched you... (Ga 3:1)

from information-augmenting observations, e.g.

(God) made us alive together with Christ (by grace you
have been saved), and raised up with him... (Ep 2:5-6)

to vocatives of personal contact, e.g.

Therefore, my beloved brothers, be steadfast... (1 Co
15:58)

from explanatory definitions of the text, e.g.

...no fornicator...or one who is covetous (that is, an
idolater) has any inheritance in the kingdom of
Christ... (Ep 5:5)

to references to the situational setting, e.g.

See with what large letters I am writing to you with my
own hand. (Ga 6:11)

Such interactional supplements tend to draw the reader/hearer
closer personally to the author, and hence also his message.

The preceding survey is sufficient to suggest the extent to which
direct speech permeates the Scriptures. It is clear that an ana=
lytical model which isolates itself from the context of communi=
cation will be of absolutely no help to the Bible translator as he
seeks to discover both the intent as well as the content of
original linguistic forms. Only a sociolinguistic method will do,
and for some preliminary background on this we turn to an overview
of the theory of semiotics as it relates to the transmission of
verbal messages.

Chapter 2 then presents a more theoretical discussion which seeks to contextualize current sociolinguistic investigations within the broader discipline of semiotics, the science of signs and sig= nalling systems. This perspective is complemented by a simple model of communication, which provides a convenient means of explaining and illustrating some of the principal issues that arise during the production of a translation which is sensitive to the sociolinguistic differences that exist between the source-language (SL) and receptor-language (RL) cultures. Translation is viewed as a process of literary composition which has as its goal the "dynamic equivalent" transmission of a message from SL to RL with respect to both content and function. A consideration of the implications of this goal and the relevance of sociolinguistic insights for attaining it constitute one of the primary objectives of this study.

Chapter 3 takes up the subject of style, that is, the characteris= tic choice of language during verbal communication, and how this relates to the object of our investigation. This includes the delineation and exemplification of sociolinguistic influences, which interact with one another in actual speech situations to determine both the forms of speech that are produced and to some extent also the communicative effect that is obtained. This clas= sification is next applied in Chapter 4 to the extratextual setting of communication as this pertains in particular to the various circumstances which may surround the establishment and operation of a viable Bible translation programme in a given RL.

In Chapter 5 we move to a consideration of discourse structure and how this necessitates a sociolinguistic point of view via the con= cept of "speech events". A speech event is a discrete segment of communication involving two (or more) participants in sustained verbal (and non-verbal) interaction. Speech events are made up of "speech acts", each of which consists of a propositional as well as an interpersonal component. A sequence of meaningful speech acts always manifests the three principal characteristics of discourse organization: segmentation, connectivity, and promi= nence, which are effected for the most part by repetition (simi=

larity/contrast) and optionally heightened rhetorically through formal patterning in the text. This model along with the socio= linguistic variables described earlier is next applied to the internal (embedded) level of literary communication, specifically translation, by means of an examination of how character conver= sations are structured in an actual biblical text (John 4:7-26). Special attention is given in Chapter 6 to the various complica= tions which may develop in the realization of speech acts in dis= course due to the influence of beliefs, values, activities, and experiences of the RL culture. Emphasis will be upon the accurate and idiomatic representation of the direct speech of Scripture within a particular sociocultural context.

Chapter 7 deals with the "quality" factor in translation: How is one to determine "success" in this endeavor? What are the main criteria that apply in the process of evaluation? The discussion is organized around four proposed parameters of quality, namely, fidelity, intelligibility, closeness and naturalness. These di= mensions are shown to interact with seven sociolinguistic polari= ties which are particularly relevant to Bible translation. Chapter 8 concludes this book with a selection of quotations from Paul's letters to the Corinthians which reiterate and exemplify the chief sociolinguistic principles presented in the previous chapters. It is important to recognize the biblical basis of these principles as they were practiced by one of the greatest cross-cultural com= municators of all time.

CHAPTER 2

Sociolinguistics, Semiotics, and Communication

Sociolinguistics is the study of language in action. Its basic
premise, simply put, is that no genuine instance of "language" use
ever exists in a social vacuum. Rather, language is always a mat=
ter of usage within specific sociocultural contexts, and usage in
turn involves purpose. Thus sociolinguistics is strongly functio=
nal in its outlook and approach to language analysis. It seeks to
elucidate the multitude of ways in which the linguistic forms of a
language are manipulated in order to accomplish the communicative
objectives of its speakers. In the process, it attempts to forma=
lize the constituents, rules, patterns and interrelationships of
verbal behavior and to predict the consequences of given instances
of language use.

In contrast to the structuralist -- from the taxonomist to the
transformationalist -- who focuses his attention upon langue, i.e.
language as an abstract system of forms (code) divorced from set=
ting, the sociolinguist studies parole, i.e. language as it is
actually realized in concrete cases of human verbal interaction. A
primary goal of the sociolinguist, then, is to investigate how
language varies in form according to shifts in the extralinguistic
context of occurrence. He must necessarily pass beyond the struc=
turalist's preoccupation with the designative aspects of meaning
in order to determine why different ways of "saying the same
thing" are in fact quite context-specific. He does this by re=
vealing how the possible formal variants are frequently the result
of differences in the social function for which each one is em=
ployed in the process of communication. The concept of synonymy,
however useful to the theorist, is not always so helpful to the
language usage analyst, who realizes that seemingly alternative
linguistic forms are not really in free variation. On the con=
trary, their choice is regularly governed by subtle social and/or
situational constraints. The aim of this study is to demonstrate
the relevance of these basic sociolinguistic principles for Bible
translation.

Since sociolinguistics involves the study of language, it may be viewed as a branch of semiotics, the general science of signs and signification. Semiotics deals with the organizing principles which underlie the structure of all signs and how these function in the transmission of messages, be they animate (e.g. the "dancing" of honeybees) or inanimate (e.g. recurrent phenomena of nature such as the seasons), human (e.g. body "language" -- kine= sics and proxemics) or non-human (e.g. animal behavior -- zoo= semiotics), verbal (e.g. writing) or non-verbal (e.g. smoke sig= nals). Semiotic structure is generally presented as being com= prised of three basic constituents: (A) the <u>sign</u> -- a physical form perceptible to the senses; (B) the <u>referent</u> -- that to which the sign points or stands for; and (C) the <u>interpretant</u> -- the system which mediates the relation between a sign and its refe= rent, namely, the code or system of signs. The relationships among these three elements is often represented in the form of a triangle, the so-called "triangle of signification" (Lyons, 1977, p. 76):

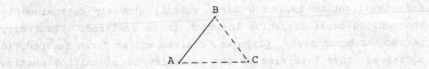

The semiotic process that relates A and B in the figure above may be termed "reference", while that linking B with C and C with A is called "interpretation". However, one cannot be too precise about this terminology since theorists vary in their explanation of the triangle depending on whether they are more "behaviorist" or "men= talist" in their orientation. I have presented the behaviorist position above. It posits a direct connection between a sign and the object, event, quality, process, etc. to which it refers in the real or experiential (conceptual) world. A mentalist approach (e.g. Lyons, 1977, p. 98) would interpose a "concept" (thought, idea, mental image, etc., i.e. point C in the figure) between the sign and its referent. In that case, the process of "refe=

rence" would follow the path of the broken line, i.e. A to C to B, while the process of "interpretation" is more or less done away with in the model.

This confusion in semiotic theory, both in terminology and in definition (which a glance at the literature will quickly sub= stantiate), is in part the consequence of attempting to represent a complex phenomenon, i.e. the way in which meaning is generated, with a model that is too simple for dealing systematically with all the factors involved. The framework below is proposed not so much as a theoretically-defensible solution to this problem, but rather to illustrate some of the additional factors that need to be considered when seeking to explain the process of "significa= tion" (in its widest sense). The relevance of this rather ab= stract discussion lies precisely in the fact that a great deal of the difficulty in semiotic theory arises due to a tacit (if not intentional) ignoring of the context within which signification takes place. And herein is found a fatal flaw in the approach, for signification is, to a large extent, strongly determined by the sociocultural situation in which it is realized. Obviously, particular human needs, purposes, desires and so forth in specific social settings give rise to the necessity of signalling meaning through the use of signs, whether verbal or non-verbal -- not the other way around.

The following diagram tries to take the factor of context into consideration in the semiotic process (see also Nida et. al., 1983, ch.1):

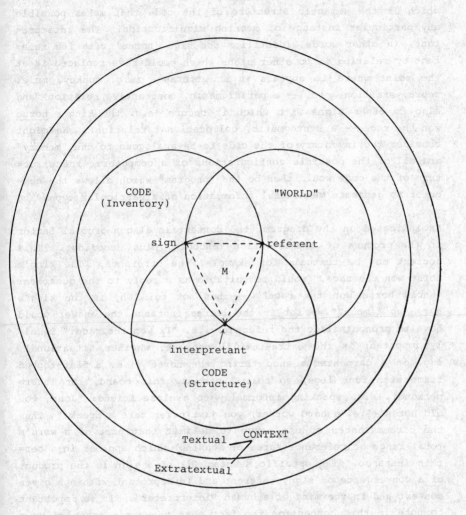

A given sign occurs only as part of a formal inventory of signs, a
code, which consists of the sum total of signs in the system along
with all of the possible rules for their combination in messages.
A verbal sign, to be specific (word, phrase), is linked to its re=
ferent, that which it designates in the "world" of reality (e.g. a

horse) or one's imagination (e.g. a unicorn), by the interpretant, which is the semantic structure of the code that makes possible any particular instance of meaning signification. The interpre= tant, in other words, identifies the sign 'horse' with its refe= rent by relating it to other signs which could have replaced it at the point where it appears in an utterance (e.g. donkey, mule, zebra, stallion, etc. -- a paradigmatic, contrastive relation) and also to other signs with which it occurs (e.g. the king's <u>horse</u> won the race -- a syntagmatic, collocational relation). We might consider the inventory of the code to be analogous to the "memory" and all of the possible configurations of a computer: the struc= ture of the code would then be the "program" which allows the com= puter to generate meaningful information of a particular type.

As indicated on the diagram, the context is also a crucial factor in the process of communication (encoding plus decoding). This context may be textual; for example, the utterance, "The king's horse won the race," would be suitable as a reply to the question: "Whose horse won the race?" -- but not to: "Why is the king's horse so famous?" -- for in the latter instance the answer would have to pronominalize the referent, i.e. "<u>It</u> won the race." Equal= ly important is the extra-textual context, whether situational, e.g. in a carpenter's shop "Bring the horse (i.e. a flat-topped frame with four legs) so that I can saw this board," or inter= personal, e.g. speaking informally to a close friend: "John, you old horse (i.e. a hard worker) you just never take a break!" Thus the circumstances of use serve to delimit that part of a word's total range of reference (area of meaning) which applies in a cer= tain instance. The specific meaning (M) of a sign is the product of a convergence of sign, referent and interpretant within a given context and in the mind of a human "interpreter". It is important to note in this connection the fact that the sense intended by a speaker (writer) when he employs a particular sign in his message does not necessarily coincide with what is actually understood by a hearer (reader). This point will be illustrated by many of the examples to follow.

Charles Morris has proposed a threefold division of the field of

semiotics into semantics, syntactics and pragmatics (1946, p. 217).
Semantics focuses upon the relations of signs to their referents,
i.e. referential (designative) and associative (including connota=
tive) meaning; syntactics studies the formal relations of signs to
one another, both on the basis of some similarity or difference
between them and as a result of their combination into utterances
(paradigmatic and syntagmatic meaning); and pragmatics is con=
cerned with the relations of signs to the non-verbal setting in
which they occur, whether personal (source/receptor) or impersonal
(i.e. social and situational meaning). This scheme is not com=
pletely adequate since the three disciplines are not entirely
autonomous, but at least it does suggest the three principal foci
of semiotic concern in relation to language analysis.

Up until the last twenty years or so, the pragmatic branch of
semiotics had generally been ignored by theorists in this field.
In recent years, however, analysts have been heeding the call of
linguists such as Hymes, Halliday, Labov, Austin, Searle, Grice,
Widdowson and Nida and are paying increasingly greater attention
to what is going on during the process of communication in addi=
tion to the transmission of text, namely, the interaction of
significant factors in the extralinguistic context. And as
studies continue, the importance of linguistic pragmatics (or
sociolinguistics) is becoming ever more apparent. Any valid syn=
tactic or semantic study presupposes a thorough investigation of
the sociocultural frame of reference. Just as purpose logically
precedes result, so also a careful examination of the total con=
text of communication, one which features a solid functional
orientation, prepares the way for an accurate description of the
way in which linguistic forms convey their intended meanings. Any
consideration of what is said (content) and how (form) can be
satisfactorily carried out only after a specification of the why
(function).

Since a semiotic approach is weakest in this critical area of in=
vestigation in that situational factors are not an integral part
of the model itself, sociolinguists have frequently turned to
another construct to help them account for the complexities of

speech in situ, and that is one derived from communications theory. In its earliest formulations as part of the new science of cybernetics (the study of automatic information transmission and processing mechanisms, see Smith, 1967), this framework, too, was limited to "meaning " in largely a referential, designative sense. But over the years it has assumed an increasingly promi= nent place in sociolinguistic theory since, with its emphasis on the process of message transmission, it explicitly takes cogni= zance of the influence of non-linguistic factors in the communica= tion event. The chief of these factors are illustrated in the diagram below (for different formulations of this approach, see Nida, Hymes, Jakobsen, Criper and Widdowson):

CONTEXT

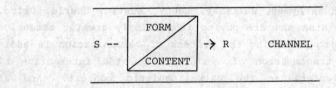

CONTEXT

In this schematization of a speech event (a unified segment of verbal interaction), the various components may be briefly defined as follows (for more detail, see Wendland, 1979, ch. 2):

Source (S): the producer of a message; he encodes it in the form of verbal signs according to the particular function (or complex of functions)that he wishes to carry out in the process of communication.

Receptor (R): the intended goal/recipient of the message; he decodes it and responds according to his interpretation of and reaction to its meaning/function.

Context: the total environmental setting: natural (climatic, to=
pographical, physical, animate), sociological (inter=
personal), technological (scientific, agricultural,
industrial), and conceptual (human values and system of
traditional/acquired beliefs), in which the message is
realized; it includes "noise", which is anything that
counteracts message transmission.

Channel: the means whereby the signs comprising the message are
apprehended by the senses; this includes the specific
mode of use (medium) that transmits the message (e.g.
writing is a medium based upon the visual channel of
communication).

These four elements are extrinsic to the text. They are not inte=
gral constituents, but do provide the occasion for producing the
message (its form and content) as well as the key for interpreting
its meaning and significance.

One may also posit four intrinsic components of communication,
i.e. those constituting the message per se. One pertains to the
content, the other three relate to form. The diagram below is an
attempt to indicate the broad relationships among these four major
message constituents:

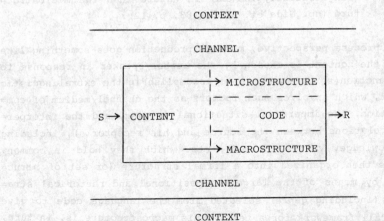

Content: the subject matter of the message; it is selected from
          the set of cultural codes which comprise the source
          group's universe of knowledge and experience, including
          their corpus of beliefs, value-system, world view, and
          so on.

Code: the total inventory of linguistic and rhetorical signs,
          together with their various possible rules and patterns
          of combination, from which the "form" of a particular
          message is constructed.

Macrostructure: the formal arrangement of content in a verbal
          discourse, constructed according to various types,
          levels, and patterns of organization (e.g. events, par=
          ticipant roles, themes & motifs, speech acts, emotive
          threads, etc.) and manifesting the three structural
          properties of segmentation, connectivity, and promi=
          nence.

Microstructure: the overt linguistic forms of language -- lexical,
          grammatical, and phonological -- which realize the com=
          plex of semantic and interpersonal (pragmatic) macro=
          structures to constitute a specific text; the macro=
          structure is broader in scope and generally less formal
          (linguistically marked) in nature than the microstruc=
          ture (cp. Nida et. al., 1983, p. 12).

From a process perspective, message production goes something like
this: the content is chosen by the author/speaker in response to
what function(s) he wants it to accomplish in the extralinguistic
context, which involves such factors as the channel/medium of com=
munication, the impersonal situational setting, and the interper=
sonal relations between the source and his receptor(s), including
the knowledge, values, beliefs, etc. which they hold in common.
This is then organized into a formal structure (or set of struc=
tures) by means of the larger compositional and rhetorical stra=
tegies (including genre) selected from the language code to give
an overall framework for a text. This macrostructure is, in turn,

manifested by a particular linguistic form, i.e. the microstruc=
ture, which is drawn from the language code in accordance with the
goals of the communication event as intended by the source and
accommodated to the medium of message transmission. The "meaning"
of a given message is in effect the product of influence from all
eight communication factors as perceived, understood, and acted
upon by the receptor. The traditional theory of semiotics has
tended to concentrate upon the four intrinsic elements of communi=
cation, i.e. content, code, macrostructure, and microstructure,
and correspondingly to overlook the four extrinsic constituents,
i.e. source, receptor, context and channel. It is this imbalance
which a sociolinguistic perspective seeks to correct, and it finds
in the communications model a useful framework within which its
analyses, descriptions, and conclusions may be cast.

As was suggested in the preceding discussion, a model based on the
communication process is decidedly functional in its orientation.
In an admittedly simplified, albeit serviceable, view of communi=
cation, it is possible to associate a primary function with each
of the eight mentioned components of speech events, as diagrammed
below:

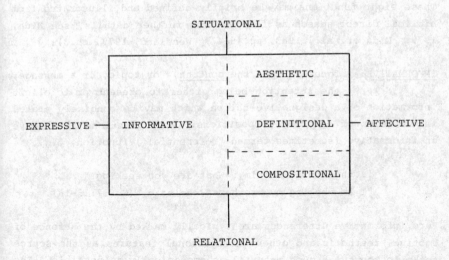

A particular function designates the effect either intended or produced when in the formulation of a meaningful utterance the speaker (writer) emphasizes one component of the system over and above the rest. In reality, of course, a function never occurs in isolation. Some situational factors, at least, will always be associated with any of the others. Certain of the functions tend to occur together, for example, the expressive and the affective, the aesthetic and the compositional, or the situational and the relational. In functional analysis, then there is bound to be some overlapping and ambiguity. Nevertheless, it is possible in many cases to determine a certain area of focus and emphasis which would support the analytical procedure of assigning a "priority" rating to the functional inventory of a particular utterance. The function (or functions) highlighted will, in turn, influence the grammatical structure, the lexical choice and the intonational features selected to convey it verbally. If, therefore, a func= tional analysis can help us to better understand the dynamics of communication within one speech setting, it can also help us to transmit messages more accurately and acceptably from one socio= cultural situation to another that is quite different. Hence its relevance for translation.

These eight functions may be briefly defined and illustrated from biblical direct speech as follows (for further details, see Nida, 1979; Nida et. al., 1983, pp.46-47; Wendland, 1979, ch.3):

INFORMATIVE: focuses upon the content, or topic, of a message, the intention being either to present or to elicit information of a designative nature which may be concisely stated in the form of semantic propositions. Real questions thus serve an informative (sometimes termed "referential") function, e.g.

> ...the man asked him, "What are you seeking?"
> "I am seeking my brothers", he said. (Gn 37:15-16)

Pure informative utterances are typically marked by the absence of emotive, aesthetic and other interpersonal features as the source seeks to convey as much material as economically as possible. The ratio of new to old information therefore tends to be rather high. The informative function is prominent particularly in directions and didactic passages, e.g.

> And God said to Noah, "...This is how you are to make it: the length of the ark three hundred cubits, its breadth fifty cubits, and its height thirty cubits." (Gn 6:14)

A distinct variety of the informative function is <u>cognitive</u> commu= nication (or "inner speech") whereby the source converses with himself, so to speak, as part of the reasoning process in order to help him formalize, clarify and direct his thinking on a particu= lar issue. This internal, mental activity (which may on occasion be spoken aloud to oneself) is often expressed as direct discourse in the Scriptures, e.g.

> "...and he thought to himself, 'What shall I do, for I have nowhere to store my crops?' And he said, 'I will do this: I will pull down my barns...'" (Lk 12:17-18)

<u>COMPOSITIONAL</u>: focuses upon the <u>macrostructure</u> of the message, i.e. the shape of its content and how this material is organized through various rhetorical techniques, repetition in particular, to serve these ends: to segment the text into units of different size and scope; to give these discrete segments internal unity and coherence; to distinguish points of special emphasis and emotive force; to create within the entire discourse a thematic progression or flow of ideas whereby the whole becomes greater than the sum of its parts. The compositional (sometimes termed "textual") function is rather difficult to illustrate concisely since it is actualized over a larger portion of text, and then primarily at the level of abstract content, though these underlying structures will always have formal/linguistic corre= lates in the surface structure of a text. However, by way of summary, it is possible to make the point with an example from chapter 3 of Genesis (a much longer text will be considered in ch. 5). The LORD God's confrontation of Adam in the Garden of Eden after the first offense assumes the following symmetrical pattern in the dialogue (sequence of speech acts):

```
    God (9) -- Accusation: why are you hiding?
        Man (10) -- Excuse: nakedness
            God (11a) -- Rejection: who told you...?
    God (11b) --Accusation: why did you eat the fruit?
        Man (12a) -- Excuse: the woman you gave me
            Man (12b) -- Confession: I ate
```

The climax of this exchange occurs right at the end where there is a shift in the alternating sequence of speakers as well as in the man's acknowledged condition, i.e. he admits, though grudgingly, his guilt.

For a larger and at the same time more intricately constructed example, consider the account of the confusion of tongues at Babel (Gn 11:1-9). This narrative is schematized below only according to its broad pattern of organization:

```
    A (v.1) setting: "the whole earth", "one language"
        B (v.2) the people are in one place -- "there"
            C (v.3-4) the people's plans (direct speech):
                        building a tower (up)
                D (v.5) Yahweh's reaction (narrative pivot/
                                            turning point)
            C' (v.6-7) Yahweh's plans (direct speech):
                        confuse human language (down)
        B' (v.8) the people are scattered -- "from there"
    A' (v.9) conclusion: "the whole earth", "confused language"
```

This introversion thus complements the general surface theme: "man proposes, but God disposes". More important, however, is the con= trast that is effected as one moves from the first half: people united, gathered together in one place -- to the second half: people divided, scattered over "the whole earth". Within the structural organization of Genesis as a whole, this account assumes even greater significance. It dramatizes the fulfilment -- against man's will -- of the command that was announced by God at the beginning of the book: "Be fruitful and multiply and fill the earth" (1:28). It thus acts as a fitting transition that links the two halves of Genesis: primaeval history (1-11) and patriarchal history (12-50). Through the apparent punishment of dispersing the population at large, Yahweh effects the blessing of continuing his saving promise, which is concentrated in the elec= tion of one man (Abraham and his descendants, chs. 12ff.)

AESTHETIC: focuses upon the _form_ of linguistic expression pri= marily on the microlevel but also on the macrolevel of discourse, whether this concerns the phonological, lexical, syntactic, or rhetorical dimension of the text. Normally this is done to heighten the effect of another speech function -- the informative, expressive, and affective in particular. The aesthe= tic (sometimes termed the "poetic") function is realized by a variety of literary devices, which may be classified into broad stylistic techniques such as repetition, contrast, deletion, re= ordering, and other shifts in expectancy (see Nida et. al., 1983). These rhetorical devices give rise to a perceptible amount of emphasis and/or surprise which result from a peak in the develop= ment of formal or semantic tension/focus or a break in some type of repeated pattern at their point of occurrence. The effect is greater if these features are compounded into mutually-reinforcing sets, e.g.

    "I will put enmity between you and the woman,
    and between your seed and her seed;
    he shall bruise your head,
    and you shall bruise his heel." (Gn 3:15)

Literary patterns of parallelism and reversal (chiasm) function to pinpoint the salient contrasts of this verse:

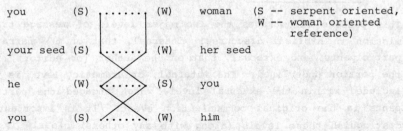

The lexical and structural patterning here, coupled with extensive

figurative language, helps to emphasize the content of the pas=
sage, whose theme, "enmity", is shifted syntactically to prominent
position at the very beginning. In addition, the operation of
this function frequently contributes to the artistic beauty of a
text, and this serves to stimulate interest and to create an
appeal which attracts the reader/hearer to what is being said,
e.g.

For as the heavens are high above the earth,
    so great is his steadfast love towards those who fear him;

As far as the east is from the west,
    so far does he remove our transgressions from us;

As a father pities his children,
    so the LORD pities those who fear him. (Ps 103:11-13)

In this passage, simile and hyperbole combine with alternating
parallelism to beautify as well as to reinforce the reiterated
theme lauding the great mercy of the LORD toward his people.

DEFINITIONAL: focuses upon the code of signs underlying the com=
              munication process. Normally this involves a
clarification or explanation with regard to a particular word or
phrase that has appeared in the discourse. The definitional func=
tion is most often manifested in the form of an equational state=
ment in which linguistic sign X is interpreted by sign Y in the
predicate, or by an explanatory (relative, causal, etc.) clause,
e.g.

> "...and I buried her there on the way to Ephrath
> (that is, Bethlehem)." (Gn 48:7)

This passage illustrates the two major levels of message trans=
mission in biblical discourse: internal, that of the narrative
participants, and external, that of the author (or editor), i.e.
the portion underlined. The internal, or dramatic, level is thus
included within the external level, which engaged the partici=
pants in the original communication event. It is important to
distinguish these levels (along with any others) clearly in the
text or the reader, and especially the listener, who does not have
access to punctuation marks and parentheses, may become confused

as to who is actually speaking, e.g. GNB:

> "...I buried her there beside the road to Ephrath."
> (Ephrath is now known as Bethlehem.)

The next example illustrates an explanatory clause having a defi=
nitional function. This, too, may be difficult to recognize since
it is based on the SL code, e.g.

> And she called his name Reuben (X); for she said,
> "Because the LORD has looked upon my affliction (Y)..."
> (Gn 29:32)

Leah here defines the name Reuben, or explains why she gave her
child this name, which in Hebrew sounds like the expressions,
"see, a son" and "he has seen/looked upon my affliction" (cf. GNB
footnote on this passage).

As the four intrinsic factors of communication show some broad
interrelationships (cp. diagram, p.19), so also their respective
functions may be grouped into pairs having a similar emphasis. The
aesthetic and compositional functions constitute the rhetorical
dimension of discourse, while the definitional and informative
deal with material that is largely designative (denotative) in
nature. In a different set of pairings, the informative and com=
positional functions exhibit much less stress upon the overt lin=
guistic forms of a language, whereas the definitional and aesthe=
tic functions depend upon them. We turn now to the functions
corresponding to the four extrinsic factors of communication.
Since these pertain to the context in which a particular discourse
is realized, they are of primary relevance to the sociolinguistic
study of language, direct speech in particular.

EXPRESSIVE: focuses upon the <u>source</u>, or producer, of the mes=
              sage and the verbalization of his own feelings,
opinions, values and attitudes. The speaker (or writer) is per=
sonally involved in what he says, for by means of his utterance(s)
he expresses his own identity, individuality and internal mental-
emotional state, sometimes with little or no regard for his
audience, that is, whether anyone is listening to him or not, e.g.

> And he recognized it, and said, "It is my son's robe, a wild
> beast has devoured him; Joseph is without doubt torn to
> pieces." (Gn 37:33)

The expressive function may manifest itself phonologically, e.g.
in volume, stress, rate of speech, and the paralinguistic quality
of voicing; lexically in exclamations, oaths and first person
pronouns; and syntactically by deliberative questions, repeti=
tion and ellipsis.

Another aspect of the expressive function is so-called egocentric
speech, which a person employs, usually in a self-serving, boast=
ful way, to make an impression upon his listeners. His intention
may be to draw their attention to his great learning and verbal
skill or to establish a particular status or position in his re=
lationship to them, e.g.

> Lamech said to his wives:
> "Adah and Zillah, hear my voice;
> you wives of Lamech, hearken to what I say:
> I have slain a man for wounding me,
> a young man for striking me..." (Gn 4:23)

Formally, egocentric language may be very similar to the purely
expressive variety, the only difference being the direction in
which the tribute is aimed -- toward self or toward others. Com=
pare the above with this typical song of praise from the Psalms:

> "I will extol thee, my God and King,
>   and bless thy name for ever and ever.
>
> Every day I will bless thee,
>   and praise thy name for ever and ever." (Ps 145:1-2)

AFFECTIVE: focuses upon the receptor of the message -- the intend=
        ed audience -- which may be either within (internal
level) or without the discourse (external level), as illustrated
by the two preceding passages. The goal of the speaker in this
case is to influence, alter or affect in some way the mental/psy=
chological state of the listener (reader), i.e. his feelings,
emotions, attitudes, values, etc. The affective (sometimes term=
ed "conative") function is typically expressed in such linguistic

forms as imperatives, rhetorical questions, vocatives, exclama=
tions, attitudinal particles, and so forth, as well as by extra=
linguistic devices like gestures, facial expressions and vocal
modulation, e.g.

> His father rebuked him and said to him, "What is this dream
> that you have dreamed? Shall I and your mother and your
> brothers indeed come and bow ourselves to the ground before
> you?" (Gn 37:10)

The above passage illustrates the emotive aspect of the affective
function. There is also an imperative, or directive, subtype where
the intention/effect is to modify the overt behavior of the
listener(s), that is to get him to do something through a command,
persuasion, admonition, etc., e.g.

> Now the LORD said to Abram, "Go from your country and your
> kindred and your father's house to the land that I will show
> you..." (Gn 12:1)

Another sub-type, the performative, has the effect of changing the
status of the receptor(s) through the actual pronouncing of an
appropriate (often formalized) utterance. This is what happens in
social and religious rituals, blessings, curses, and so forth,
e.g.

> "Cursed be Canaan; a slave of slaves shall he be to his
> brothers..." (Gn 9:25)

> "Blessed be Abram by God Most High..." (Gn 14:19)

There is obviously a continuum between affective and expressive
speech, for in many instances it is not possible to distinguish
between asserting one's own feelings, desires, and moods, and
influencing those of other people. Similarly, both functions
often stand in contrast to the basic purpose of informative
speech. In expressive and affective utterances (as opposed to the
purely informative variety), the communication of emotions and
opinions becomes paramount in an effort to modify the thoughts and
actions of the receptor, while the denotative aspects of the mes=
sage are clearly subordinated. However, nothing prevents these
two disparate types of discourse from appearing in the same con=
text, e.g.

> (Reuben) returned to his brothers, and said, "The lad is gone (informative); and I, where shall I go?" (expressive) (Gn 37:30)

RELATIONAL: focuses upon the channel of message transmission, in particular, that means of "contact" between the source and receptor which must be maintained if communication is to take place effectively. This contact may be physical, pertain= ing to the medium over which the verbal signals are being convey= ed. In this case, the relational (also termed "phatic") function serves to check up on whether the message is being received ade= quately, or whether there is some distortion or interference due to "noise", e.g. "Can you hear me now?" -- "Loud and clear!" More important is the psychological contact that continually needs to be reinforced and encouraged in order to ensure message transmis= sion. This is effected by forms such as vocatives and conven= tionalized formulae and routines which operate mainly to keep the lines of communication open and interpersonal relations in good repair. Special verbal markers of a phatic nature are necessary to open or close a normal conversation in any speech community. The following are some typical examples from the Old Testament:

> (God) said to him, "Abraham!" (a vocative opener)
> And (Abraham) said, "Here am I." (the phatic response) (Gn 22:1)

> And Jethro said to Moses, "Go in peace." (Ex 4:18, the Hebrew equivalent of "Good-bye")

There is very little concern for the transmission of either infor= mation or emotion in such connective utterances; rather, the pur= pose is almost exclusively one of personal interaction via the spoken word, e.g.

> He said to them, "Is it well with him?"
> They said, "It is well..." (Gn 29:6)

Utterances having a purely relational function are not very common in the dialogues of Scripture due to the condensed and selective nature of the conversations recorded there. The lack of such pha=

tic filler, however, can sometimes cause a literal translation
sound unnatural to receptors of a face-to-face (oral-aural orient=
ed) society, where this verbal "touching" is an essential part of
maintaining harmonious social relations. Examples will be given
later in the book.

SITUATIONAL: focuses on the context "surrounding" the source and
                receptor as communication takes places. This func=
tion serves to orient the interlocutors (in the case of direct
speech) with respect to each other and the conditions that pertain
during the speech event in which they are engaged. It parti=
cularizes the message with respect to the temporal, spatial, phy=
sical, cultural, social, linguistic/textual, and channel-related
aspects of the total environment in which it is found. Such spe=
cification usually takes the form of textual modifications (this,
that, thee, thou, etc.) which are made according to a set of
variables selected during the process of message "contextualiza=
tion". As these variables will be discussed at length in the next
chapter, it will not be necessary to go into detail here, except
to consider a brief example:

> (She) said to the servant, "Who is the man yonder,
> walking in the field to meet us?"
> The servant said, "It is my master." (Gn 24:65)

The words "yonder" and "to meet" reflect the spatial setting of
the speech act: "It", or better, "He" (GNB) results from the
linguistic context (i.e. anaphoric reference to the pronoun's
antecedent); while "my master" places the speaker and the refe=
rent into a specific social-role relationship that could well be
different were someone else speaking.

The situational function is obviously very broad in scope, and
there may be disagreement over its precise range and constitution.
However, its importance to effective communication cannot be
overestimated, for every utterance, in addition to its principal
functional thrust, will always evince a varied degree of influence
from both the linguistic and the extralinguistic context of use.
Hence this function is of special relevance to the sociolinguist

in his study of the nature and operation of speech acts in discourse.

The Functional Dimension of Non-Verbal Communication

The central concern of this book is verbal communication, direct speech in particular. But it is worth noting, for completeness' sake, that there is a significant non-verbal aspect to communica= tion in the Scriptures. Normally this occurs in conjunction with the verbal element (on the internal level) so that messages are reported as being transmitted via several channels at once -- by means of sound and sight at a minimum. This nonverbal component comprises all actions which are performed, whether voluntarily or involuntarily, to convey a certain meaning to those who observe them (e.g. facial expressions, gestures, body movements and posi= tioning, etc.). Such behavior is usually of a culturally-specific nature, and it is always manifested in a particular social setting under clearly-defined interpersonal circumstances. It is this situational context which both elicits the action in the first place and then enables the observer to interpret its significance correctly. The problem facing the translator is similar to that presented by any form arising from the SL setting. The people of his own culture may not see anything noteworthy in such symbolic actions at all, or they might construe a given piece of behavior as they would in their own social environment, where the meaning may be different to varying degrees. In either case, misunder= standing is bound to result.

Like verbal, so non-verbal message transmission involves the same type of semiotic activity, and therefore it may be analyzed according to a functional communication model. The components are the same: source, receptor, channel, context, etc., and so are the associated functions: expressive, affective, relational, si= tuational, etc. The four extrinsic components/functions tend to be the most important in terms of incidence and applicability, e.g.

> ...(Abraham) <u>ran</u> from the tent door <u>to meet</u> them, and <u>bowed himself to the earth</u>, and said, "My lord, if I have found favor in your sight..." (Gn 18:2-3; situa=

tional: honorific)

> Greet one another with <u>a holy kiss</u>. (2 Co 13:12; phatic/relational)

In the case of the expressive and affective types, which are the most common, one can be even more specific and assign particular intentions to the individual actions, e.g.

> All who pass along the way <u>clap their hands at</u> you; they <u>hiss</u> and <u>wag their heads</u> at the daughter of Jerusalem. (Lm 2:15)

All three types of behavior mentioned in this passage are affec= tive in nature. They convey the doers' mockery and disgust which is directed at the objects of their scorn, namely, the people of Jerusalem. Even the subtypes of the expressive and affective functions are frequently encountered in the Bible, usually in dramatic contexts, e.g.

> And Pharaoh said to Joseph, "Behold, I have set you over all the land of Egypt." Then Pharaoh took his <u>signet ring</u> from his hand and <u>put it on Joseph's hand</u> and <u>ar= rayed him in fine linen</u>... (Gn 41:42)

Pharaoh's actions serve a performative (affective) function since they visually testify to his official appointment of Joseph to the post of prime-minister of the land.

Non-verbal communication involving the intrinsic functions is generally not as important to the biblical message, but a number of instances do occur, chiefly with an informative intent, e.g.

> ...cry aloud for them; <u>wave the hand</u> for them to enter the gates of the nobles. (Is 13:2; cp. Lk 1:22, 62)

Non-verbal communication can be made more complex in ways similar to those found in verbal messages. The same communicative func= tion may be effected by several different behavioral "signs". The expression of sorrow, for example, is conveyed by tearing one's clothes and wearing sackcloth (Gn 37:34), by weeping (Gn 50:1), by lying/rolling on the ground (Mi 1:10, Js 7:5), and by putting dust upon one's head (Js 7:6). Conversely, the same sort of behavior

may communicate different things depending on the context. A He=
brew woman, for example, might cover her face as a sign of respect
and modesty (Gn 24:65), or, under certain circumstances, to indi=
cate that she was a prostitute (Gn 38:15). There may be a con=
vergence of symbolic actions in a given context, usually all
having a similar function, as shown in Lm 2:15 and Gn 41:42 cited
earlier. There are also many gestures, etc. which have a compo=
site function, that is, several communicative purposes are effect=
ed simultaneously, e.g.

...and lifting up his hands, (Jesus) blessed them. (Lk 24:50)

The uplifted hands was in this instance indicative of Christ's
status, i.e. a position of power and authority, and it also un=
doubtedly had both a performative (i.e. blessing) and emotive
intent (i.e. to strengthen the spirits of his disciples). Perhaps
the latter would also incorporate the relational function, namely,
to demonstrate his solidarity with those whom he was thus bles=
sing.

Occasionally culturally significant behavior is highlighted by the
biblical writers for a rhetorical-compositional purpose to stress
a dramatic contrast in the text; for example, David's actions
before and after the death of his first son by Bathsheba (2 Sm
12:16-16 versus 12:20), or those of the Pharisee (Lk 18:11 --
highly egocentric in word and deed) as opposed to the behavior of
the Publican (Lk 18:13 -- expressive of deep humility) at prayer
in the Temple.

When translating, then, one handles these non-verbal signs just as
the verbal ones. First, their precise significance must be deter=
mined in the context of use, and the sum total of settings in
which a given gesture, for example, occurs serves to delineate its
range of "meaning". Then the translator must discover what that
gesture would mean (if anything) if it were transferred "lite=
rally" into the sociolinguistic environment of his language. In
instances where misunderstanding or meaninglessness would result,
the functional intention of the gesture must be made explicit

somehow in the text or, less preferably, in a footnote. The same
caution concerning the possibility of cultural transposition in
the use of equivalents needs to be observed, especially when
actual historical (narrative) references are involved.

It will not be possible to treat this subject in detail, but the
following examples should suggest some of the main factors that
ought to be kept in mind when dealing with such culturally-symbo=
lic actions in a translation:

> (Tamar) <u>laid her hand on her head</u> and went away crying.
> (2 Sm 13:19)

This expressive gesture conveys the impression that the agent is
in great sorrow and perhaps a state of shame as well. A similar
action with a partially similar meaning occurs among the Tonga
people, the difference being that both hands are placed together
at the back of the person's head. However, this is normally done
only during the time of a funeral to show bereavement. But the
textual and extratextual context would undoubtedly suggest the
significance of this gesture to the reader. The GNB replaces the
original form with an action that would be equivalent in meaning
in Western culture:

> ...and <u>with her face buried in her hands</u> went away
> crying.

In the next example, the original has no close correspondent in
English or Tonga culture:

> Balak's anger was kindled against Balaam, and he <u>struck
> his hands together</u>. (Nu 24:10)

Depending upon how many times it was done, this particular action
in Tonga society would be carried out to demonstrate one's
humility when making a request or when receiving a gift from
someone. Their equivalent is to pound the chest once with the
fist. GNB renders it this way:

> Balak <u>clenched his fists</u> in anger and said to Balaam...

This is another example of cultural transposition which was prob=
ably introduced in order to retain the same level of emotive
impact. Notice that in this passage the original author marked
the meaning of the gesture (i.e. anger) overtly in the text. This
strategy contrasts with that of the first example, where the sig=
nificance was quite apparent from the narrative context.

A real difficulty is found in Gn 29:11 where from the Bantu point
of view two misleading non-verbal signs occur together:

> Then Jacob kissed Rachel and wept aloud.

Traditionally, at least among the Chewa and Tonga peoples, adults
do not kiss in public (or even in private). Women, rarely men,
will occasionally kiss babies and small children, but that is as
far as it goes. The implication conveyed by this passage would
then be that Rachel was a small girl -- but if that were true, why
was she out tending the flock by herself? And why did Jacob weep
upon meeting her? There is no funeral mentioned in the context
which might cause a grown man to cry. Certainly no close rela=
tives would ever greet one another in that way. GNB marks the
intended meaning by translating: "...began to cry for joy," but
this only introduces a paradox into the text (i.e. cry -- joy) for
the uninitiated Bantu receptor. In this case, a footnote is prob=
ably the only solution -- if the average reader knows how to use
it!

We have thus far considered two different, but complementary,
approaches toward a description of the functioning of direct
speech in society, namely, semiotics and communication. Our work=
ing model has been applied to both verbal and non-verbal behavior.
We now take up the theory of Bible translation to see how some of
the central sociolinguistic issues that have been raised relate to
the process of interlingual message transfer and a definition of
translation itself.

Bible Translation as a Communication Event

Bible translation is a complex act of verbal communication. It is an instance of "communication" since all eight components of speech events are activated. It is "complex" because not only one, but at least two distinct events are operative: the primary, which refers to the original creative act when the message was first composed, and the secondary, which is a literary process that attempts to convey the full communicative value of the origi= nal message in a new, and often quite different, audience setting. Herein lies the testing point of the translator's task: the lin= guistic and sociolinguistic context of the SL message generally has relatively little in common with that of the intended RL mes= sage. This state of affairs may be illustrated by the diagram below in which the two basic figures are meant to portray the two disparate communicative situations:

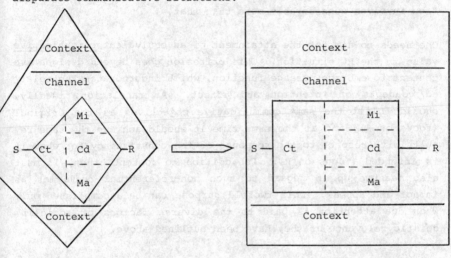

SL Setting (primary)   RL Setting (secondary)

What is different about these two settings? Obviously the micro= structure (Mi) and the macrostructure (Ma) of the two messages will not be the same because the respective linguistic codes (Cd) do not correspond. The original source (S - author) and his re= ceptors (R - readers/hearers) differ from those who participate in the translation event, and this includes their level of linguistic and biblical competence as well as their cultural background,

whether material or, more important, cognitive and emotive, i.e.
encompassing their beliefs, values, experiences, expectations,
presuppositions, and so forth. The individual contexts of commu=
nication also vary greatly in most instances: physically, social=
ly, temporally, spatially, situationally, etc. As for similari=
ties, the channel, in the case of a translation, will be much the
same: predominantly a written medium with varying degrees of in=
fluence from oral discourse. Secondly, it is a basic principle of
idiomatic translation that the content (Ct) of the message, ought
to be duplicated in the RL text. If that were indeed achieved in
a given version, it would certainly be a significant accomplish=
ment. But the transmission process should not be limited to the
goal of reproducing referential information. Effective communica=
tion involves considerably more than that.

One needs to aim for the attainment of an equivalent <u>communicative
value</u> in the RL situation. This criterion goes beyond designative
content to embrace message function, which incorporates the relat=
ed concepts of intention and effect. A translation, ideally,
should fulfil the same communicative objectives as the original
(focus on S), and at the same time it should achieve the same re=
sults with respect to the response of the constituency for whom it
is intended (focus on R). In addition to content, then, it must
also measure up in regard to such non-referential qualities as
impact and appeal. This twofold purpose can be accomplished only
when due attention is paid to the diverse factors of sociolin=
guistic relevance as they have been outlined above.

To illustrate some of the more intricate aspects of the problem,
consider this seemingly straightforward passage:

> And a man found (Joseph) wandering in the fields; and
> the man asked him, "<u>What are you seeking</u>?" (Gn 37:15)

We are primarily interested in the translation of the underlined
quotation. The first thing that needs to be investigated is
whether the RL employs direct speech to the same degree (quantity)
and for the same purposes (quality), and in the same contexts
(distribution) as the SL does. To determine this, a thorough com=

parative analysis is required, one that is not only statistical, but which also explores the sociolinguistic functions of dialogue in the RL. A study of this nature reveals that Chewa, for ex= ample, has an affinity for direct discourse that is similar in most respects to that of the original Hebrew. The degree of embedding allowed is somewhat less, but there are relatively few other situations where biblical conversation does not transfer easily into Chewa. In fact, there are occasions when indirect speech is employed in the original, narrative particularly, where the Chewa would prefer a direct quotation, e.g.

> ...and (Jesus) directed that <u>something should be given to her to eat</u>. And her parents were amazed; but he charged them <u>to tell no one what had happened</u>. (Lk 8: 55-56, RSV)

Here is a back translation of a possible Chewa restructuring of this passage:

> ...and Jesus commanded, "<u>Give her something to eat</u>." Now her parents were surprised, but Jesus told them saying, "<u>Do not tell anyone what has happened here</u>."

However, such a shift from indirect to direct speech should nor= mally be avoided until a complete discourse analysis of the entire pericope reveals that matters of thematic emphasis, participant focus, plot progression in relation to narrative peak, etc. would not be distorted by this procedure.

Returning to the Genesis passage (37:15), one finds that it is not difficult to translate the form of this informative (perhaps also phatic) oriented query into Chewa, viz.:

> "<u>Kodi   ufuna ciani</u>?" (as the old Bible puts it, i.e.
> "What do you (sg.) want?")

That is a pretty accurate representation of the propositional con= tent of these words. Situationally, however, it's all wrong. To ask a stranger "what he wants" in this manner is a grave insult in Chewa social culture. In place of that, an expression that con= veys the same meaning and fits the interprersonal setting would sound like this:

"<u>Kodi bambo, mumati nkwabwino?</u>" (pl)
"(Question marker) mister, do you/say, in everything
well there?"

The form (and the designated content) of that question is obvious=
ly quite a bit different from that of the original. Functionally,
however, the two utterances are communicatively equivalent.

Similarly, if we reconsider the passage cited as an example of the
expressive function above, Gn 37:33, we find that a literal rende=
ring presents no apparent difficulties. The original (at least
the English version from which the translators work) slips readily
into Chewa:

> "<u>Ndiwo malaya a mwana wanga: wajiwa ndi cirombo; Yosefe
> wakadzulidwa ndithu.</u>"

> "It is the coat of my son: he has been devoured by a
> wild beast; Joseph has truly been torn to pieces." (a
> back translation)

Again, referentially, the information is all there. A comparison
with the original Hebrew would reveal little, if anything, mis=
sing. Nevertheless, the Chewa (as well as the RSV) sounds rather
inappropriate in this particular context: a father has been led
to believe that his beloved son has been horribly destroyed (with=
out even a body to bury), and he reacts as if he were a medical
examiner announcing an official report on the incident. There is
thus a clash, not so much in the form or content of the transla=
tion, but in its situational import. Sociolinguistically, it is
an unacceptable rendering of this segment of communication.

The new Chewa translation corrects this error (and it is an error
despite the correspondence in content) with the following text:

> "<u>Ha! ndi akedi! Yosefe wajiwa ndi chirombo! Mwana wanga
> wapita, kalanga inee!</u>"

> "Ha! (exclamation of shock/surprise)

> it's his indeed! (the robe needs no mention)

> Joseph has been devoured by a wild beast! (it would not
> sound natural for a father to mention the "tearing to

pieces" of his own son; therefore this information is
left implicit under the verb phrase "devoured by a wild
beast")

My child is gone!

Woe is meeee!" (a climactic expression of great personal
grief)

The Chewa here seeks to duplicate an actual cry of mourning which
would be true to the dramatic context. Even the rhythm and other
paralinguistic features (e.g. syllable lengthening) are taken into
consideration in an effort to reproduce the power and poignancy of
the original. This includes several lexical additions which func=
tion as discourse type markers, i.e. the initial exclamation and
the final outbreak of sorrow. The latter is particularly approp=
riate since it acts as a compensatory substitute to replace the
bitter sound play that is found in the Hebrew at this point:

   tārof toraf Yōsef!

This pair of examples has drawn attention to two major problems
that are encountered in the translation of biblical dialogue in
particular. The first concerns the source language. We find that
a lack of access to the original text can sometimes put the trans=
lator at a rather serious disadvantage when it comes to rendering
utterances of special sociolinguistic significance, some of which
are clearly marked in the Hebrew/Greek (e.g. through the use of
transitional particles, rhetorical questions, word order varia=
tions, phonological patterning, and so on). The interposition of
an English text, especially a literal one, obligates the trans=
lator to work within a context that is at least one step removed
from that of the original. A portion of the communicative import
of the SL text invariably gets filtered out in the process.

Secondly, as far as the receptor language is concerned, one fre=
quently notices a hesitancy, even a reluctance, on the part of
translators to contextualize the utterances which they are try=
ing to recreate: "What would we actually say in such and such a

situation -- never mind the form, or even the content, of the text that we are translating from?" And there's the rub. A capable translator can be taught the need for changing the forms of the SL in order to convey the meaning of the message in the RL. But what constitutes "meaning"? Does it include the situational connota= tions that have been briefly illustrated above? Is one justified, then, in altering propositional content in order to transmit some interpersonal aspect of the situation -- one that may even be implicit in the original, but which may require some formal mark= ing in the RL? A "neutral", middle-of-the-road rendering is not always possible, or desirable. The translator may have to travel one road or the other: he can simply ignore these sociolinguistic features and allow the unnaturalness of his translation to in= crease as the incongruence between text and context grows, or he can allow these factors to shape the form and, on occasion, also the content of his translation, with the inevitable result that the gap between the SL text and the RL text widens (i.e. in the degree of correspondence of their surface features). And no mat= ter how "right" the latter option may be, it can sometimes be a very difficult position to defend in a meeting of casual reviewers and church leaders -- particularly those literalists who regard translation as being essentially a process of direct transfer from the forms of the biblical languages into the forms of their own language.

The answers to questions such as these have serious implications for one's definition of translation. One of the more tried and tested of the many definitions that have been proposed -- one which aims to achieve "dynamic equivalence" in the process of message transfer -- reads as follows:

> "Translating consists in reproducing in the receptor language <u>the closest natural equivalent</u> of the source-language message, first in terms of meaning, and second= ly in terms of style." (Nida and Taber, 1969, p. 12 -- emphasis mine)

These same authors later define the term "dynamic" like this:

> "...a translation of the Bible must not only provide
> information which people can understand but must present
> the message in such a way that people can feel its rele=
> vance (the expressive element in communication) and can
> then respond to it in action (the imperative function)."
> (ibid, p. 24)

This explanation is clearly based on a model of communication
similar to the one which has been discussed above. It is a defini=
tion which takes into consideration the three principal aspects of
texts, namely, their form, content and function (the latter two
under the term "meaning").

A major practical difficulty develops, however, in trying to
determine exactly what constitutes "equivalence". This in turn is
related to the priority which the definition establishes: first
"meaning", then "form". But what priority is to be given in cases
(as we have seen above) where there is some dissonance between the
propositional and situational aspects of meaning? This issue
concerns the matter of evaluating a translation, a topic which
will be taken up later (ch. 7). In the next chapter the subject
of style is introduced, with a focus upon the varieties of
language that may appear in response to factors of a sociolin=
guistic nature. This is done in order to highlight some of the
principal features of the complex process of cross-cultural com=
munication, particularly as these relate to the re-creation of the
biblical message in a unique situational environment -- the con=
textual setting of a translation.

CHAPTER 3

Sociolinguistics and Style

It is not the intention here to provide a full-scale exposition of
the subject of style (see Wendland, 1979, ch. 3) since much of
that would not be germane to the present study. Rather, after a
simple working definition has been presented, the chapter conti=
nues with a survey that outlines the various ways in which the
field of stylistic investigation relates to the communications
model discussed earlier. This furnishes the basis for a more
specific application of stylistic theory to a sociolinguistic
approach towards the analysis of direct speech in the Bible.

Style may be generally defined as the sum total of linguistic
characteristics (phonological, lexical, grammatical, and rhetori=
cal) which interact to distinguish any one instance of language
use from another. The study of style, or stylistics, is thus a
comparative activity which seeks to specify those recurrent (not
random or occasional) features of language form which serve to
characterize one text as being either different from or similar to
another. Stylistic analysis may be conducted according to an ob=
jective (text-oriented) or subjective (response-oriented)
approach, using a quantitative or a qualitative based methodology
(or both), on many different levels of verbal organization --
within a single text, between texts, or encompassing a number
(corpus) of texts, genres, or even complete linguistic codes
(languages) and sub-codes (dialects).

In order to delimit the area of literary analysis which is of
special interest and importance to the Bible translator, the
communications model will be employed as a framework for segment=
ing the field, to distinguish one stylistic methodology from
another. This means of classification is subdivided into a number
of dimensions according to the eight factors which may be viewed
as operating, or influential, during the process of communication.

In other words, an analytical emphasis on any one (or combination)
of these aspects of message transmission results in an approach
that is "stylistic" in the sense that it is to one degree or
another concerned with variations in the form of the text or texts
being considered. The four intrinsic factors are presented first
-- those that constitute a "message": microstructure, macrostruc=
ture, content, and code. Then the four extrinsic factors are
applied -- those that are external to, yet operative upon, the
message which is conveyed: source, receptor, channel, and
context.

MICROSTRUCTURE: All expositions of biblical style must begin
with an examination of the linguistic form
(microstructure) of the Scriptures since this is the vehicle
whereby the total message was communicated, namely, through the
verbal signs encoded by an author and decoded by his readers (or
hearers). In the present analytical model, then, the designation
"microstylistics" will be restricted to those studies whose focus
of attention is directed primarily to matters of linguistic and
literary form on the sentence level and below and an elucidation
of what has been termed the aesthetic, or poetic, function of
language. Most traditional Hebrew and Greek grammars have at
least something to say about style on this level, though they may
prefer to designate it by the term "rhetoric" or "literary tropes"
(e.g. Gesenius-Kautzsch, 1910; Robertson, 1934). Perhaps the
best available description (in English) of the linguistic styles
of the various authors of the New Testament is that of Turner
(1974). But he does not distinguish the rhetorical dimension of
discourse from the accumulation of lexical and grammatical data
characteristic of a particular writer (for an excellent introduc=
tion to Greek NT rhetoric, see Nida et. al., 1983). Most micro=
stylistic studies are deficient for one or more of the following
reasons: (a) they do not deal with the subject systematically
within a unified linguistic framework; (b) the presentation is
for the most part ad hoc and not very well integrated to show the
formal interrelationships between categories; and (c) as a rule
the description of form is not complemented by a consideration of
function, even in the most general terms (an exception here with

reference to synoptic sayings is Tannehill, 1975).

MACROSTRUCTURE: Stylistic studies of the macrostructure focus upon the form of discourse content and the compositional function of communication. These investigate the various devices whereby the content of a text, or set of texts, is organized as one or more abstract constructs which are realized in turn by the linguistic forms of a language (a study of the macro= structure should, ideally, be based on a thorough analysis of the microstructure of discourse). A description of this kind may be generic ("universal" types) or particular (language/genre/author/ text-specific) in scope, and they are usually either paradigmatic (content-oriented) or syntagmatic (form-oriented) in technique. The former approach is exemplified in the "Structuralist" method (e.g. Calloud, 1976; Polzin, 1977; Leech, 1969), and the latter by the literary school of "form critics" (e.g. McKnight, 1969; Tannehill, ed., 1981). A macrostylistic emphasis is clearly evident in the works of biblical scholars who espouse the literary methodology known as "rhetorical criticism" (e.g. Jackson and Kessler, 1974; Dewey, 1980). It may also appear in studies of a more linguistic nature which stress the so-called "discourse structure" of texts (e.g. Longacre, 1979; Louw, 1982).

CONTENT: The thematic content, or subject matter, has not pro= voked much interest among stylisticians, biblical or otherwise. Many, in fact, would deny that this possibility exists, maintaining that style is purely a formal attribute of texts, and that content has nothing to do with it. Other analysts disagree, however, and propose that the choice of subject matter, certain diagnostic themes in particular, is a stylistic option open to an author just as is his selection of verbal form. Should this theoretical position be granted, then one might indeed posit a stylistics of content for biblical literature as well, notably in the methodology of the "source critics" who do differentiate distinct general styles at least partially on the basis of pre= ferred theological themes, for example, the so-called Priestly vis à vis the Yahwist "documents" which are said to co-exist in the book of Genesis (cf. Eissfeldt, 1965; von Rad, 1966). The work of Northrup Frye on images, themes and archetypes in literature (e.g. 1957) and possibly also that of Kenneth Burke (1961) would fall under this category as well.

CODE: A study of the linguistic code as manifested in the Scriptures was quite a bit more popular in the first half of this century than it is nowadays. This earlier view placed emphasis upon delineating the distinctive characteristics, in particular, the theological implications, of an entire language system (langue) and the world of thought that this was supposed to reflect, as distinct from those properties manifested by a speci= fic arrangement of forms (parole), whether a single text or a corpus of texts. Thus the Hebrew "mind" or ethos (world view) was typically contrasted with Greek thinking on the basis of assumed diagnostic features of the respective languages, such as verbal morphology, the construct state, and the etymology of selected lexical items (e.g. Knight, 1953; Bowman, 1960). One of the great difficulties with stylistic studies of this nature, and a source of valid criticism which has since largely silenced this generic approach, was the tendency to depend upon one's subjective impressions of language (often biased, naturally, in favor of one's academic specialty) instead of hard linguistic facts of a sufficiently broad and detailed comparative variety (cf. Barr, 1961). Of far more value are investigations of a narrower scope into the particular uses or manifestations of a given linguistic code in biblical literature, for example, the "interference" caused by a Semitic substratum (Hebrew, Aramaic) on the form of New Testament Greek (e.g. Black, 1967; Turner, 1976).

We come now to the four extrinsic components of the communication model and the respective stylistic studies associated with each one. These are of greater relevance to the sociolinguist since they all, in one way or another, deal with the extralinguistic setting, both personal and impersonal, that obtains when a mes= sage is transmitted.

SOURCE: A focus upon the source (speaker/writer) of a message leads to an effort to find a relationship between the

formal linguistic features of a text and various associative mean=
ings which may be attributed to the personality, character, atti=
tude, bias, perspective, preoccupation, value-system (or whatever)
of the person that produced it -- le style est l'homme même. Sty=
listics then becomes a more or less intuitive search to discover
the mind of the man (or men) behind the message, i.e. the psyche
of the source. This approach is founded on the premise that
stylistic preference, even the selection of genre reflects cogni=
tive preference and particular modes of perceiving reality. The
danger of such studies is that the further the investigator departs
from the concrete language of a text and its own semantic organi=
zation, the more subjective and speculative his observations
become. We discover the mind of the analyst instead of that of
the original author, described, of course, in terms of the parti=
cular theoretical perspective that has been applied, e.g. psycho=
analytical, structuralist, and so on. The Apostle Paul seems to
be the biblical writer most often subjected to this type of ego=
centric analysis. Among the most prominent (and capable) practi=
tioners of the ideational method is Luis Alonso Schökel (e.g.
1967).

RECEPTOR: In this instance the spotlight of critical scrutiny
swings full circle from the origin to the object of the
act of communication as the analyst seeks to reveal the effects,
both cognitive and emotive, of a literary work on the mind of the
receptor(s). Biblical studies of this type range from crass beha=
vioristic stimulus-response style descriptions to more sophisti=
cated interpretations of how readers/hearers verbalize their psy=
chological experience with a particular text. More important,
then, than the form of the message is the form, or nature, of the
reaction on the part of the audience. Thus, as in the case of the
source-centered approach, so also the effect-oriented method tends
to blur the integrity of the literary object itself with subjec=
tivism, where more depends upon the artistry of the analyst than
that of the author himself. A number of receptor-based methodo=
logies have been applied to biblical literature in recent years,
from Barthes' Structuralist-influenced analysis (see description
in White, 1975) to the phenomenological position of critics who

view the text from a "process-perspective" (e.g. articles in
Semeia 24, 1982). A legitimate area of research where studies of
this kind might prove to be more beneficial in revealing the dyna=
mics of a text concerns investigation into the nature of "antici=
patory feedback". This refers to the literary device whereby an
author builds into the discourse certain comments derived from
either real or hypothetical responses to his message on the part
of his audience. A great deal of the impact and significance of
books like Malachi and Galatians, for example, stems from this
interpersonal, affective aspect of meaning.

CHANNEL: An emphasis upon the channel of communication, the
physio-sensory means whereby messages are conveyed, is
observed in all studies where there is an explicit or implicit
comparison between media of transmission, in particular, between
oral and written varieties of the language. The stylistic rele=
vance of comparisons of this type generally appears more by impli=
cation than design, for in most cases the media (i.e. distinct
modes of use within a given channel) are not the object of a sepa=
rate analysis, but instead form part of some larger investigation
of a topically-related subject, e.g. the influence of oral tradi=
tion upon the written word (i.e. literary style). This is true
also of biblical studies that explore the possible influence of
the channel/medium of transmission upon the form of the message,
or set of messages. For example, as part of his delineation of a
certain generic pattern that appears in the literature, a form
critic will attempt to determine whether or not any part of the
received text once existed in oral form (e.g. Koch, 1969). This
will necessarily entail a stylistic analysis which aims to dif=
ferentiate the extant text from its preliterate, oral substra=
tum. Where this includes a comparison of underlying variants, we
enter the realm of "tradition history" (Catchpole, 1977).

CONTEXT: A contextually-oriented stylistics tends to be for the
most part a generic as opposed to a specific study in
that it describes the conditions which characterize groups of
texts, both literary and non-literary, rather than individual,
unique compositions. The goal of such analysis is to postulate a

correlation between certain message forms and variables in the situation of encoding. Style is thus viewed as a link between text and context -- between linguistic forms and the extralinguis= tic setting in which those forms are elicited. A contextual sty= listics in turn endeavors to correlate and to classify (according to general function) elements of form and associated aspects of environment, in particular, those linguistic features ("style markers") which are more or less restricted to specific kinds of non-verbal context, e.g. temporal, spatial, physical, social, etc. In its application to the Scriptures, a situational stylistics is represented again in the work of the "form critics" who seek to determine the interrelationships between form, circumstance, and function in the generation and transmission of the texts of the Bible (e.g. Dibelius, 1971; Bultmann, 1968). Thus distinctive categories of literary tradition are viewed as the product of the setting in which they arose and the purpose for which they were used. This determinative setting is termed Sitz im Leben ("life-situation"). Many studies of this nature include a consideration of channel-related influences as well.

This survey has shown the variety of perspectives with which one might approach an analysis of the biblical message. There is cer= tainly no single "sanctified" way of looking at things. Some pro= cedures are generally more reliable and insightful than others, and thus it is a good idea to test the results of one method by applying those obtained from another method, e.g. the macro= linguistic by the microlinguistic. From a sociolinguistic point of view, however, of the eight stylistic approaches outlined above, the one that has the greatest relevance is the last, the contextual. But the rest cannot be ignored in any analysis, especially studies associated with the other three extrinsic factors i.e. source, receptor and medium. In the next section we shall consider a more detailed inventory of sociolinguistic fea= tures, which should make possible a correspondingly more precise exposition of the influence that context, taken in its widest sense, has upon the text of a message.

Sociolinguistic Variables and Varieties of Speech

Within the broad functional model of communication, we might
distinguish nine primary sociolinguistic parameters. Any one of
these factors may operate in a given context, normally in con=
junction with others, to influence the shape of individual utte=
rances. This system, albeit tentative and at times arbitrary,
does permit a more precise description of the complex phenomena of
speech acts than the communications model applied by itself would
allow. As a result, the various constituents may be analyzed in
greater detail, both formally and functionally. This preliminary
grid of compositional and contextual variables provides a means
for investigating the individual speech styles (varieties) of dif=
ferent participants in the drama of biblical dialogue, the lite=
rary style of one author compared to that of another, and indeed
the "style" of the translation as a whole in its sociolinguistic
context. Not every factor will be diagnostic in any given speech
event, but there will normally be at least one feature present
which serves to differentiate the verbal output of the respective
speakers, on whatever level of discourse this may be. The task of
isolating and classifying these sociological and situational
properties is to some degree a rather subjective analytical exer=
cise, for in reality every segment of direct speech is a composite
realization of most, if not all, of these factors in mutual inter=
play. They are treated more or less individually in this section
merely as a heuristic procedure to highlight the special influence
that a given variable may have in verbal interaction. In conclu=
sion, then, we will take a brief look at those features which tend
to cooccur to form bundles or sets of interrelated sociolinguistic
pressures that act in concert to structure the speech event and to
shape its constituent speech acts in a particular way.

The nine sociolinguistic variables singled out for discussion
range considerably in their scope and stability. Some are nor=
mally characteristic of entire speech situations, while others
often shift in "value" from one speech act to the next since they
are the product of an individual's chosen communicative tactic at
the moment. It should be pointed out that the more general a

given variable is in scope, the harder it is to specify its effect on the linguistic form of dialogue in the Scriptures. In an actual speech situation, the variation would be much more obvious. But due to the loss of the phonological component as well as all extralinguistic communication, this influence is not always apparent in the "represented" (imitative) speech such as we have in a written text. The versimilitude of such speech representa= tion varies from writer to writer (or literary school): some cha= racter conversations actually <u>sound</u> more realistic and true-to-life than others, which may be hardly distinguishable from the voice of the author. All visualizations of speech, however, are truncated or reduced from reality to a greater or lesser extent. It is simply not possible (nor would it be aesthetically practi= cal) to represent every oral/aural characteristic of an actual conversation, not only with regard to linguistic form, but especially the paralinguistic and extralinguistic features that always accompany speech to modify the message in a variety of ways.

The different points of sociolinguistic interest and importance surveyed below will be illustrated with passages selected from the RSV (Revised Standard Version), which gives a fairly accurate (and yet readable!) reflection of the SL verbal form. Certain problem areas will be emphasized by discussing them in terms of the addi= tional potentials and limitations that one encounters when trans= lating these passages into a Central African language. Examples will be cited from the Chewa and Tonga Bibles, both the old (missionary) and the new (mother-tongue) versions. This compara= tive approach involving several languages will help us to focus more clearly upon the diverse issues concerned in the complex process of communicating God's Word both interlingually (across boundaries of language and culture) and intralingually (across social, situational, and other stylistic boundaries). We will concentrate on the "internal", or embedded, level of verbal trans= mission, that is, direct discourse among participants within the text itself. This is of special concern in the present study. However, where pertinent, mention will also be made of the rele= vance of these features to the "external" level of communication in the SL, that is, the speech of the original author. In the next chapter, this external level will be considered again, but then from the perspective of the situational setting in the RL and the establishment of a sociolinguistically viable translation pro= gramme in that particular context.

There will be a certain amount of overlapping of a general nature in this section with the material presented earlier under the eight communication functions, the extrinsic ones in particular. But any reiteration is not gratuitous in view of the sociolinguis= tic importance of these topics and the value of considering them from a different perspective -- one that permits finer distinc= tions to be made, which in turn encourages greater accuracy in the analysis and description of the speech phenomena of Scripture.

1.   <u>SPATIAL-TEMPORAL SETTING</u>: Influence from the factors of place and time upon speech production are undoubtedly the most stable and obvious to the ordinary language user. Because of where he lives and in what period of history, a person normally acquires an identifiable dialect, one that is shared with many other speakers. It is a manner of talking which colors everything he says ,and to a lesser degree also writes. Since the locative and chronological aspects of speech operate quite independently of each other, they are treated separately in the discussion below.

The <u>temporal</u> dimension comprises all those linguistic modifica= tions in dialogue which are the result of a shift in time as it relates to the form of expression. Such variation is best viewed as a continuum ranging from archaisms (e.g. fossilized literary or liturgical language) sprinkled throughout the conversations of elders to colloquial slang, which frequently functions as a badge of linguistic identity to give a sense of solidarity to the younger generation. Other possible stages along this continuum include a more or less standard or conventional style of the language (employed in more formal situations, in written lite= rature, radio and television broadcasts, etc.), obsolescent speech (forms which are passing out of sociolinguistic favor), and obso=

lete language (characteristic of an earlier speech generation). It is important not to posit a one-to-one correlation between the age of a speaker and the temporal quality of his language, for at best there is only a general tendency linking the two. Other situatio= nal factors (see below) operate to modify and even counteract this tendency. During a church worship service, for example, the youth may be quite content to use a speech style which in other contexts they would disdain as being completely out of date.

It is not easy to find unambiguous examples of the influence of time on the formal aspects of direct speech in the Bible. Sup= posedly "rare words" (old) and Aramaisms (new) have proved to be unreliable indicators (Archer, 1974, ch. 10). Apparently any direct discourse that was embedded into the narrative, prophecy, or whatever, was conformed to the speech style in common currency at the time of writing. However, there are a number of interes= ting instances of poetic speech which reflect an earlier form of the language than the general literary context in which they occur (for details, see Goss and Freedman, 1950; Geller, 1979). By and large these appear in dramatic and/or climatic situations and are manifested as direct speech, for example: the exultation of Lamech (Gn 4:23-24), the blessing of Jacob (Gn 49), the song about Pharaoh's defeat (Ex 15), the oracles of Balaam (Nu 23-24), the blessing of Moses (Dt 33), the song of Deborah (Ju 5), David's lament (2 Sm 1), and the psalm of Habakkuk (Hk 3). The oral, poetic nature of these texts no doubt accounts for their preser= vation of older features of the language.

The temporal factor is much more important on the external level of communication, i.e. author -- audience, as well as in the derived setting of a translation. The Old Testament historians, for example, sometimes make explicit mention of the passing of time in relation to linguistic usage, particularly with reference to proper names, e.g.

> He called the name of that place Bethel; but the name
> of the city was Luz at the first. (Gn 28:19)

But significant common nouns may also be distinguished for this same reason, e.g.

> ...for he who is now called a prophet was formerly
> called a seer. (1 Sm 9:9)

The importance of employing a correct temporal dialect in a trans=
lated text will be discussed in more detail in the next chapter.

A special problem relating to temporal variation is <u>anachronism</u>,
that is, the use of a RL expression which does not fit the socio-
historical setting of the SL. This is especially noticeable when
it appears in the direct speech of biblical participants. Usually
an anachronistic word, phrase, etc. is of relatively recent origin
or reference, and therefore it clashes with the temporal context
of the original document, e.g. "the main city of the empire" (LB -
Living Bible) for "the great city" (Gn 10:12); "political group=
ings" (LB) for "nations" (Gn 10:31); "highway to hell" (LB) for
"road" (Mt 7:13); "20 dollars a day" (LB) for "one denarius" (Mt
20:2). Anachronism is, of course, a matter of degree, and it is
inevitably also a cultural issue. The use of modern equivalents
may be unavoidable as a means of conveying concepts which were
traditionally not part of a people's world of experience. But at
other times a translation team will have to decide between refe=
rential precision in the search for RL equivalents and fidelity to
the original historical-cultural setting. For example, in looking
for a suitable word to express "cubit" (Gn 6), the Chewa transla=
tors decided to employ a traditional form of measurement, <u>mkono</u>
'arm', which designates the distance between the elbow and the top
of one's hand (roughly 18" in an adult male, but not standardized
by any means). This was utilized instead of the more exact -- and
anachronistic -- <u>mita</u> 'metre'. Sometimes the decision boils down
simply to which RL term is going to sound least jarring and con=
spicuous in the context of occurrence. In this case, the use of
<u>mkono</u>, an obsolescent word, suits the (ancient) historical nature
of the text, whereas <u>mita</u> would inject a contradictory contempo=
rary flavor due to its relatively recent official introduction
into the vocabulary (i.e. when the countries of Central Africa
"went metric").

The _spatial_ factor has to do with the diverse influences that a persistent location has upon the linguistic production of a speaker, whether this be current, i.e. the area where he is living at the time of speaking, or antecedent, i.e. some place where he lived or visited prior to the present speech situation (e.g. Mt 26:73). One normally employs the specific variety of language spoken in the area where one grows up. This basic "dialect" may be modified if one moves to a new linguistic environment, or if speakers of another language or dialect come to live in close proximity, particularly if these aliens possess a certain amount of prestige which would influence others to want to emulate them verbally. It lies beyond the scope of this study to attempt to differentiate between "language" and "dialect". For our purposes, it is sufficient to note under this dimension any formal variation which is a product of the speaker's geographical origin. This would include differences such as those often observed between the rural and urban varieties of a given language.

Differences in geographical dialect do not play a large role in the direct speech of Scripture. However, a few notable examples occur, each of which presents a rather unique translation problem. The earliest instance is recorded in Genesis 31:47:

> Laban called (the heap of rocks) _Jegar-sahadutha_;
> but Jacob called it _Galeed_.

The former name is Aramaic, a close cognate of Hebrew, which encodes the second name. However, the meaning of the two names is essentially the same, namely, "a pile to remind us" (GNB), cf, verse 48. The usual translational solution is to simply transli= terate both names and to indicate their common meaning in a foot= note. This practice places emphasis upon the form of the message. Another solution, one which highlights the meaning and signifi= cance of these terms in the context, is this:

> Laban named it _in the Aramaic language_, "a pile to remind us," and Jacob named it _in the Hebrew language_, "a pile to remind us."

This may be effected very economically in a Bantu language, i.e.

the underlined portions in Chewa would be: m'Chialamu...
m'Chiheberi. It can then be left to a footnote to supply the
original forms in a transliteration.

That brings up the matter of the wider use of Aramaic in the Old
Testament. Are these shifts of language form away from the Hebrew
significant? In some cases it does not appear so (e.g. Ez 4:8-
6:18), while in others it does (e.g. Ez 7:12-26). The latter pas=
sage quotes a letter written by Artaxerxes, the king of Persia, on
behalf of Ezra the scribe. This letter would naturally have been
written in Aramaic, which was the official medium of communication
throughout the polyglot Persian empire. But in such an extensive
passage, to shift to a dialect of the RL for the sake of formal
correspondence would probably only be confusing for receptors, and
so the switch in dialect is best merely noted in a footnote.

Perhaps the best known instance of geographical, or spatial, in=
fluence on the text concerns the phonological difference between
"shibboleth" and "sibboleth" (Ju 12:6). Here the position of the
tongue in the formation of the initial spirant distinguishes the
local Semitic dialects of Gilead and Ephraim respectively. The
difficulty is to determine whether the significance of these two
words rests upon sound alone, or whether their common meaning was
involved as well, i.e. 'a stream in flood' (cf. Ps 69:2), as the
context would indicate. Both the Chewa and the Tonga versions are
limited to reproducing the sound variation in the transliteration
of these words. This solution works out reasonably well in Chewa
since the /s/ palatal fricative is foreign to its normal sound
system, though it is familiar from English loanwords. In Tonga,
however, a phonologically compatible palatal glide, i.e. /sy/,
must be used instead, and thus the slight distinction of dialectal
strangeness that is present in Chewa is lost completely.

Moving to the New Testament, we find that the use of Aramaic,
though not extensive, nevertheless occurs in some significant
contexts. Here, of course, we are no longer dealing with a geo=
graphical factor, but a codal one since distinct languages, i.e.
Greek and Aramaic, rather than spatial dialects are involved. How=

ever, these two aspects of linguistic variation may well be treated together since they are so often related sociolinguisti= cally in actual use, i.e. in so-called "code-switching" from one dialect/language to another in certain contexts. Christ, for example, was undoubtedly bilingual in Aramaic, the language of the home and marketplace, and Greek, the language of wider communica= tion (higher education, commerce, government, etc.). Which code he used and when probably depended for the most part on whom he was speaking to, e.g. Aramaic to his disciples and the Pharisees, Greek to the Roman centurian and to Pilate. A unique case of "code-combination" indicates the extent to which these two languages permeated the everyday speech of Palestine. One would expect the language of prayer to reflect communication on a most personal level, hence use of the mother tongue:

> And (Jesus) said, "Abba, Father, all things are possible to thee..." (Mk 19:36)

The introductory address is a bilingual doublet composed of the Aramaic and the Greek words for "father". The phrase cannot be easily translated. The closest one can come in Chewa is to dupli= cate some of the emotive intensity of the expression through the use of an initial vocative pronoun: Inu Atate 'You, Father'.

Otherwise the presence of Aramaisms in the direct speech of NT personages does not pose too much of a translation problem since the biblical author invariably interprets the meaning for the reader in an aside, e.g.

> Jesus cried with a loud voice, "Eli, Eli lama sabach- thani?" that is, "My God, my God, why hast thou forsaken me?" (Mt 27:46)

In such instances the Aramaic is simply transliterated (as in the RSV) and the meaning conveyed afterwards in the authorial digres= sion.

The one genuine example of spatial dialect influence in the NT cannot be translated since it apparently existed only on the pho= nological level and was therefore not recorded by the Evangelist:

> (Peter) denied it with an oath, "I do not know the man."
> ...The bystanders came up and said to Peter, "Certainly
> you are also one of them, <u>for your accent betrays you</u>."
> (Mt 26:72-73)

Thus since the formal modification effected by the dialectal
difference was not distinguished in the original, the translator
is not under obligation to do so either.

A final point worth noting in connection with the subject of
dialect concerns both the internal and the external levels of
communication. The Aramaic mother tongue of most of the New
Testament writers must have occasioned a certain degree of lin=
guistic "interference" which was manifested in their production of
Greek, whether spoken or written. The result was a distinct style
of Koine, very evident in the gospel of Mark, for instance, which
has been termed "Semiticized Greek" after the probable source of
the variation (e.g. paratactic syntax, word order, asyndeton, use
of verbal auxiliaries like "begin to", impersonal plural, prolep=
tic and resumptive pronouns, etc.). This Semitic influence was
certainly reinforced by the Hebrew Old Testament Scriptures and/or
its translation into Greek (Septuagint).

2. <u>EXTERNAL SETTING</u>: This dimension takes up those extralinguis=
tic features of a communication setting
which interact with sociological factors to modify the formal pro=
perties of direct discourse. There are two aspects to this vari=
able, the dramatic and the physical. In each case we are dealing
with external circumstances which exert pressure to change the
normal register or speech style that would be expected in a given
situation.

The <u>dramatic</u> setting refers to the series of events in which
people are caught up in life. These influence the mental outlook
(evaluation, attitudes, opinions, etc.) of the individuals so
affected -- how they "feel" about one another -- and this, in
turn, may alter their verbal behavior with regard to one another.
This type of external pressure is most clearly seen in cases where
the same persons interact with each other in completely changed

circumstances, especially when this involves some sort of crisis situation. The role relationships of the persons may be no diffe= rent, but their respective status levels can be drastically affected. Isaac, in Tonga for example, on account of his deceit= ful behavior with Abimelech is demoted from an honorific (his expected position) to a familiar, or even pejorative, status as far as direct reference to him is concerned (Gn 26:9-10). This particular station is only confirmed by Isaac's economic prospe= rity, which the inhabitants of the land suspect has been gained to their own disadvantage (26:16). Once, however, that Abimelech realizes that Isaac's well-being is the result of Yahweh's bles= sing, he again reverts to the system of respect forms that he originally used when speaking with Isaac (e.g. 26:28). Similarly, in the confrontation between Jacob and Laban -- a man and his father-in-law -- over the latter's stolen "gods" (Gn 31:25-42), the Chewa must reflect the mounting tension provoked by the situa= tion which threatens to severely damage their interpersonal rela= tions. In particular, the increasing anger and frustration of Jacob over Laban's failure to prove his accusations has to be signalled morphologically by a shift in his pronominal references to Laban, from honorific plural to familiar singular forms. This subtle form of verbal rebuke is subsequently reversed again after Laban indirectly "apologizes" (Gn 31:43-44).

The dramatic circumstances also have a predictable effect upon the emotive tone that colors a given speech event. Normally in the Bible this marking does not extend beyond one or two utterances, perhaps to keep one's personal feelings from dominating the account, e.g.

> Esau said to his father, "Have you but one blessing my
> father? Bless me, even me
> also, O my father!" (Gn 27:38)

The normal harmony between Esau and his father has been upset by the clever machinations of Jacob and Rebeccah. The feeling of extreme bitterness and discouragement that must have been felt by Esau in this situation (suggested in the original by the paralle= lism climaxed by two utterance-final vocatives) is conveyed in

Tonga by an initial exclamation plus a particle of urgent request,
which are added to the first utterance:

> "Aaaaw, pleeease (<u>Acuuu, kaka</u>), is there not just one
> more blessing, Father?"

Notice the impersonal mode in which this plea is made -- out of
deference to the aged patriarch. The implication here, i.e. "I
would have expected a better deal from you," is one which the cir=
cumstances lead the Tonga reader to arrive at. The translation
thus communicates what he would be moved to express were he in
that same situation.

The dramatic context may also suggest a sharpening of emphasis
when conveying a statement from the original. When Sarah is
detected laughing to herself over the improbability of the LORD's
promise of a child, she tries to cover up with the denial: "I did
not laugh" (Gn 18:15). But that would be an unnatural response if
rendered literally in Tonga, for it is too "flat" emotively; it
manifests no particular point of stress as the reader/hearer would
expect under these circumstances. Thus the Tonga is "contex=
tualized" to read:

> "<u>No</u> (to introduce the denial), I haven't laughed,
> <u>no</u> (to emphasize her innocence in the matter)."

When adapting the form of speech to the situation of use, a trans=
lator must take care not to fashion the original haphazardly and
risk an inappropriate style in the RL. For example, as the women
rush excitedly from Christ's empty tomb to report what the angels
there told them, we read:

> And behold, Jesus met them and said, "Hail!" (Mt 28:9)

But listen to how this event is reported in the Living Bible:

> ...suddenly Jesus was there in front of them!
> "<u>Hello there</u>!" He said.

The infelicity here is jarring. The casualness of this form of
greeting clashes with the dramatic circumstances in which it is
uttered.

The _physical_ setting includes all those environmental variables of a personal or impersonal nature that can modify the production of speech. The personal factors may be either transient (e.g. smok= ing, alcohol, physical pain, strenuous exertion, etc.) or per= sistent (e.g. speech impediment, old age, mental deficiency, demon possession, etc.). As a general rule, these influences do not play a part in the rendering of biblical discourse even though they are recorded as being part of the extralinguistic context of dialogue. For example, what the "man who was deaf and could hardly speak" (Mk 7:32, GNB) actually said after his healing by Christ is not recorded. The Gerasene demoniac is reported to have hailed Christ "with a loud voice" (Mk 5:7). But any physical/ linguistic impediments which may have been associated with his affliction are not manifested verbally.

The impersonal factors are somewhat more important to the transla= tor. They include such things as the number of people being addressed (i.e. whether a single individual, several, or a large crowd); the proximity and spatial relationship of the speakers to one another (e.g. Jesus' private conversation with Nicodemus (Jn 3) in contrast with his instruction of a crowd while sitting out in a boat on the lake (Mk 4:1ff.)); the use of non-verbal commu= nication (e.g. the breaking of bread in Lk 24:30 which apparently functioned as a signal of personal identification); and "noise", that is, anything which disrupts, distorts, or disturbs the verbal transmission process (e.g. the wailing over the death of Jairus' daughter in Mk 5:38-39).

Generally, the influence of these environmental factors is restricted to phonological modifications (we presume), and these are not registered in the original. However, there are certain aspects of the setting which do make an impression upon dialogue through deictic and/or spatial references, e.g.

> "...see, Rachel his daughter is coming with the sheep!" (Gn 29:6)

This statement has to be reworked in Tonga in order to take the physical setting into consideration:

"That one (i.e. at a significant distance from both speakers, yet within eyesight) the one coming over there (i.e. you can see her now, the words being accompanied by a gesture of pointing) with the flock of sheep, it's his daughter, Rachel."

Notice how the Tonga speaker must first set the stage by clearly identifying the referent, for that is the information of primary importance. The actual name, Rachel, in contrast with the Hebrew, is really of minor significance, for Jacob is presumed not to know her anyway. For such "deictic speech" to turn out naturally in the RL, the translator must be able to imagine for himself the setting as specified in the original and then render the dialogue as if he were actually there on the scene speaking the words him= self (or hearing them spoken) in his own language.

Temporal and spatial distinctions can be made with fine precision in the demonstrative system of most Bantu languages. Both aspects are combined in the following quotation, which thereby makes explicit an attitude is undoubtedly implicit in the SL text:

They said, "Is not this Joseph's son?" (Lk 4:22)

In Chewa this utterance requires three distinct demonstratives:

"Kodi uyu si mwana uja wa Josefeyu?"

i.e. "Is not this one (who is standing here in our pre= sence) that son (the one we have known for some time now -- with a certain overlay of depreciation) of Joseph here?" (again emphasizing the contrast between now and then, here and there, as it is focused in the person of Christ).

3. INTERPERSONAL SETTING: This dimension introduces the personal factor into the setting. It encompasses a diverse assortment of properties which pertain to the social circumstances that apply during a specific speech event, in parti= cular to those alterations in a message that result from the social relationship between source and receptor(s). As far as dialogue is concerned, such modifications would include the indi= cation of relational qualities like respect (or the lack of it), familiarity, role interaction, relative status, level of formali=

ty, degrees of power and solidarity, etc. in conversational exchanges. Adjustments in the type of language employed vary according to different levels of appropriateness with respect to the prevailing _social_ situation, i.e. what are the interpersonal features which characterize the act of communication that is taking place. There are three principal aspects to this socio= linguistic variable (frequently referred to as "register" in the literature), namely, class membership, degree of formality and role relationship.

a) <u>Class Membership</u>: This category includes a variety of compo= nents which contribute to the formation of a distinct type of language that relates to the social group to which an individual belongs. Among the most important of these factors are distinctions made according to factors such as a per= son's birth (patrician vs. plebian), degree of education (litera= te vs. illiterate), economic standing (rich vs. poor), type of employment ("white collar" vs. "blue collar"), or ethnic back= ground (superior vs. inferior, depending on one's socio-political situation and the source of the evaluation). These pairings are not intended to be interpreted as strict polar opposites; they merely indicate the extremes of a hypothetical scale which stretches from one quality to its opposite. The so-called "classes" of society which are often referred to in sociological studies, i.e. upper - middle - lower, are in fact constituted according to a complex interaction of these factors within a given speech community. At the lowest level this concept might be extended to include an individual's own unique idiolect, that is, his idiosyncratic manner of speaking -- a "personal" sub-dialect. Different class varieties, or "codes", may be distinguished linguistically by the characteristic selection of vocabulary, pronunciation, intonation and other paralinguistic features, sen= tence length/complexity, fluency, and so on. Oftentimes these differences reflect the relative level of influence and authority ("power") that its speakers have in the community. These criteria and the resultant language codes always overlap in the organiza= tion of a speech community into distinct groups based on social class. There are three mutually-interacting subcategories to con= sider:

i) <u>sex</u>: There is probably a difference between male and female
             styles of speaking to a greater or lesser extent in all
societies. This variation, which may be manifested on all levels
of linguistic organization, will naturally be greater in groups,
such as Chewa and Tonga, where the social and spatial mobility of
women is relatively restricted in comparison with men. It no
doubt existed also in Hebrew/Jewish culture as well, though the
biblical text does not give much formal evidence of this. The
variations that do appear in the dialogues involving women are to
be attributed rather to the degree of formality of the situation
in which they are communicating (see below). In translation,
then, there is not usually a great need to cater for a special
female sub-dialect due to the comparatively small amount of dis=
course initiated by the female personages in the Bible. A book
such as Ruth, however, should definitely be considered with this
possibility in mind, for many of the conversations recorded there
are engaged in solely by women, Ruth and Naomi in particular.

ii) <u>age</u>: This variable overlaps to a certain extent with the
             Spatial-Temporal discussed above in that the various
age groupings in a society may be partly, at least, distinguished
according to the relative amount of lexical conservatism/innova=
tion which their respective speech styles manifest. However, this
is not the only characteristic to be observed, for it constitutes
but one aspect of linguistic organization. Other relevant factors
requiring attention would be those of a phonological nature, e.g.
pronunciation with paralinguistic attributes such as rate of
speech, use of pause, volume, and voice quality being prominent
components, though there may be some idiolectal features involved
here as well. Variation in the use of grammatical features also
needs to be considered, for the youth may well show a preference
for certain novel morphological forms and syntactic constructions,
perhaps due to the influence of a major world or regional
language.

iii) <u>interest group</u>: A third sociological aspect of "class" may
                  be posited according to the particular as=
sociation of speakers that one finds himself habitually interact=

ing with. Such an affiliation ("in-group"), whether it be formal=
ly constituted or not, results from a mutual interest or viewpoint
which all members share, such as a common trade, education,
occupation, guild, religion, research, hobby, sport, political
party, etc. A distinctive, sometimes technical, vocabulary and
diction, which in extreme cases is referred to as "jargon", is
perhaps the most obvious evidence for this type of specialized
background upon one's conversation. This mode is closely related
to that of subject matter (see below), for the specific company a
person keeps, as well as any particular evironment which he either
restricts himself to or is socially confined in, will always af=
fect both what he talks about and how he talks about it.

One will notice a conspicuous lack of examples under this aspect
of communication. It is not because class is not relevant to an
analysis of the sociolinguistics of biblical dialogue. On the
contrary, the topics under this heading in themselves would
suggest the importance of this subject as a whole to the formation
of speech. The problem lies rather with our lack of information
about both the nature and the operation of such sociological vari=
ables in the community at large, that of the SL as well as that of
the RL. Without an adequate understanding of the form and func=
tion of these varieties in conversational interchange, it is not
possible to make a reliable application to the activity of trans=
lation. One can readily think of areas where such considerations
might be germane, for example, in the speech styles of socio-
religious groups like the prophets of the OT, or the Pharisees and
Sadducees of the NT. But detailed lexico-statistical studies
would have to be made either to substantiate or to disprove such
broad categories. It is likely that in the process of literary
composition, these sociological distinctions were smoothed over or
harmonized into a single relatively homogeneous style. In the RL,
too, much research is necessary before one is able to differen=
tiate such varieties with confidence and then to utilize them
appropriately in translation.

There are two areas in Scripture, however, one largely extratex=
tual, the other intratextual, where one may be able to discern the

sociological factor operating to modify the form of linguistic production. The more obvious influence is felt in the language which the NT writers used to convey their message, especially in the epistles. Here we find considerable evidence of a special "Christianized" code which was distinct from standard Koine Greek. Pressure from the Semitic languages and the theological termino= logy of the OT (including the Septuagint) also contributed to this particular variety of Greek. Thus there developed a unique reli= gious vocabulary out of the need for the Christian community to express its spiritual concepts and experiences, involving prima= rily a redefinition or extension in meaning of extant terms, such as: euangelion (referring to the content of the "good news" of salvation through Jesus Christ), ekklesia (individual local Chris= tian fellowship/universal community of believers), charis (in Paul: God's benevolent disposition/behavior towards a hostile and unworthy humanity), kurios (as a designation of Yahweh in the OT and Jesus in his divinity), agape (God's loving relationship and behavior toward man), kosmos (especially in John: everything which is at enmity with God), parousia (the second coming of Christ) (see Turner, 1981, for detailed comments on these and many other "Christian words").

The second example is more speculative, but further investigation may demonstrate that it, too, is a factor of considerable socio= logical importance to biblical communication, namely, the speech of God in the Old Testament, particularly in pronouncement con= texts (i.e. blessings, curses, formal instructions, promises, oaths, etc., cf. also the category of discourse genres below). The rhetorically heightened (often poetic) utterances of Yahweh are a regular feature of the narrative portions of the Pentateuch, especially in Genesis. But this hypothetical "divine code" also appears in some of the later historical books as well. Here is a passage picked out at random from 1 Chronicles:

And when David again inquired of God, God said to him,

```
(A)    "You shall not go up after them; (6)
         (B) go around and come upon them
                     opposite the balsam trees. (15)
         (B')And when you hear the sound of marching
                     in the tops of the balsam trees, (15)
(A')  then go out to battle, (7)
```

```
            For God has gone out before you (9)
            to smite the army of the Philistines." (7)
                       (1 Ch 14:14-15)
```

In addition to the obvious structural patterning of this text, which features a chiasm in the command portion (A:B::B':A') as well as an antithetic separation in the promise of God (God... Philistines), the passage is unified by its rhythmic (syllable) structure (as indicated in the parentheses) and also by line-final sound similarity, i.e. in Hebrew:

  -hem/ -'Īm / -'Īm / -chāmāh // -chā / -ttĪm

which audibly links the two functional portions together. Granted, one would probably not want to equate this with Hebrew poetry (the spatio-temporal progression is too pronounced), but neither is it ordinary prose (with such a high degree of poetic patterning). It stands somewhere in between -- perhaps to distinguish the code/ dialect of God, who is in a "class" by himself! This literary phenomenon probably also reflects the theological expectations and norms of the Hebrew community concerning how best to represent "divine" language.

b) Formality depends both upon the interpersonal factor of who is speaking to whom (class membership, status, etc.) and also upon the impersonal setting or circumstances which sur= round the communication event. It may be viewed as a sliding scale, with different levels possible, ranging from strict rigidi= ty to complete intimacy in verbal interaction. Several hypotheti= cal stages along this continuum of formality have been proposed by different investigators, though all recognize that the boundaries between them are very difficult to define with any precision. The following is a brief exposition of five categories that are quite generally accepted among sociolinguists (for more detail, see Joos, 1962):

i)   frozen: This is the most inflexible type of communication.
There is little or no opportunity (or demand) for modifications in form, content, or situation of use. This class consists of formulaic, stereotyped, or ritualized utterances of chiefly a phatic or performative nature, for example, greetings:

> Jesus came and stood among them and said to them, "Peace be with you." (Gn 20:21)

ii)   formal: This is also a very impersonal variety since verbal exchange with the receptor(s) is either absent or kept to a minimum. While there is more freedom of form and con= tent than with the frozen type, stereotyping is still relatively common, especially in the use of expressions which appear fre= quently in the oral or written tradition. The grammar is charac= terized by its complexity and explicitness, and the vocabulary manifests a tendency toward abstraction in both form and content. Formal discourse in the Bible is normally didactic (informative/ affective) in nature, and frequently it belongs to a distinct genre of literature, e.g.

> "Truly, truly, I say to you, (a typical marker of formal speech) a servant is not greater than his master; nor is he who is sent greater than he who sent him." (Jn 13:16)

iii) consultative: This variety concentrates on the transfer of information between two parties (the norm in biblical dialogue). The receptor thus actively participates in the verbal exchange, which distinguishes the consultative from the preceding two types. The participants do not share the same back= ground information and/or level of understanding, however, and therefore this material needs to be supplied by one of the spea= kers so that the conversation might continue. In addition to the dominant informative function, there is also an increasing propor= tion of expressive and affective elements, which have their lin= guistic correlates, as were noted in the preceding chapter, e.g.

> Peter said to him, "Lord, do you wash my feet?"
> Jesus answered him, "What I am doing you do not know now, but afterward you will under= stand." (Jn 13:6-7)

iv) <u>informal</u>: Informal, or casual, speech is used between friends and relatively close acquaintances. It is not necessary to provide much background information since the spea= kers are well known to each other. The functional focus shifts from the informative to the expressive and affective types; there is also an increase in the amount of relational speech. The aesthetic function is realized in the formal and consultative varieties by forms of a more literary and rhetorical nature, whereas in informal speech it is manifested more through idioms and other colloquial expressions. Grammatical constructions tend to be looser, and there is an increase in the proportion of anaphoric reference and ellipsis, e.g.

> Simon Peter said to him, "Lord, not my feet only but
> also my hands and my head!"
> (Jn 13:9)

> ...Simon Peter beckoned to him and said, "Tell us who it
> is of whom he speaks." (Jn 13:24)

v) <u>intimate</u>: Intimate language is employed only between the best and closest of friends, especially male and female. There is a special emphasis on the sharing of personal feelings rather than information, and therefore one observes a high percen= tage of expressive utterances with a good deal of phatic filler thrown in to ensure the closest possible verbal "contact" between speakers. Ellipsis and anacolutha reach their highest concentra= tion in intimate speech, while the vocabulary gives evidence of some highly restricted, even idiosyncratic, usages, e.g.

> (John) said to him, "Lord, who is it?" (Jn 13:25)

> Jesus said to her, "Mary." (Jn 20:16)

The ways in which these hypothetical registers are formally indi= cated will vary from one language to another. It is difficult sometimes to specify exactly what these markers are since other sociolinguistic variables cannot always be factored out of the data. Roughly, however, the levels vary between these poles: elaborate, complex, explicit grammar and diction versus an abbre= viated, simple and implicit manner of expression. The degree of formality is very much dependent upon the social occasion of the discourse (e.g. public speech vs. private conversation) as well as upon the role relationships between speakers. Since the latter tends to be more overtly marked in languages, we shall turn to that for some more concrete illustrations of how the interpersonal setting affects the translation of direct discourse.

c) The formality of a given situation is very closely related to the interpersonal relationship between speakers. Frequently, as the circumstances change, so do the respective participant roles. Other factors which interact to specify the particular interlocu= tionary role pattern operating in dialogue are the speakers' several ages, sex, status, kinship relations, and mutual rapport as well as the content of what is being talked about. Often these roles may be described in terms of paired relational sets. Christ, for example, played many different roles during his ministry; here are some of them: friend -- friend (disciples), son -- parents, teacher -- students, religious leader -- adherents, king -- sub= jects, citizen -- government authorities, savior -- saved.

One of the most important verbal markers of role (and hence "regi= ster") in a Bantu language is the mode of personal address. The choice of a "relational register", that is, the appropriate level of honorific (or depreciatory) expression to employ in conversa= tion, is not an optional matter. It derives from sociolinguistic stimuli that may be implicit in the original, but which must be explicitly acknowledged and indicated in a translation. Genesis 24, for example, presents a variety of social relationships which have to be marked in Tonga, i.e. (R) - respect forms, (F) - fami= liar forms:

reference	participants	role factor involved
24:4-5	Abraham (R) -- servant (F)	a matter of status
24:12	servant (F) -- God (F)	mutual familiarity

> Notice that in Tonga respect for the deity is not marked linguistically in formal address; in Chewa, however, honorific forms must be used when talking to God or one of his agents.

reference	participants	role factor involved
24:17-18	servant (R) -- Rebekah (F)	age, sex, perhaps also the status of the servant as a stranger and guest in the land
24:31, 49	servant (R) -- Laban (R)	mutual respect forms due to their equal status

The servant derives his status by association, i.e. as a representative and emissary of his master Abraham.

| 24:58, 60 | Laban (R) -- Rebekah (F) | sex, kinship, age |

In addition to pronominal usage (i.e. plural - honorific, singular - familiar), which is highlighted by concordial agreement pat= terns, there are some additional, more subtle ways in which a social register may be manifested. In Gn 24:23 the servant asks Rebekah: "Tell me whose <u>daughter</u> you are." The GNB modifies this to read: "Please tell me who your <u>father</u> is." But the latter would be sociolinguistically inappropriate in Tonga since refe= rence to her father would automatically increase her status. Thus the translation reads: "Tell me, whose <u>child</u> are you?" The Tonga does not have to specify that Rebekah is a "daughter" (i.e. female) since that was noted earlier in the discourse (v. 16). Moreover, since the terms for "son" and "daughter" are rather long in the language, the component of sex is left implicit in conver= sation whenever possible. In 24:58 Rebekah is asked: "Do you want to go with <u>this man</u>?" A literal translation would turn out to be rather depreciating in Tonga since "this man" (equivalent to "this somebody") is used as a reference to the servant in his very presence. The polite way of putting it would be: "Do you want to go <u>with them</u>?" (i.e. indirect plural of respect).

Embedded quotations naturally complicate things still more. In 24:18-19, for example, when saying: "Drink, my lord," in Tonga, Rebekah employs the honorific plural, as was already observed. In 24:44, however, the servant is reporting this same speech from his own perspective, before the words in question were actually utter= ed. Therefore, he must employ familiar terms in order not to at= tribute too much respect to himself when conversing with Rebekah's family. Then, when he comes to quoting what she did in fact say (24:46), he is able to move back into the honorific register.

The dialogues of Scripture are filled with instances where the interpersonal relationship between speakers, whether or not these are overtly signalled in the SL, calls for specialized linguistic forms of appropriateness in the RL. Take conversation openers, for example. In Genesis 24:17 Abraham's servant, after running over to meet Rebekah, blurts out: "Pray give me a little water to drink from your jar." Despite the particle of entreaty in the original ("Pray"), this utterance still sounds too abrupt in Chewa, where a man in such a situation would have to properly introduce any request to a stranger, especially a woman: "Zikomo mai..." -- "Excuse me, ma'am..." Such expressions, generally of a phatic nature, are undeniably lexical additions to the text, and yet they are definitely demanded by the context of use, where to omit them would sound unnatural. The degree of directness, or explicitness, thus needs to be carefully studied from a sociolin= guistic perspective.

In many cases, the reported Hebrew manner of making a request or a proposal is entirely too blunt for Tonga ears as well. When Jacob comes to Laban with an offer to work for Rachel, he says: "I will serve you seven years for...Rachel" (Gn 29:18). Cultural incon= gruities aside, a man could never be so forthright with a prospec= tive father-in-law. His proposal would have to be softened with an introduction like: "How would it be if..." (Ino mbuti kuti...). Similarly, when the stipulated time period has elapsed, Jacob brashly (if rendered literally in Tonga) demands: "Give me my wife that I may go in to her, for my time is complete" (29:21). The acceptable way of saying this is: "The days that we agreed upon are complete (i.e. reason before result), so how would it be if (a polite transition to the request) we got married to one another (this is the general expression to use when speaking in a formal situation) now?" (a word which supplies the necessary urgency to the request, tactically positioned right at the end of the utterance).

Obviously, the cultural component is a major factor in determining a person's speech strategy in any given situation. This background includes the community's world view and system of beliefs as well as the overt material aspects of their environment and way of life. This culturally-specific outlook on interpersonal relation= ships and the resultant effect on direct discourse is evident in the following example:

> And (Rachel) said to her father, "Let not my lord be angry that I cannot rise before you, for the way of women in upon me." (Gn 31:35)

In the old Chewa Bible the final clause is translated literally, with unfortunate results: "The things that happen to women are upon me," -- some sort of ill-fortune or malevolent action is implied. The search for a suitable sociocultural equivalent in the new translation took many turns. A very euphemistic circum= locution that draws heavily from local custom had to be rejected (by church leaders) because of its allusion to traditional religious belief: "...for I cannot salt the stew at this time." That would have been the most natural in this situation. Another reference turned out to be too general in its implications: "...for I am feeling ill these days," -- an expression denoting physical sickness or pregnancy in addition to menstruation. Another was too specific in its application: "...for I have fallen down/in the dirt," -- which refers to the first menses. Other possibilities were felt to be too provincial in usage: "...for I am crossing over the river at this time;" "...for I am sleeping at the back of the hut." An idiomatic alternative was too explicit and hence inappropriate for a daughter to use in direct conversation with her father: "...for I am one who is washing" (i.e. an oblique reference to the menstrual flow). Even a com= paratively neutral allusion to the regular passage of time which marks this physical phenomenon was too overt under these circum= stances: "...for I am at the month" ("month" is the same as "moon"). The ultimate solution allowed only the faintest mention of this "illness" (for that is how the Chewa view it) peculiar to women: "...for I am not well according to the things of us women."

One final example illustrates an interesting instance of a clash between the three aspects of the interpersonal variable: class membership, degree of formality and role relationship. In John 9:31-33, a poor uneducated and (formerly) blind beggar (near the bottom of the Jewish social hierarchy) corrects some faulty think= ing on the part of the religious leaders of the day in a brief, but pointed, apologetic discourse. In the original, the beggar's speech assumes the formal phraseology and diction of a teacher (and the translation ought to reflect this level of language) -- similar to that of Jesus himself, in fact. The incongruity of the situation was so intolerable to the learned theologians that they could not help but refer to this striking role reversal in their attempt to shut the man up:

"You were born in utter sin, and would you teach us?" (Jn 9:34)

The typical response of a person of high status to a social infe= rior who has upstaged him is verbal abuse, and that is what we have here. It is important that the insulting nature of the reply be manifested also in translation so that it does not sound merely like an ecclesiastical judgment on the part of the synagogue lea= ders. Chewa signals this by leading their reaction off with an exclamation of disparagement: "ha!"

Many more examples could be cited, for the influence upon dialogue of interpersonal situational relations is pervasive and particu= larly strong. There is hardly a speech that occurs (in real con= versation anyway) where its presence is not indicated formally in one way or another -- lexically, grammatically or even phonologi= cally. The dilemma facing the translator concerns the degree to which he must depart from the formal shape of the SL message in order to capture its meaning in the RL with an impact that is equivalent with respect to the sociocultural context in which it occurs.

4. LANGUAGE MEDIUM: This variable concerns the vehicle of message transmission, to be specific, the difference between oral-aural communication and the visual channel as employed by the medium of print. The present focus is upon the

various social and linguistic factors which operate during the literary representation of speech -- when the fluidity of oral discourse becomes fixed on the printed page. The question of medium is crucial, for we are obviously dealing with a transposi= tion from one mode of communication to another, from the oral to the written. What changes took place in the process?

Generally one would expect that the shift from speech to writing involved alterations to the linguistic form such as these: a written style is more regularized grammatically, with fewer "per= formance errors"; it is at the same time less redundant, having an aversion for repetition, especially exact reiteration; it is more complex syntactically, exhibiting longer sentences and embeddings which are intended to present ideas in a more "logi= cal" array; its clause, sentence, paragraph, etc. transitions are more explicitly marked; it avoids certain typically colloquial forms and localisms, aiming for a more formal, dignified and wide= ly understood manner of expression; it introduces additional textual attribution and description, including colorful terms, figurative language and special sound effects (alliteration, assonance, rhythm, etc) -- depending upon the genre -- in order to provide extra verbal animation to compensate for the absence of sound (intonation, voice quality, etc.), non-verbal communication (gestures, facial expressions, etc.) and personal participation (including "feedback") by receptors in the communication event.

Now to what extent does direct discourse in the Scriptures mani= fest modifications along these lines? The problem is that we do not have any actual transcriptions of dialogue from that time to use as the basis for a comparative analysis. The only texts avail= able are those which have, to varying degrees, been shaped by the written medium in which they appear. In the case of the Old Tes= tament, this is more or less limited to the remainder of the bib= lical text. The poetic, oratorical nature of many "official pro= clamations" in the Scriptures has already been pointed out, both in the OT as well as the NT. In what measure is this feature a product of the shift from speech to writing? Have scribes and editors been responsible for the formation of a distinct "lite=

rary" style in the Bible, or could these obviously stylized forms simply be a reflection, with uncertain clarity, of an original oral, formulaic and rhetorical mode of presentation?

The majority of scholars tend to support the former position -- that the direct discourse of Scripture is the end result of a long process of literary editing which has shaped the text into the form that we now have it. For example, with reference to the sayings of Jesus, the position of the form critic and redaction critic alike is:

> "...that the christology of the New Testament, including the Gospels, does not spring from the authentic teach= ings of Jesus himself, but from the response to Jesus made by the first Christians." (Smalley, 1977, p.187)

The implication is that this "response" was progressively modified over the years until it was finally codified in the form of the text as we now have it. A rather different perspective is assumed by Alter, this time with respect to dialogue in the OT:

> "...literary convention requires writers to make all their characters follow in their speech the decorum of narrative literary Hebrew, allowing only the most frag= mentary and oblique indications of a personal language, of individual tics and linguistic peculiarities..." (1981, p.72)

Thus Hebrew conversation is essentially basic narrative style enclosed in quotation marks, i.e. preceded by the obligatory speech introductory formula, and manifesting a distinct "bias of stylization" which affects the words of virtually all speakers (ibid., p.70). The implication for translation, if this is true, is that rather than to seek a model for rendering the direct speech of Scripture from RL patterns of dialogue, the translator should instead retain a general literary mode of presentation throughout.

Objections could be raised against both positions cited above. Dialogue in the Scriptures, particularly in the Old Testament, manifests a wide variety of formal characteristics which would seem to establish it as having a strong oral base. Among such

features, one might observe the following which are concentrated
in the speeches of the biblical participants: repetition, voca=
tives, exclamations, intensifiers, dramatic infinitives, ellipsis,
verbless predication, asyndeton (minus conjunctives), the emphatic
use of the personal pronoun, word order variations, and subtle
sound effects, among others. This is not to say that we are
dealing with naturalistic transcriptions of complete speeches.
There must have been some amount of literary representation -- of
altering an oral mode of communication to writing, including the
selection of what is actually "said", in order to give the "illu=
sion" of speech. But the end result appears to be closer to the
original oral substratum than is generally assumed.

To give but one example, here is how Reuben reacts to the dis=
appearance of Joseph:

"The lad is gone; and I, where shall I go?" (Gn 37:30)

We cannot enter upon a full stylistic description of these two
clauses, in which a diversity of linguistic devices -- phonologi=
cal, lexical and grammatical -- converge to heighten the expres=
siveness of Reuben's cry of anguish, but notice the following:
first of all, there is a striking syntactic balance in the origi=
nal which foregrounds the principal participants in the drama at
this moment:

'The boy, he is not; and I, where shall I go?'

In each case, the subject, which is emphasized, is placed outside
of its clause, as it were, in initial position. A pair of idioma=
tic expressions add to the emotive force of Reuben's lament:
"he is not" - he's gone/dead; "where shall I go?" - a rhetorical
question, i.e. he can now "go" nowhere to escape the blame that is
sure to fall on his head. Even the sound level of discourse is
fully utilized to help convey the speaker's deep despair:

'anī 'ānāh 'anī bā'.

This utterance gives the impression of being a realistic oral
reaction of the speaker to the situation he is in, at least from
the point of view of the writer. It seems rather difficult,
therefore, to attribute a quotation like this either to a redac=
tor's pen or to view it simply as expressing "the decorum of
narrative literary Hebrew"! The translation of such passages does

not present too much of a problem, for a Bantu language anyway, if
the full resources of the RL are consulted, in particular, the
stylistic repertory of actual dialogue. And it may even turn out
in a significant number of instances that literalness is idiomatic
when it comes to matching device for device (cf. Wendland, 1984):

> "The boy, inside (i.e. the pit) he is not; and now I,
> what am I to do?" (Chewa draft back translation)

The factor of language medium also played a part in shaping the
form of the NT text through the influence of the Septuagint, as
was noted earlier. Due to the literal nature of this translation,
many "hebraisms" found their way into the speech of Christ and his
apostles (among many others). In addition to the obvious instances
of a correspondence in vocabulary, we also observe, for example,
that the Hebrew infinitive absolute is often rendered in the LXX
by means of the finite verb with a dative of the cognate noun --
so also in Luke:

> "...they went to the chief priests and elders, and said,
> "We have strictly bound ourselves by an oath (literally:
> 'with a curse we have cursed ourselves') to taste no
> food till we have killed Paul..." (Ac 23:14)

It is possible that Luke employed this construction here as a
deliberate literary device in order to contextualize the utte=
rance, i.e. to emphasize the "Jewishness" of the speakers. John's
gospel betrays a particularly strong Semitic tendency, in syntax
as well as diction, e.g. prolepsis of the subject of a subordinate
clause (a form of topicalization): "...look at the fields, for
they are white for (the) harvest" (Jn 4:35); the use of ou mē
with the aorist subjunctive or future indicative to convey a
forceful negation: "Whoever drinks of the water which I will give
him, never again will he thirst forever..." (Jn 4:14).

5. SUBJECT MATTER: The content, or topic, of a discourse is
chosen by the source as part of his overall
communication strategy in a given context. This topic (also
termed "field", "province", or "domain"), on whatever level of
generality it is considered, obviously affects the linguistic form

of an utterance in the selection of vocabulary. A discourse on the theme of water and worship (John 3) will manifest a completely different lexical constituency (semantic range) than one which speaks about bread and authority (John 6). However, there may be an even more subtle manner of influence, namely, with respect to the prevailing grammatical structures of a text. Topics falling under the general category of existence of possession will tend to favor syntactic constructions that differ from those required by topics exhibiting primarily movement and location (cf. Halliday, 1980, p.60).

For example, in the parable of the sower (Mk 4:3-8), the subject matter has to do with what happens when a farmer broadcasts seed in his field, and the linguistic form consists mainly of simple, past predications within predominantly transitive verb construc= tions. On the other hand, when presenting Christ's interpretation of this parable (Mk 4:14-20), where the topic shifts from one that is progressive and eventive (the figure) to one that is relational and descriptive (the meaning), Mark employs a much higher percen= tage of copular, participial and relative constructions in the present time. Normally, one would expect these features to be accompanied by a greater incidence of intransitive clauses as well, but in this case there is a thematic emphasis upon the "word", and so it is reiterated in various transitive frames throughout the text. There is considerable overlap in this re= gard with the typological factor (see 6 below) since the two passages exemplify distinct discourse types (i.e. narrative and expository). That is one of the problems the analyst faces in trying to evaluate the effect of the choice of topic on the message: it is virtually impossible to hold the other contextual factors constant to permit a relatively unbiased judgment to be made.

To give another example of the interaction of the subject matter of discourse with other factors in the communication event: when a typical parson discusses a religious topic -- as opposed to his hobby, which may be gardening -- he invariably speaks a different type of language, especially in its phonological features. As

Fowler describes them:

> "...the overall pitch level of the voice is high, and the frequency band through which the voice ranges is artificially narrowed, resulting in distortion of the normal intonation tunes of the language." (1974, p.227)

Now to what is one to attribute this particular effect -- to the religious content alone (i.e. a "formal" topic necessitates a for= mal style), or to the social role of the parson, the type of dis= course being engaged in, the degree of formality, or to the spe= cial interest group that he represents and his status over against that of his audience in the interpersonal setting (i.e. theologi= cally trained clergy)? Clearly, to one degree or another each of these situational variables is involved. A sociolinguistic perspective, then, certainly does not make the translation task any easier. But by pinpointing various possible extralinguistic influences upon speech, it at least has the potential to enlighten the translator as to why in a particular passage he is having trouble, and in many cases it can also through this factorized approach toward the analysis of direct discourse assist him in finding an appropriate solution in the RL.

As far as the actual translation is concerned, the topic of dis= course is a matter requiring attention only with respect to the degree of difficulty that it presents during message transfer. Generally the process is less complicated if the thematic concepts are objective (concrete), designative and factive as opposed to being subjective (abstract), emotive and symbolic (cf. Nida, 1981, p.26). For example, the first of the two related passages below is more readily converted into Chewa or Tonga than the second, not only due to its structural simplicity, but also because the second exhibits a degree of abstraction and semantic complexity which necessitates a considerable amount of formal modification in order for it to be correctly comprehended in the RL:

> "Other seed fell among thorns and the thorns grew up and choked it, and it yielded no grain." (Mk 4:7)

> "...they are those who hear the word, but the cares of the world, and the delight in riches, and the desire for other things, enter in and choke the word, and it proves unfaithful." (Mk 4:19)

The latter has to be rendered in Chewa this way (a back transla=
tion):

> "...those are the people who really hear the Word of
> God, but they are shaken about (i.e. upset) by the
> things of down here (i.e. this life), riches deceive
> them, and they hanker after many other things. Now
> these things act as if they cover up (i.e. destroy the
> effectiveness of) that word, and it produces nothing."

Ease of perception is also related to the receptor's cultural
background and experience. Certain subjects in Scripture, NT
eschatology for example, will be more difficult for Bantu in
contrast to Western receptors to understand since such themes have
not figured prominently in their traditional system of beliefs
(cf. Mbiti, 1971, p.183). Conversely, other topics, such as levi=
rate marriage, will be easier for an African than a Westerner to
comprehend since they are part of the former's traditional way of
life. This matter of cultural convergence to and divergence from
the biblical record affects, in addition to the translation pro=
cess itself, the nature and distribution of explanatory footnotes
which may be introduced to supplement the content of a text.

6. <u>DISCOURSE TYPES & GENRES</u>: This dimension concerns the formal
qualities which are superimposed
upon direct speech that simultaneously encodes one of the major
discourse types or genres. The "type" of text is an etic (univer=
sal) category, that is, one which may be expected to occur in any
language. Nida (1981) posits four basic types: narration,
description, argument, and dialogue. Longacre (1968), employing a
different set of criteria, also describes four types: narrative,
procedural, expository, and hortatory. "Genre" is an emic cate=
gory (Pickering, 1980, p.74) since its formal varieties are defin=
ed according to criteria that are language-specific (with RL names
being generally assigned to each). A given genre may be composed
of several discourse types; "story-with-song" (<u>nthano</u>) in Chewa,
for example, may contain all of the four types proposed by Nida.
One genre can be distinguished from another by higher level rheto=
rical schema, or patterns of organization, as well as by a set of

lower level linguistic (primarily grammatical) characteristics, such as: major sentence type and linkage, amount of relative-descriptive clauses and attributive constructions, tense usage, word-class preference, intonational and rhythmic patterns, and so forth. The diversity, density, and distribution of literary embellishments (figurative language, rhetorical questions, irony, etc.) may also be an important factor to take into consideration. The point is that these same features will be carried over into direct speech, which may incorporate any genre. It is for this reason that Nida distinguishes between the mixed text-form "conversation" and pure "dialogue", the latter consisting only of sequences of questions and answers or affirmations and negations (1981, p.15). Thus the choice of genre (or type), which depends on various other situational and functional factors, becomes a sociolinguistic variable that may have considerable influence on the ultimate shape of any piece of direct discourse. If this capacity of genre-embedding (usually within narrative discourse) is not recognized by translators, it is likely that their render= ing of dialogue in the RL will turn out to be considerably less than natural.

The book of Genesis, for example, contains a wide selection of potential discourse types/genres. These are designated as "poten= tial" pending further comparative investigation which is required to establish them as being formally distinct from one another (the work of the "form-critics" is quite useful in this regard). The majority of these types and sub-types do occur in the speech of the narrative personages. Among them we find: praise (panegyric) poetry (Gn 4:23-24); formal instructions (procedures) (Gn 6:14-16); judicial pleas (Gn 18:23ff.); prayers (Gn 24:12-14); vows (Gn 28:20-22); predictive prophecy (Gn 25:23); expressions of mourning (Gn 42:36); dream reports (Gn 40:10-11. 16-17); offi= cial proclamations (Gn 41:44); blessings (Gn 27:27-29); and curses (Gn 20:3). A given RL will probably not make the same generic distinctions as the SL, i.e. it may be over- or under-differentiated in comparison with the original, or else the cate= gories may not correspond in every respect. Even where there are functional correspondences, the respective linguistic markers will very likely be different.

In the case of translation, the important thing is that whenever possible an equivalence of function be maintained between SL and RL typological categories, particularly when direct speech is involved, for here is where the functional aspect of communication becomes foregrounded in a text. Taking Old Testament curses, for instance, one notices that this special type of discourse normally involves two parts: the pronouncement of evil or punishment to come (sometimes signalled by the word "cursed" -- 'rr e.g. Dt 27: 15-26); and secondly, the reason for the curse (occasionally this element occurs first, e.g. Gn 3:14, 17):

> God...said to (Abimelech),
> "Behold, you are a dead man,
> because of the woman you have taken;
> for she is a man's wife." (Gn 20:3)

Here is how this form is realized in Chewa, where curses pro= nounced publically are also very significant, both socially and linguistically (as shown by a distinct verbal pattern):

> God...said, "You shall see (udzaona, i.e. a genre-fixing introduction to an imprecation; here formal correspon= dence, i.e. with "behold", is quite idiomatic), surely (ndithu, i.e. often employed as an emphasizer in oaths) you shall die because this woman whom you have taken is already married!"

A good example of the importance of correctly marking an embedded genre occurs in Judges, chapter 9. The first part of Jotham's inflammatory public address to the citizens of Shechem consists of a traditional folktale (or the adaptation of one). If the bounda= ries of this sub-discourse are not clearly demarcated in the RL text, i.e. opening in v.8 (e.g. "Once upon a time...", or in Tonga: Kaindi kaindi... 'Long ago long ago'), closing in v.15, explanation in v.16, not only will Jotham's speech be difficult to follow (especially for listeners), but it is likely that receptors will miss the punch-line, namely, the application of the climax of the tale to the current situation (i.e. vs. 15 and 20). In parti= cular, the transition between verses 15 and 16 needs to be indi=

cated in an appropriate manner, e.g. Chewa (back translation):

> "...devour the cedars of Lebanon," <u>so spoke Jotham</u>.
> <u>Then he explained saying</u>, "Now if you have acted
> honorably..."

A crucial aspect of function which must be taken into considera=
tion when searching for equivalence between SL and RL on the level
of genre concerns the particular kind of reality and the nature of
the truth claim that is made. A fictive account, such as the par=
able of the Good Samaritan, cannot be disregarded simply because
it was apparently not based on an actual historical event. The
translator needs to make sure that what appear to be corresponding
genres in the SL and RL literatures really do match up in this
regard. The parable of Nathan (2 Sm 12:1-4), for example, has a
much greater didactic impact and moral import than the historical
narrative from which it was derived (2 Sm 11). In this case,
then, the closest functional equivalent in Chewa is not the
folktale (<u>nthano</u>), but the proverbial anecdote (<u>mwambi</u>), which is
used to illustrate a particular proverb. The equivalence is not
exact, for the truth claim of the <u>mwambi</u> is always derived, being
a reflection, so to speak, of the proverb on which it is based.
Nevertheless, the <u>mwambi</u> genre is the better choice as a formal
pattern to follow in translation since it tends to depict events
that are close to reality and everyday human experience in con=
trast to the fantastic elements which typically enliven <u>nthano</u>.
Indeed, Nathan's story was so realistic that it was initially
interpreted as being literally true by David (cp. his reaction to
the telling, 2 Sm 12:5). Therefore, its incriminating effect was
so much the greater when its fictionality and pointed application
were dramatically revealed (2 Sm 12:7).

7. <u>IMPLICIT INFORMATION</u>: This dimension concerns not so much what
is said, but what is <u>not</u> said during
speech. This is information which is part of or derived from
either the linguistic or the extralinguistic context of the commu=
nication event but which is not overtly stated. We might distin=
guish three general types of such implied material according to

relative scope and perspective: presuppositions, assumptions, and implications. All three refer to content which is taken for granted by the speaker to be understood by the hearer during verbal interaction (note: the definitions below are somewhat narrower than these terms are popularly used).

a) Presuppositions: These are broad, culturally-based assump= tions about what is true, valid, correct, and appropriate with regard to reality and man's situation in life. They constitute the foundation of a society's world view. In a non-complex community they are generally taken for granted and therefore not explicitly referred to in, or even linguisti= cally recoverable from, a text since they are not debatable issues. But because societies are usually not simple and undiffe= rentiated in today's world, the degree of acceptance of these cul= tural presuppositions and the strength with which they are held and serve to guide people's thinking varies depending on the degree of homogeneity/heterogeneity of the social group involved. There are two major aspects to all presuppositions, relating pri= marily to designative and associative meaning respectively:

i- beliefs: These concern particular areas of life in the "real world" of experience or imagination to which pre= suppositions relate. They may be associated with any aspect of the culture: religion, social institutions, cosmology, ontology, ecology, forms of artistic expression, recreational activities, life style, and so on. Such beliefs are presumed to be true since, at least in the minds of the people, there is, or has been, no tangible evidence to the contrary, either in their living memory or in recorded (oral/written) tradition.

ii- values: These are the expectations, attitudes, opinions, norms, evaluations, connotations, etc. which are attached to or associated with the various beliefs mentioned in (i) above. They concern the objects/persons, events/states, abstracts, and relations that constitute a people's culturally-specific world and way of life. Such values are interdependent and they vary in "potency" (intensity held), "range" of applica=

tion, and in the different "groupings" or networks of relations which they form.

b)   Assumptions: Assumptions are based on those cultural, so=
                     cial, and linguistic factors that relate to a
particular speech event and the shared knowledge which interlocu=
tors may "assume" to be relevant, appropriate, true, etc. in a
given situation. Since they are contextually more specific and
individually oriented than the presuppositions discussed above,
there is more room for disagreement and debate over the issues
involved. These are normally hinted at and at times explicitly
referred to in the discourse, i.e. for the sake of emphasis or to
provide background information or the logical basis (premises) for
an argument or debate. They may also be modified, sometimes con=
siderably, by a speaker's frame of mind (cf 9 below), that is,
one's personal attitudes and emotions. Thus one can often deter=
mine a speaker's assumptions and feelings from the words which he
utters, just as one can predict certain typical characteristics
about the discourse which will be produced in a particular situa=
tional context, for there is a mutual interaction between the two.

Implicit information at the level of the speech event, namely, the
assumptions held or the knowledge shared by the speakers, would
incorporate also that content which is linguistically recoverable
from the text. In other words, every discourse includes certain
information which is formally and/or semantically entailed by what
is said, for example, by figurative language, or grammatical con=
structions such as ellipsis, passives, rhetorical questions, or
lexical items like proforms and nominalizations.

c)   Implications: Generally speaking, an implication refers to
                    information that is even more specific in
nature than that conveyed by an assumption. Another difference is
that this information may also be of an associative variety, such
as connotation, whereas an assumption normally involves strictly
designative meaning. Furthermore, there is a subtle shift in
perspective between the two terms. An assumption regards the pro=
cess of message transmission primarily from the point of view of

the source. This is content which he takes for granted to be an unspoken part of the message that he is communicating and which, therefore, does not have to be stated explicitly. An implication, on the other hand, refers to this same process more from the pers= pective of the receptor. It is meaning which the source (S) consciously intends that the receptor (R) will understand, or experience, from the message, but which for one reason or another (e.g. to avoid redundancy, for politeness' sake, the level of discourse formality, divine avoidance, etc.) he chooses not to mention overtly. Diagramming this dual relationship we have:

$$S \xrightarrow{\text{assumption}} //MEANING// \xrightarrow{\text{implication}} R$$

Implication is thus also related to the intentional (illocutio= nary) function of an utterance, which will be considered in grea= ter detail in the next section (8).

An examination of the following passage from the book of Job may help to clarify the importance of these three related types of implicit information:

> And the LORD said to Satan, "Have you considered my servant Job, that there is none like him on the earth, a blameless and upright man, who fears God and turns away from evil?"
>
> Then Satan answered the LORD, "Does Job fear God for naught? Hast thou not put a hedge about him and his house and all that he has, on every side? Thou has blessed the work of his hands, and his possessions have increased in the land. But put forth thy hand now, and touch all that he has, and he will curse thee to thy face."
>
> And the LORD said to Satan, "Behold, all that he has is in your power; only upon himself do not put forth your hand." (Job 1:8-12)

Below are listed two major cultural (specifically theological) presuppositions which underlie this speech event:

(1) God is all-powerful; therefore, he may bring special blessing or punishment upon a person during his lifetime.

(2)   God may delegate this power to bless or to punish to another spiritual being, be he an angel or a devil.

One also detects a pair of conflicting assumptions about these presuppositions. This is information which is situationally more specific and thus of more immediate relevance to one's interpre= tation of the significance of the message in its present context:

a)   A righteous person, if made to suffer enough, will eventually repudiate God.

b)   A truly righteous person will not reject God no matter how much he is tested (i.e. suffers).

Several important implications may also be derived from this passage:

text	implication
"Does Job fear God for naught?"	Job remains upright merely because he personally benefits from this relationship with God and this way of life.
"Hast thou not put a hedge about him...?"	Like Job, so too God is a sham, for he has "bribed" Job into obedience, not only by blessing him, but also by protecting him from evil.

(Notice that there is an implicit accusation here; it is Satan's position that God does not "play" fairly -- rather, he plays "favorites" in order to ingratiate himself with his chosen ones.)

"...all that he has is in your power..."	Satan has permission to harm Job -- to deprive him of his blessings from God; thus God's "hedge" has been removed.

All this information, the presuppositions and assumptions in par= ticular, provide the initial tension for the drama of Job and serve as the conceptual framework within which the thematic argu= ment of the book is developed. Three more fundamental presupposi= tions later furnish the rationale for the speeches of Job's "friends":

(3) If a person suffers in life, he must have done wrong --
     the greater the sin, the more severe the punishment.

(4) If a person is righteous, God will reward/bless him in
     his life.

(Notice that (4) is the converse of (3); they might be combined
in the maxim: "a man reaps what he sows".)

(5) If a sinner repents and confesses his wrongdoing, God
     may relent and remove his punishment/suffering.

It should be pointed out that it is not always possible to distin=
guish the presuppositions and assumptions of the narrative parti=
cipants (and the society at large for whom they often act as types
or representatives) from those of the author. In this preliminary
study I have not attempted to do so. Indeed, the moral position
or viewpoint of the narrator may color in various shades the
events and speeches that he is reporting.

In their discourses, Job's companions adopt a perspective based
upon presuppositions (3) and (5), which is in direct conflict with
Job, whose viewpoint is determined by a variant of presupposition
(4), i.e. God does not punish just persons by causing them to
suffer unduly in life. This conflict gives rise to another
opposing pair of assumptions which develops the position of God
and Satan revealed earlier (i.e. a-b):

(c) Job's friends (who represent the traditional religious
     establishment: Job is suffering; therefore, God must
     be punishing him for his sinfulness.

(d) Job: I am suffering even though I am just/innocent;
     therefore, God is treating me unfairly.

These thematic tensions are emphasized by reformulation and reite=
ration throughout the dramatic dialogues which comprise the main
part of the book (ch.3-31). Finally, after the transitional
discourses of Elihu (ch.32-37), God intervenes to enunciate the
climax as well as the conclusion of the debate (ch. 38-42). His
address advances the following "divine" presupposition which
corrects all of the others (i.e. 1-5):

(6) God's power and wisdom, which are clearly evident every=
     where in nature, surpass all human undertanding. This
     is true in the moral sphere as well. Man is simply not
     competent to assess the motives and methods of God's
     works in the world, particularly with regard to their
     appropriateness and justice.

Thus God's actions cannot be mechanically evaluated according to a
simplistic CAUSE-EFFECT model of viewing reality, a system of
rewards and punishments, as Job's friends tried to do. Rather,
God's operations and dealings may be more profitably viewed and
interpreted (who can fully explain his doings?) on the basis of a
MEANS-END model. God controls all things in the universe, the
evil as well as the good, and only he has the power to transform
the former into the latter. Thus, his tolerance of evil in the
human sphere is purposeful: morally therapeutic, prophylactic,
didactic, corrective, etc. for the righteous -- punitive,
restraintive, etc. for the unjust. It is presupposition (6) to
which Job ultimately responds in a positive manner (42:2-6), thus
bringing his own will into conformity -- and harmony -- with the
benevolent purpose of his Creator.

We have discussed this passage at some length (of course, we have
just scratched the surface of Job!) simply to illustrate the
important role that implicit information plays in the interpreta=
tion, and hence also the translation, of the biblical message. It
should be pointed out that the preceding has been a simplification
of a complex and at times rather confusing issue in linguistic-
logical theory (see, for example, Cooper, 1974; Kempson, 1975).
This treatment is motivated by the need to apply the insights of
the theory to translation. Consider, for instance, just one of
the utterances cited above: "Does Job fear God for naught?" Al=
though presupposition, assumption, and implication deal with what
is left unsaid in the SL, there is an obvious relevance for trans=
lation in that a literal rendering may not convey the same infor=
mation, whether explicitly or implicitly, in the RL text. And if
such information is not recoverable by the reader/hearer in the
context of use and is therefore lost to him, then, in the case of

significant content, it is the responsibility of the translator to provide it concretely in his text. If this is done, the form of an utterance in the translation may be different from that of the original, but the total meaning inventory will be the same (or at least equivalent in nature).

Returning then to our example, it turns out in Chewa that the principal presupposition and assumption underlying this rhetorical question as well as its implication have to be overtly acknow= ledged in the text:

"<u>Yes</u>, <u>but</u> Job does not obey God <u>for no reason at all</u>."

The initial "yes" makes special reference to the faulty presuppo= sition (4), namely, Satan grants God's right to "reward" the just with prosperity. However, the adversative "but" marks the be= ginning of a challenge to God's characterization of Job as "blame= less and upright". The basis for this contradiction is Satan's assumption (a) that a person remains upright only while things are going well for him in life. The shift from a (rhetorical) question form to a direct assertion, coupled with the Chewa double negative construction (i.e. "not...for no reason at all"), then clarifies the implication of Satan's words, viz. Job is willfully profiting from his special relationship to God -- he has been "bought" with God's blessings.

Another example may help to demonstrate the importance of a tho= rough understanding of presupposition and implication for the translator:

> Then the LORD God said to the woman, "What is this that you have done?" The woman said, "The serpent beguiled me and I ate." (Gn 3:13)

God's question presupposes the fact that any disobedience to his command (i.e. not to eat of the fruit) was an offense against him. The consequent assumption, leading up to his question, is that since she did eat, she was guilty, morally answerable to him, and subject also to the punishment stipulated. Again in this instance, as in the Job passage, a rhetorical question is utilized to high= light the function of the utterance. Thus, information is not

really being requested; it is being emphatically conveyed. The
implication then of what amounts to an accusation is this: explain
why you disobeyed me. At this point a language such as Tonga must
make explicit whether the woman's response was a genuine admission
of guilt or not. The context suggests the latter option since her
words seem to indicate that she rejected the implication of wrong=
doing and hence intended to smooth over what she had done. The
translation reads (via English):

"No, the snake deceived me and so I ate."

By asserting "no", the woman denies the fact that she was fully
culpable for her action, and her unstated assumption is: it was
not entirely my fault. This contrary position may have been based
on a presupposition which differed radically from God's, namely,
that a transgression of his law, if instigated by another party,
does not bear the same degree of guilt or deserve the same measure
of punishment. A possible implication is: I ought not be
punished, at least not as severely. God does not dignify such
depraved reasoning with a reply. Since the same combination of
presuppositional elements appeared in the preceding verse, the
point is doubly stressed: man (or woman) patently refuses to
accept full responsibility for his (or her) wicked behavior. It
is up to the translator to ensure that this same information is
conveyed also by the RL text, if not implicitly, then explicitly.

Some of the most complex instances of linguistically marked
assumptions in the Bible are attached to conditional construc=
tions. The problem in the New Testament, for example, is that
there are four kinds of assumption depending on the type of con=
ditional clause that is used in Greek. They are summarized on the
table below (after Loos, 1978, p.59):

Type	1 ACTUAL	2 CONTRARY-TO-FACT	3 BELIEVABLE	4 CONCEIVABLE
ASSUMPTION expressed:	reality	unreality	probability	possibility
premise is:	true	untrue	uncertain	doubtful

Many languages, including English, do not have this diversity of conditions. Chewa, too, distinguishes only assumption types 2 and 3-4 (4 is comparatively rare in the NT). This presents difficul= ties when one must render type 1 in translation, e.g.

> "...if you do not believe (Moses') writings, how will you believe my words?" (Jn 5:47)
>
> assumption: you do not believe now
>
> implication: you will not believe in the future

The usual Chewa conditional particle ngati 'if', when used with no modification of the verb, results in a type 3-4 condition, and in the case of this passage a wrong implication is conveyed by the text, i.e. it gives the antagonistic Jewish leaders the benefit of a doubt, whereas Christ himself is not so optimistic. The solu= tion here is to shift to a causal conjunction, popeza 'since'.

A further complication arises in instances where there is an apparent clash between text and context -- where the speaker cannot possibly agree with the implication suggested by what he seems to have said (as indicated by the textual and/or extra= textual setting). In John 15:20, for example, Christ says, refer= ring to the "world": "If they kept my word (type 1 condition), they will keep yours also." However, the assumption, since they kept my word, is manifestly not true to the situation. Therefore, this utterance must be interpreted as a contrary-to-fact (type 2) condition -- perhaps utilized here as a rhetorical device, a type of negative hyperbole -- and consequently translated in such a way that this same implication will be apparent in the RL text, i.e. "Since they did not do what I taught them..."

8.   COMMUNICATION FUNCTION: This sociolinguistic dimension of
                              dialogue concerns the aim or purpose
for which the speaker utters his words as well as the result that is thereby achieved. In its most general terms, we are referring to the eight communicative functions described earlier. Thus it is possible to classify any utterance or group of utterances according to which function, or combination of functions, it performs in the message transmission process: informational, com=

positional, aesthetic, definitional, relational, expressive, af=
fective, or situational. As these have already been illustrated,
it is not necessary to do so here. It is essential to point out,
however, the complex nature of motivational interaction in verbal
(as well as non-verbal) communication. We are not dealing with
absolutes and sharply defined boundaries. Rather, as earlier
examples have shown, functional analysis is a matter of compara=
tive probability ratios, with considerable fuzziness at the edges.
These sociolinguistic distinctions can be defended, and they are
useful in describing the organization and operation of speech in
society. But the analyst must never lose sight of the fact that
in reality there is considerable convergence and overlapping of
categories which must be taken into account. The reliability of
his interpretations and predictions is only as strong as the
objective basis according to which they were made, and the latter
often leaves much to be desired. This indeterminancy, which is a
consequence of the implicit nature of much of the data, will again
be apparent in some of the passages cited below.

The intentional factor is also a very important component of
sociolinguistic study on a more specific level -- that of the in=
dividual speech act. This has been the subject of increasing
research in recent years, and in this section we shall consider
its relevance to the activity of translation. The speech act is
itself a complex of several closely interrelated components. Four
of these are discussed here under the heading of function; the
two other aspects will be treated later under the heading "state
of mind" (9).

First of all, it is necessary to distinguish three levels of
speech organization: (the following definitions are my own; other
analysts may interpret these same terms somewhat differently):
speech situation, which involves a given speaker with the full
range of possible conversation-mates and contexts; speech event,
i.e. one particular pair (or group) of speakers in a given socio=
cultural situation; and speech act, which is the basic functional
constituent of speech events. The linguistic features associated
with a speech situation are less subject to change and hence more

characteristic of a person's idiolect, while just the opposite is true in the case of speech acts.

The four basic constituents of speech acts may be described as follows (for additional detail, see Austin, 1962, and Searle, 1969, where the terms enclosed in parentheses are used):

1. FORM (locution): This is the overt, linguistic part of a speech act (roughly, a clause unit of discourse). It comprises the words, grammar, and sounds whereby an utterance is produced, that is, transmitted by the speaker and perceived by the addressee. (This presentation of speech act theory will be made in terms of oral verbal communication; written communication may be analyzed along similar lines.)

2. CONTENT (proposition): This is the sense of the utterance, that is, its designative meaning. The basic unit of content, the proposition, may be factored into fea= tures of reference (i.e. persons, objects, concepts) and predica= tion (i.e. properties, actions, states, and processes) along with the semantic "case" relations whereby the propositional consti= tuents are joined together as well as the coordinate and sub= ordinate relations which link propositions (and groups of propo= sitions) together to form a discourse (see Nida, 1975, chs. 4-5).

3- INTENTION (illocution): This is the purpose of the utterance as intended by the speaker -- what he wants to accomplish by saying what he does. The three basic types of intention in speech are assertions, interrogatives, and imperatives as conveyed by the generic forms statement, question, and command respectively. The intentional (illocutionary) "force" of an utterance/proposition, however, is normally stated in terms of functional distinctions that are more specific, e.g. rebuke, promise, warning, instruction, demand, etc. The category of in= tention will be the focus of our attention in this section.

4. EFFECT (perlocution): This refers to the consequence of an utterance as far as the receptor is

concerned, that is, what it actually accomplishes in terms of influencing his behavior and/or thinking. For example, an utte= rance with the intentional force of an order may effect a perlocu= tionary effect of obedience, disobedience, fear, respect, anger, etc. or any combination of these. In other words, there may be either a physical, cognitive, or emotive response to what is said.

There are a number of contextual requirements that have to be met before a speech act has even the potential for a reasonable degree of success. No act of message transmission is ever 100% success= ful due to the factor of "noise", which may be physical (e.g. channel interference) or conceptual (e.g. different levels of ver= bal competence between source and receptor, varying emotional states, disparate or even incongruent presuppositions, assump= tions, etc.). Since the mental "grid" for perception and inter= pretation differs from one individual to the next, no one ever "receives" the same meaning, whether designative or associative, that another person "transmits". The communication process always involves at least some measure of skewing or message distortion. Consequently, it is that much more imperative that certain speech conventions be observed in order to keep this error factor to a minimum. Some of the more important requirements for satisfactory verbal communication are listed below (cf. Austin, 1962, pp. 14-15). This listing is an idealization, of course. In actual speech situations there is always some bending, if not breaking, of the "rules" of conversational etiquette. However, there are limits, and successful communication depends on a certain degree of conformity to these unwritten appropriateness conditions. When any of these norms are either unintentionally not realized or deliberately disregarded, then message transmission is partially or even entirely blocked. These contextual stipulations are of a very general nature. Obviously, every distinct speech community and cultural group will have many other, more specific patterns, strategies, and customs of interacting via language -- all in= tended to facilitate the attainment of definite functionally-based objectives (cf. Farb, 1974).

a)   The speech act must generally fit into an accepted pattern of convention for conducting the procedure or purpose that is intended;

b) the speakers should be qualified, i.e. have the necessary verbal and mental competence, and the physical and emotional circumstances should be conducive for obtaining the desired results;

c) there may be no errors or omissions of factual content during performance, that is, in the realization of the speech act (sequence of acts);

d) the act of communication must be motivated by sincere and appropriate ideas, attitudes, and emotions on the part of both speaker and hearer(s);

e) the prior and subsequent behavior of the participants, source as well as receptor, should be consonant with the primary objective of the communication event as a whole.

Other principles could undoubtedly be added to the above, but these are sufficient to illustrate the importance of sociolinguis= tic factors such as we have been discussing in determining the success or failure of individual speech acts and their combina= tions.

It is important for the purposes of analysis to distinguish between the content and the intention of speech acts. For example, in response to Peter's request: "Explain the parable to us," Christ replies: "Are you still without understanding?" (Mt 15:16). In the old Chewa Bible the latter is rendered as a real question, i.e. one requesting information -- in this instance: "yes" or "no". But in the passage above the question is rhetori= cal and like most rhetorical questions it serves to convey meaning of an illocutionary nature. Here the intent communicated by the original in its context is one of surprise, perhaps also rebuke, viz. you ought to know better! The point is that whether we translate this passage in the form of a question or a direct statement, the propositional (truth-value) content remains the same, i.e. you are still ignorant (with regard to this matter). But the intention does not; it varies along with the form (in this case). Additional formal marking is usually needed therefore in the RL to signal the particular type of illocution that is demanded by the situation. In both Chewa and Tonga, this is done by means of an initial rhetorical particle (i.e. kani/ani - "so it is that..."), which accents the fact that the speaker did not expect the reaction which he has just received; the particle further suggests that a reprimand may be forthcoming.

The significance of this issue for translators is that every pro= position ("kernel" clause) of the SL text carries its own inten= tional force in addition to a particular segment of designative content. Intentions vary widely in their range of aims and objec= tives; they include everything that a speech community can do with words: praise, bless, inform, apologize, greet, advise, explain, ridicule, mourn, and so forth (these are subtypes of the various functions discussed earlier). It is not enough, there= fore, for one to reproduce merely the sense of the original in the RL. In addition, the complete and correct communicative intent must be transmitted. Sometimes this will require the introduction of overt linguistic markers as we saw in the preceding example. Thus the situational variable of functional intent exerts its influence along with all the rest to determine the realized form of speech in a given language. The following are a few more examples to demonstrate the importance of this sociolinguistic principle for an idiomatic rendering of direct speech in the Scriptures.

The first passage illustrates the need for a wider, discourse perspective when translating speech acts:

The serpent said to the woman, "You will not die." (Gn 3:4)

Propositionally, or content-wise, that is a faithful rendering of the original Hebrew. Sociolinguistically, however, it is not. That is to say, the RSV translation fails to capture the emphasis and the intentional force of Satan's words. The concept of death is foregrounded and this is negativized, literally: 'not dying you shall die,' cf. 2:17. But more than that: these words are not simply a statement of fact, as they sound when considered in isolation. Rather, they are a direct contradiction and a denial of what the woman has just quoted God as saying (i.e. "...lest you die"). The Chewa translation brings out this motivation of the original:

"<u>Iyai</u>, kufa simudzafa konse!"

"<u>No</u> (an initial response, i.e. what you have said is not true), <u>to die you will not die</u> (an emphatic cognate construction formed from a finite verb and its related "infinitive" which confirms the initial negative) <u>at all</u> (a final repudiation of what was implied by the previous speech act)!"

Somewhat later in the story, it is God himself who addresses the woman with regard to his earlier prohibition:

"What is this that you have done?" (Gn 3:13)

This is no mere request for information or an explanation (as the old Chewa Bible implies). It is rather a demand, in particular, one whose purpose is to elicit a full confession from the woman. This comes out quite clearly in the Chewa:

"<u>Say you</u> (familiar address, the vocative signals a shift in the addressee along with an indication of the nega= tive tone of the utterance to follow), <u>what you have done</u> (this topicalized clause throws the spotlight upon the woman's sinful deed and her culpability -- <u>why have you done it</u>?" (the final rhetorical question conveys the LORD's emphatic negative evaluation of her action; i.e. you don't realize the consequences of what you have done).

Often the linguistic form of an utterance must be altered quite drastically in order to preserve its intentional implication as well as its propositional content in translation, for example, in the Parable of the Two Sons:

...and he answered, "I go, sir,"... (Mt 21:30)

A literal transfer of this into Chewa would imply that the son is going somewhere else (other than to the field) and is talking to someone other than his father. The idiomatic equivalent is:

"<u>Chabwino, abambo</u>." -- "Alright, father."

At times even the propositional content must be modified somewhat in order to retain the essential illocutionary force, e.g.

> (Peter) began to invoke a curse on himself and to swear, "I do not know the man." (Mt 26:74)

The words here quoted are problematic in that they make a simple assertion; no curse is suggested at all. Thus a literal transla= tion can even sound contradictory since the intention referred to in the quote margin is not realized in the subsequent words of direct speech. This apparent contradiction may be resolved in two ways, e.g. GNB:

> Then Peter said, "<u>I swear</u> that I am telling the truth!"

Here the intention is incorporated into the quotation itself as a performative verb, i.e. "I swear". This constitutes a speech act which is "performed" by literally pronouncing that this is what is being done. Another, more dynamic possibility is exemplified in the Chewa (draft):

> Peter began to swear and say, "<u>By God</u>, this person whom you are referring to, I don't know him at all!"

In this rendering, which sounds more natural to the listener (though anachronistic in the English translation), we have the inclusion of a traditional RL curse formula within the speech act itself, i.e. <u>Mulungudi</u> lit. 'God indeed!' (often accompanied by the gesture of pointing upward with the right hand). The implica= tion, which gives the words a special power and authority, is that God himself will punish the speaker if he is not telling the truth. The original intention has been made explicit by this alteration of the form, and perhaps also the content, of the message. The communicative "meaning", however, remains the same.

Rather more controversial are those situations which require the addition of an entire proposition in the RL in order to faithfully convey the full intentional force of the original. Consider the following example:

> Then the foremen of the people of Israel came and cried
> to Pharaoh, "Why do you deal thus with your servants?"
> (Ex 5:15)

In the Chewa cultural context, no subject, let alone a foreigner, would ever address the chief in this way. The utterance would be regarded as an intolerable insult in spite of the trying cir= cumstances that provoked it. Rather, the Israelites would have to preface their complaint as follows in order to receive any kind of hearing at all (and to avoid the criminal charge of malediction):

> "Pepani amfumu, timati tingodziwako chabe, kaya chifukwa
> chiani..."

> "Sorry O Chief, we say we were just wondering merely, we
> don't know why..."

Six ameliorative devices plus an honorific vocative are required to "soften" their plea prior to making it. Now this may sound a bit overdone in English, but in terms of traditional Chewa social culture such a self-depreciating preface would be an essential part of the foremen's request as a whole. It is necessary in order to gain a hearing in the first place and also to avoid giving a wrong impression of the character and status of the speakers as well as the genuineness of what they had to say. This is an extreme example, perhaps, but it does indicate the extent to which the original form/meaning may have to be modified so as to achieve functional equivalence. Whether or not this degree of restructuring would be allowed in a translation depends very much on the nature of the version envisioned for the receptor consti= tuency and its guiding principles (see ch. 7).

These passages exemplify the need for carefully considering the sociolinguistic implications of the covariation of content and intention in speech. One thing is clear: a translation which is preoccupied with the expression of the former at the expense of the latter in a given situational context will often fail to reproduce the full functional significance of direct discourse in the RL text.

9.   <u>STATE OF MIND</u>: This dimension concerns the psychological state of the source with regard to both the message that he is encoding and also those with whom he is commu= nicating. This variable has two aspects: attitudinal stance and emotional condition. Despite their obvious interaction in verbal discourse, the two will be discussed separately in order to better illustrate the contribution that each factor makes to the produc= tion of speech.

a)   <u>Attitudes</u>: A speaker generally reveals to a greater or les= ser extent his personal involvement in the words that he utters, and this self-participation is reflected at all levels of linguistic organization: lexico-semantic, grammatical, and phonological. He does not mechanically generate sentences in response to some external or internal ("innate") stimulus. Rather, he develops a particular communication strategy, formulating his speech acts in planned succession according to the specific pur= pose(s) that he wishes to accomplish through them in the situation of use. In the process he also reveals certain opinions, biases, feelings, values, etc. with regard to what he actually does say or think (the emotive component of speech will be discussed below). The functional (intention-effect) aspect of his involvement, as we have seen, is conveyed mainly by his choice of vocabulary, its syntactic arrangement in the utterance, and the particular sen= tence type he selects to encode the information, i.e. statement, question, or command. The speaker's attitude, on the other hand, is principally conveyed by a variety of modal expressions (e.g. to be sure, if i am not mistaken, beyond the shadow of a doubt, it would seem, etc.), particles, and functional auxiliaries, both separable (e.g. possibly, indeed, perhaps, surely, must, might, should, ought, etc. in English) as well as inseparable (e.g. cer= tain verbal prefixes and suffixes in a Bantu language). These verbal markers in conjunction with the general content and context serve to indicate his personal evaluation or impression of what he has to say -- its certainty, uncertainty, validity, potentiality, conditionality, desirability, or necessity. Intonational modifi= cation also plays an important part in the "subjectivization" of speech. This psychological "mood" thus pertains to the underlying point of view that colors every act of communication.

It is helpful to distinguish between (at least) two levels of attitude: i- those which lie close to one's psychological "sur= face", so to speak, and shift according to the constantly changing situations and circumstances of life, such as the ones mentioned above (certainty-uncertainty, desire-aversion, etc.); and ii- those of a much more stable and permanent nature which are more deeply rooted within one's personality -- the ones which reflect a person's value system, stem from a hierarchy of felt needs (food, protection, companionship, physical activity, mental stimulation, aesthetic release, spiritual experience, etc.), constitute a part of his world view and ideology, and reveal his fundamental cultu= rally-determined presuppositions. Among the latter would be included positions adopted (consciously or subconsciously) with regard to such universal human characteristics and experiences as: greed vs. generosity, dominance vs. subservience, suspicion vs. credulity, optimism vs. pessimism, conservatism vs. liberalism, and so on. These underlying ideologically-based attitudes are revealed in one's overall pattern of behavior, which encompasses also one's characteristic manner of speaking. This central modal stance or perspective on life in turn controls a person's more superficial and transitory opinions and influences also his current behavior, including how a speaker evaluates a particular speech situation and develops a strategy of verbal expression to fit the context. The latter is of special concern to us in this section, but it is necessary to recognize the deeper system of belief from which it originates, for this conceptual-attitudinal base will naturally vary from culture to culture.

It is the responsibility of the translator, then, to take note of the various attitudinal devices employed in the SL text, such as modal verbs (e.g. doubt, desire, wish) and auxiliaries (e.g. can, could, should, would), verbal mood markers (e.g. for indicative,

subjunctive, desiderative, optative), rhetorical questions, con=
ditional constructions, and the particles referred to above. This
must be done along with a thorough study of the context of use,
for most modal forms have a wide range of application depending on
the particular extralinguistic situation. Then, once a specific
attitude has been identified, whether this is explicitly marked in
the SL text or not, the search for a suitable RL equivalent
begins.

Various degrees of correspondence are possible. It may be almost
complete, as in the case of the Hebrew dubitative particle _ulay_
'perhaps' and the Chewa correspondent _kapena_ (or the Tonga
ambweni), e.g.

> Sarai said to Abram, "...it _may be_ that I shall obtain
> children by her." (Gn 16:12)

It is more often the case, however, that any correspondence in
word class is only partial at best. Take the Chewa hypothetical
particle _ngati_: it may function like the Greek _ei_ to indicate a
potential condition, e.g.

> "_If_ you continue in my word, you are truly my
> disciples..." (Jn 8:31)

But _ngati_ can (or should) not be employed like _ei_ to introduce a
real condition, e.g.

> "_If_ you are the Christ (i.e. if it is true that you
> are!), tell us plainly." (Jn 10:24)

This passage is another interesting case where the linguistic form
is partially contradicted by the situational context. The speakers
of these words, Jewish skeptics, demonstrated both by their
actions (10:31) and also in their subsequent speech (10:33, cf.
also v.20) that they did _not_ accept Jesus as the Christ (Messiah).
Their attitude was manifestly one of denial. Then why did they
use a real condition here, giving Christ the benefit of the doubt,
at least linguistically? We may have a case of sarcasm, or more
probably this was a strategic choice, i.e. feigning to be
believers, so as not to prejudge his reply, they employed this

request simply as a test to see if he would say something worthy
of condemnation (cf. 7:26-27, 41-42, 8:6).

The most frequently encountered situation is where there is no
formal correspondence between the SL and RL at all. Nevertheless,
it is possible to remain equivalent on the functional-attitudinal
level through the use of different, yet contextually appropriate
forms. To express contrary-to-fact conditions, for instance, the
basic Greek conjunction _ei_ becomes a verbal prefix in Chewa, i.e.
-_kada_-. e.g.

> Martha said to Jesus, "Lord, _if_ you _had been_ here, my
> brother _would_ not _have_ died." (Jn 11:21)

Finally, one can also find passages where either the SL or the RL
(usually the latter) makes a distinction in attitude which the
other language does not formally indicate, i.e. the psychological
stance is left implicit. In Tonga, for example, a reason proposi=
tion, if prominent by virtue of speaker certainty, is frequently
transformed into a rhetorical question introduced by the marker
Tee (kayi)... 'Isn't it true that...' Since the original does
not distinguish this particular attitudinal perspective, the
translator must be able to deduce it from signals in the situa=
tional context. Thus, in place of the RSV's "... for the LORD is
not among you" (Nu 14:42), the Tonga reads:

> "_Isn't it true that_ the LORD is no longer with you
> anymore?"

In this passage a more emphatic form is necessary in order to give
the causal relationship a prominence which corresponds to that of
the original (note its reiteration at the end of v.43). Similar=
ly, in Chewa a speaker has the option of superimposing an extra
element of obligation to requests, commands, recommendations, etc.
by means of the verbal prefix -_zi_-. This appears especially in
contexts where a repeated or habitual action is being referred to
(thus it partially corresponds to the Greek distinction between a
present and aorist imperative), e.g.

> "Pray (mu_zi_ti) like this..." (Mt 6:9)

In a subtle interpretive insight into the question of attitude and how it influences one's speech, the Chewa translators rectified what they sensed to be a deficiency in a literal rendering of the angel's announcement of Christ's resurrection to the women who came to the tomb:

> And he said to them, "Do not be amazed; you seek Jesus of Nazareth, who was crucified. He is risen, he is not here; see the place where they laid him." (Mk 16:6)

Keying on the initial imperative, the Chewa shapes the text to continue to reflect an attitude of complete certainty, which was intended to allay the women's potential doubt, suspicion and fear over what had happened. The angel is not a neutral observer -- a disinterested bystander -- and he ought not sound that way. The appropriate tone is conveyed very simply lexically by a short, utterance-final attitudinal particle, and then grammatically by a rhetorical question indicating assurance, as shown in the back translation below:

> But the young man told them, "Do not worry. You've come seeking Jesus of Nazareth, the one whom they crucified, <u>isn't that right (ati)</u>. He has arisen, he's not (in) here. <u>Have a look, wasn't it right here where they placed him?"</u>

The boundary between attitude and emotion (see below) is not always clearly defined in formal terms. Fortunately, the transla=tor, in a Bantu language at least, normally does not have to make this distinction. However, it is useful at times to observe the specific psychological/emotive factors involved in the original so that a more precise reproduction may be effected in the RL text. The following passage, for instance, expresses a mixture of several attitudinal and emotive constituents (i.e. surprise, most likely combined with doubt, skepticism and possibly even scorn. These overtones converge to heighten the impact of the query's content, the very first words that Pilate apparently addressed to Jesus:

> ...and the governor asked him, "Are <u>you</u> (the pronoun is emphatically fronted in the original) the King of the Jews?"

Some kind of marking of the modality may be necessary in the RL (which was overlooked in the RSV), or the question might be under= stood as a real one (as it is in both the Chewa and Tonga old translations, i.e. Pilate was really desirous of finding out who Jesus is). The new Chewa version, for example, utilizes a stressed initial separable pronoun (a depreciatory, familiar/ singular form, as in the Greek) along with a back-shifted question particle (kodi) to accurately convey Pilate's puzzled and probably cynical point of view with respect to the content of his inquiry, i.e. how could this pitiable person be a genuine "king"; and why was it that the "Jews" themselves wanted him dead? (notice that in their accusations against Christ, the Jewish leaders never claimed him as their king, cp. Lk 23:2):

> "Iwe ndiwe mfumu ya Ayuda kooodi (with characteristic intonation)?"
> "So you, you are the king of the Jews, huh?"

Also related to attitude is the expression of tactical overlays such as degrees of politeness, sincerity, authority, integrity, and intensity. When, for example, Judas come up to Jesus in the Garden saying, "Hail, Master" (Mt 26:49 -- better rendered: "Greetings, Teacher"), we immediately sense a sham sincerity there which contradicts everything else in the interpersonal and situa= tional contexts. It is perhaps for this reason, to draw attention to the incongruity of these words, that GNB translates: "Peace be with you, Teacher" (emphasis mine). Factors of politeness and authority are closely related to the sociological and interperso= nal dimensions discussed earlier, while increased intensity is usually connected with the expression of one's emotions (the emo= tive variable below). It may be useful, however, to differentiate between emotive intensity and the stress given to certain elements of content. The latter we might term "emphasis", and this feature, too, is part of what we have been referring to as a speaker's attitude over against his message. He continually monitors the discourse in order to select those aspects of meaning to which he wants to give special prominence in relation to both the surround= ing text and the reaction that he anticipates from his audience.

Normally it is not too difficult to duplicate the effects of
increased intensity in the RL text, provided that the translator
realizes that linguistic forms entirely different from those found
in the SL may be required, as a comparison of the two passages
below indicates. The first, the RSV, closely imitates the form of
the original Greek:

> "If then the light in you is darkness, how great is the
> darkness!" (Mt 6:23)

The second is a back-translation from Chewa into English:

> "Now if that which ought to enlighten you has turned
> into darkness, that darkness is indeed black-black-
> black!"

In the Chewa, a reduplicated ideophone (bbi-bbi-bbi!) is introduc=
ed to emphasize the contrast which lies at the heart of this com=
parison.

Another important subjective attitude which may be superimposed
upon speech is irony (and its more caustic cousin, sarcasm).
Irony, often criticism disguised as a compliment, is a device that
is used frequently by the Apostle Paul in his letters and from
time to time also by Christ in his discourses, especially with
reference to the Pharisees, e.g.

> "You have a fine way of rejecting the commandment of
> God, in order to keep your tradition!" (Mk 7:9)

Irony is difficult to translate because its effectiveness so often
depends on subtle situational cues coupled with the use of
language-specific lexical items and a marked intonational pattern.
A literal rendering often turns out to convey the opposite meaning
intended (in the old Chewa Bible, for instance, Christ sounds as
if he is praising the Pharisees here!). But other rhetorical de=
vices are usually available in the RL to transmit the desired
critical attitude forcefully, yet also in the socially-appropriate
oblique way. The new Chewa translation of Mark 7:9 utilizes
figurative language to do this:

"Your path is clever to make a detour around the
commandments of God in order to follow along after your
own customs!"

b) Emotions: The emotive element in speech, which includes what
is often termed "connotation", incorporates not only
the verbalization of one's attitudes and opinions regarding what
is being said, but it encompasses also the expression of a
speaker's concurrent feelings and aesthetic reactions. A persons's
attitudes, which are dependent upon his underlying world view and
value system, are relatively predictable since they are based on a
more or less consistent way of thinking and perception. One's
emotions, on the other hand, are more unstable and unpredictable
since they so often depend on external circumstances which lie
beyond the control of the individual. A particularly strong emo=
tion, such as grief over the death of a loved one, may modify
one's attitude, e.g. from a sense of security to one of insecu=
rity, but usually the shift is temporary, and with the passing of
time one returns to "normal".

Human emotions may be conveyed by a diversity of verbal techniques
such as rhetorical questions, word order modifications, exclama=
tions, intensifiers, oaths, vocatives, intonation, and related
paralinguistic accompaniments. The translator's problem is not
usually one of finding suitable emotive equivalents in his
language -- he has plenty of those to draw upon -- but rather it
lies in determining exactly when to employ them. There is little
difficulty when the speaker's feelings are overtly indicated in
some way in the SL text, e.g.

        ...and in all the streets they shall say, "Alas! alas!"
        (Am 5:16)

A local dynamic equivalent is normally readily available for ex=
clamations such as these, e.g. Maawe! (exclamation) in Tonga or
Kalanga ife! (expressive oath = "may we be punished") in Chewa.
But when there is no explicit emotive signal(s) in the SL text,
then the translator must make a decision: should he follow the
form, and to some extent also the content, of the original and

simply disregard the emotive impact which the extra-linguistic
sociocultural context favors -- or should his intention to commu=
nicate the latter to the reader override the former concerns, as
long as this can be done in a succinct and unobtrusive way. One
method would involve the introduction of figures of speech, a more
dynamic manner of expression, in place of non-figurative language,
e.g.

> "O Lord God, forgive, I beseech thee!" (Am 7:2)

In Chewa, this highly expressive (i.e. anguish, pity-evoking) plea
of intercession would turn out this way, following the pattern of
traditional prayers to the deity:

> "<u>Inu</u> (a), Chauta Mulungu, akhululukireni <u>ana anu</u>
> (b), <u>ndapota nanu</u> (c)!"

> "<u>You</u> (a), Chauta God, forgive them <u>your children</u>
> (b), <u>I beg of you</u> (c)!"

This utterance features (a) an emphatic initial vocative pronoun
of respect to draw the addressee's attention to the words that
follow; (b) a specification of the objects of God's forgiveness
as his "children" (since he created them); and (c) a figurative
form of request, lit. 'I have twisted (like a string is made, i.e.
in petition) with you.'

In the Chewa language, exclamations represent one of the most
effective ways of indicating slices of the diverse array of senti=
ments that permeate the dialogue portions of Scripture. Normally,
these occur right at the beginning of an utterance, e.g.

> And (Jacob) was afraid and said, "How awesome is this
> place!" (Gn 28:17)

In idiomatic Chewa this quotation would be rendered:

> "<u>Ih-ih!</u> pano mpoopsa!"

> "Ih-ih! at this spot it's terrifying!"

These short, emotion-laden words can also perform a larger rheto=
rical function in the text, e.g.

> And Sarah said, "God has made laughter for me; everyone
> who hears will laugh over me." (Gn 21:6)

Sarah's poetic expression of unbounded joy is conveyed this way in Chewa:

> Now Sarah said, "Hedee! this laughter of mine has come from God. Indeed (Ndithu), everyone who hears about this will laugh together with me!"

The initial exclamation sets the exultant tone for the words to come. This plus the intensifier that begins the second utterance emphasizes the thematic play on Isaac's name, i.e. 'he laughs' (cf. 21:5), which links the major speech act intentions: praise and prediction. Such foregrounding, which is absent from the RSV (and most other) texts, is also justified due to the artistic mode of expression in the original Hebrew (i.e. rhythmic balance, lexical parallelism, and key word placement: laughter/laugh at opposite ends of the utterance) and perhaps also to heighten the obvious allusion to the situational contrast present in 18:15.

There are occasions, on the other hand, where a minimum amount of feeling should be generated by the text. This is usually the case with euphemisms, which are the linguistic equivalent of disinfec= tant -- intended to remove all the possible unpleasantries and emotive irritants of speech, e.g.

> Ephron answered Abrahm, "...Bury your dead." (Gn 23:15)

The impassivity of the Hebrew is easily duplicated in Chewa:

> "...Ikani maliro anu."

> "...Place your funeral."

Notice that in both languages reference to the deceased is kept as general as possible; not even the place of burial (which is the topic of discussion) is mentioned. Thus a literal rendering of the GNB would be both inappropriate and impolite:

> "...Bury your wife in it."

The danger of employing emotive marking in a translation is the tendency to overdo it -- to "overcharge" the dialogue. Consider this passage:

But Hannah answered, "...Do not regard <u>your maidservant</u> as a <u>base woman</u>...(1 Sm 1:16)

Here is how the Living Bible (LB) colors Hannah's words:

"Please don't think that <u>I</u> am just <u>some drunken bum</u>!"

In addition to problems of reference (i.e. "bum" generally refers to a male person), LB has injected an emotive element, along with a level of colloquialism, which many would find unsuitable in this context, namely, a pious parishioner addressing a priest in the house of God. Similarly, in the following passage, LB de-euphe= mizes the more oblique expression of the original and therby distorts the emotive level of the utterance. First the RSV trans= lation is given, then LB:

(The Jewish leaders) answered him, "You were born in utter sin, and would you teach us?" (Jn 9:34)

"You <u>illegitimate bastard</u> you!" they shouted. "Are you trying to teach us?"

The underlined portion may indeed fit the context from a twentieth century Western perspective (though its informality could be ques= tioned), but this is not really what the Jewish leaders said -- or meant, nor is there any suggestion of "shouting" in the SL text. The connotative levels of the SL and RL do not match in this case; the translation has been over-done.

The emotive component is a crucial sociolinguistic factor in translation, and yet as we have seen, it is one which can be easily skewed out of line with the original if one gets carried away in his enthusiasm to have the biblical participants speak idiomatically. One control on such possible distortion is to limit the introduction of connotative elements to those which are formally signalled in the SL text or definitely implied in the situational or larger discourse context. Furthermore, when deal= ing with emotive implication, it is best to restrict any additions to those which are necessary in order to accurately convey the illocutionary and wider functional properties that are focal in the original. This principle is illustrated in the next example:

Joseph...spoke roughly to (his brothers), "Where do you come from?" he said. (Gn 42:7)

This is how the Chewa conveys the underlying sense of Joseph's question:

"<u>Anthu inu</u>, mulikuchokera kuti, <u>eh</u>?"

"<u>You people</u>, where are you coming from, <u>huh</u>?"

The addition of the initial vocative (with the vocative pronoun, <u>inu</u>, in post-nominal position to give a depreciatory tone) as well as the final exclamation is justified for two reasons: (a) from the SL perspective, the speech act is given explicit characteriza= tion in the quote margin (i.e. "spoke roughly"); (b) from the RL perspective, a literal transfer would most likely be understood as a simple request for information, a phatic-like expression typical of initial polite conversation between strangers.

Summary: the Interaction of Situational Variables

The preceding survey has shown that the nine sociolinguistic dimensions of speech usage may be of considerable relevance when one is translating the dialogue portions of Scripture. Although the different "variables", each of which contributes to a distinct "variety" of speaking, have been presented more or less indivi= dually, at a number of points in the discussion the mutual inter= action of these factors has been emphasized. The attempt to iso= late one from the other is useful only as a practical procedure to facilitate an analysis of the diversity and intricacy of verbal communication in society and to increase our awareness of what changes need to be made during the transfer of speech acts from one sociolinguistic context to another. The whole is, of course, more significant from a communications point of view than the sum of its parts. Nevertheless, a factored study of the whole enables one to get a better understanding of the contribution of each specific component as well as their integration into a meaning-ge= nerating complex during the process of message transmission.

In connection with the overlapping of these variables, it is important to call attention to a number of their principal inter= relationships, a feature which, as we have seen, makes it diffi= cult to extract and describe their individual contributions to the speech event. These connections are summarized in the figure below:

A. <u>MATRIX</u> ------------> B. <u>MESSAGE</u> --------------> C. <u>MIND</u>

1. Spatial-Temporal   4. Subject Matter   7. Implicit
   Setting   Information

   2. External Setting   5. Language Medium   8. Communication
                                                     Function

      3. Interpersonal   6. Discourse Types   9. State of
         Setting   & Genres   Mind

The sociolinguistic variables thus tend to converge to form bundles of situational influence upon the process of verbal com= munication. One possible way of grouping these nine dimensions is illustrated above. Accordingly, there are three sets of logical dependencies in which the initial member of each triad appears to involve a strategic decision or option that is somewhat more basic in the progression than the others. Of course, strict lines of demarcation cannot be drawn for a phenomenon as complex as speech (or the conceptual process itself), and yet there are some broad tendencies that are worthy of note. There is a general narrowing of focus -- scope, sphere of influence, degree of stability -- as one moves from (1) to (9), that is, from those variables which pertain primarily to the matrix, or setting, of the communication event through those attached to the message itself and finally to those that arise in the minds of the interlocutors. The matrix encloses the message and both circumscribe the situational factors associated with the mind. Further relationships among the diffe= rent constituents of this process may be briefly described as follows:

A.   Those relating primarily to the circumstances surrounding the speech event -- the <u>MATRIX</u>:

1.   SPATIAL-TEMPORAL SETTING: This factor involves the most general type of contextual in= fluence pertaining to the speaker's respective linguistic and environmental backgrounds. It is therefore static and fixed, a matter relating to the broader features of one's dialect.

2.   EXTERNAL SETTING: This dimension takes into consideration the everyday events which continually impinge upon people's lives and which, in turn, modify their ver= bal behavior. It is a dynamic factor, one that is ever in flux, and due to its impersonal nature and complexity, the results of external setting and circumstance upon the speech event cannot often be predicted with certainty.

3.   INTERPERSONAL SETTING: This aspect of the setting is established by the dyadic relations between source and receptor(s) within the static and dynamic back= ground (1 + 2) in which they are interacting via speech. The relationships involved may be based upon similarity, when one is linked to others of the same dialectal group (e.g. age, sex, class, status, etc.), or they may be based on various contrasts among those of different sociological groups, resulting in dis= tinctions in their respective speech styles. The interpersonal setting is circumscribed by the external setting, which is itself encompassed by the spatial-temporal setting.

B.   Those relating primarily to the verbal MESSAGE:

4.   SUBJECT MATTER: The content to be communicated generally precedes the choice of a channel, though it is also true that most kinds of content may be conveyed via any channel as long as the appropriate formal adjustments to the message have been made. The selection of a topic for discussion is to a great extent influenced by the particular setting in which the communication event is to take place.

5.   LANGUAGE MEDIUM: This factor concerns the choice of language as opposed to some other semiotic mode of

communication (e.g. music, mime) as well as the interaction of verbal and non-verbal methods of message transmission. It also deals with the alterations in form which are necessitated by a shift either in the channel of transmission, e.g. from sound to sight, or in the medium of the message, e.g. from television to the printed page (or vice versa).

6. <u>DISCOURSE TYPES & GENRES</u>: The variables of subject matter and medium within a given context normally operate to determine the generic form-type that is best suited to communicate the message to the intended audience.

C. Those relating primarily to the <u>MIND</u> of the speech partici= pants:

7. <u>IMPLICIT INFORMATION</u>: This dimension concerns what one does <u>not</u> have to mention during speech. It is based upon the speaker's knowledge (or estimation) of the pre= suppositions, assumptions, and personal background of his hearers. There is thus a focus on what the source and receptor(s) have in common, conceptually as well as experientially.

8. <u>COMMUNICATION FUNCTION</u>: This aspect refers to <u>why</u> one says what one does; it concerns the speaker's reason or purpose for saying something. There is a focus on the receptor, specifically, what the message is intended to accomplish and what it actually does achieve in relation to R during the communication process.

9. <u>STATE OF MIND</u>: This factor deals with <u>how</u> one presents the message. There is a focus on the source and the psychological (attitudinal-emotional) setting in which a par= ticular speech act (or sequence of speech acts = speech event) is realized, for this, too, affects the form of the message. The reasons for saying something in a particular way (9) are thus superimposed, as it were, upon both (7) and (8) and, indeed, the other sociolinguistic dimensions as well. This is undoubtedly the most unstable and unpredictable of them all, for one's frame of

mind varies constantly according to a host of factors -- personal
and impersonal, linguistic and extralinguistic, and so on.

We shall conclude this chapter with a concrete example which
illustrates how a number of these speech variables interact with
one another to shape a conversation. To abbreviate the discussion
somewhat, our consideration will be limited to those points which
affect a specific Bible translation, namely, Chewa and Tonga. The
passage under investigation is from Genesis 30:14-16:

> In the days of the wheat harvest Reuben went and found
> mandrakes in the field, and brought them to his mother
> Leah.
>
> Then Rachel said to Leah,
>
> (a) "Give me, I pray, some of your son's mandrakes."
>
> But she said to her,
>
> (b) "Is it a small matter that you have taken away my
>   husband?
>
> (c) Would you take away my son's mandrakes also?"
>
> Rachel said,
>
> (d) "Then he may lie with you tonight for your son's
>   mandrakes."
>
> When Jacob came from the field in the evening, Leah went
> out to meet him and said,
>
> (e) "You must come in to me, for I have hired you with
>   my son's mandrakes."
>
> So he lay with her that night.

In order to properly understand this conversation, one must be
familiar with the situational context, which includes in particu=
lar the information from Genesis 29:15 to the point where our text
begins. An essential part of this background information as it
applies to the immediate context is the meaning of "mandrakes". A
footnote in the GNB defines these as follows: "Plants which were
believed to produce fertility and were used as love charms."

Moving then to the dialogue itself, from the point of view of translation the primary consideration in utterance (a) is to adopt the appropriate register for co-wives to use with one another. The degree of formality should be casual, but certainly not intimate due to the brooding hostility that existed between these two women. In Chewa, this interpersonal factor is manifested primari= ly in a shortened verbal form, i.e. from <u>undipatseko</u> to <u>patseko</u> (i.e. a deletion of subject and object prefixes). The familiar second person singular form is employed together with the colloquial suffix <u>-ko</u>, which suggests, for politeness' sake, that only a portion of what has been requested need actually be given. An emphatic request introducer, <u>Chonde</u>, somewhat more intensive than "please", is used to strengthen Rachel's case. The dramatic situation, namely, one issuing from an intense rivalry between co-wives, prevents her (in Chewa) from mentioning the specific nature of the "charm" that she wants. That would be the verbal equivalent of the proverbial "waving a red flag". So she uses the generic term <u>mankhwala</u> = 'medicine, potion, etc.'; that was spe= cific enough in this context. Another situationally-related im= plication must be clarified, and that is tied up with the phrase "your son's mandrakes". A literal rendering of this implies that Reuben still has them in his possession. Chewa corrects this by saying: "the medicine which your son found (<u>-peza</u>) and gave to you" -- indeed, somewhat longer, but substantially more precise. An earlier draft which made explicit an incorrect assumption also had to be revised, i.e. "the medicine which your son found for (<u>-pezera</u>) you," which suggests that Reuben deliberately went out to look for mandrakes for his mother.

Leah's two rhetorical questions, (b) and (c), on one level func= tion as intensified accusations, i.e. You have <u>already</u> done that -- <u>now</u> you want to do this. But on a deeper intentional level, by implication perhaps, they act together to express a refusal of Rachel's request. In Tonga, this implicit refusal, which is phrased indirectly in this face-to-face situation, must be given due prominence:

> "<u>Now what do you want (i.e. or expect) from me</u>, isn't it true that you've robbed me of my husband?"

From the point of view of both speakers, the immediate focus of
attention may have been the fertility charm, but the primary bone
of contention was the husband they shared. Tonga reinforces this
underlying attitude with the assertive introductory clause, "isn't
it true that..." In Chewa the same idea is put somewhat diffe=
rently: "Are you still not satisfied that you have stolen away my
husband?" Notice that just the opposite preference seems to be
expressed by the GNB: "Now you are even trying to take away my
son's mandrakes." The topical and functional emphasis upon
"husband" is also indicated by selecting a verb that is stronger
in its negative connotation, i.e. "stolen away" vis à vis "taken
away" (a literal translation, as in the old Chewa Bible, implies
that Jacob is now lost to both women). When referring to the
current situation and the charm, on the other hand, proper verbal
decorum (i.e. to avoid an overt insult which could derail the
conversation) demands that Leah utilize an emotively more
"neutral" verb, "take away". The designative meaning is, of
course, the same, but situationally, as part of her conversational
strategy, there is a significant difference between the two
options. Leah, it should be pointed out, specifies the exact
nature of the "medicine" in question (in Chewa: mankhwala a
kondaine 'medicine of love-me') in order to make it clear to
Rachel that she knows exactly what she is up to and the value
which this charm holds for her. The expression thus strengthens
her bargaining position in preparation for the offer that she
knows Rachel will have to make.

In (d) Rachel reacts to Leah's implied refusal with an offer, or
more precisely, a payoff. It was a calculated move: Rachel knew
what she was giving up and considered that to be worth what she
was getting in return. In a Bantu, as well as the Hebrew, cultu=
ral setting, children are the purpose and foundation for a
marriage; in both childlessness is cause for drastic action --
divorce, concubinage, polygamy, etc. Thus, there is nothing in
the text or context that would suggest that Rachel made her deal
"sadly" (LB).

In most, if not all, Bantu languages the logical order of the original: consequence -- condition, must be reversed in order to conform to the expected order of events. Here again the topic of conversation, the interlocutors, and the dramatic situation all interact to modify the manner in which the proposition is stated. There is also a presupposition that motivates Rachel's expressed position of authority in the matter, namely, she controls the actions of Jacob. In Tonga, like Chewa, reference to the fertili= ty charm must be made indirectly since the two women are in direct conversation on the topic of their shared husband:

"<u>Alright</u>, if you will give me <u>the fruit of your son</u>..."

"Fruit" is a generic term denoting some type of natural produce (in preference to <u>musamu waluzyalo</u> = 'tree/potion for childbear= ing'). The initial "Alright" is often found in an argument or a debate when one speaker concedes a point raised or challenged by another; here Rachel grants Leah's refusal to part with her charm for nothing.

Reference to sexual intercourse is normally veiled by some sort of euphemism or another, with variations possible depending on who is speaking to whom and under what circumstances (the most explicit form of expression would be to a prostitute, e.g. Gn 38:16). A literal reproduction of the Hebrew, as done in the old Chewa and Tonga Bibles, sounds rather vulgar in this context. Thus Chewa goes with: "he will stay with you," while Tonga employs a speci= fic technical term that denotes the action whereby a polygamist spends the night with one or another of his wives: "...my husband will <u>turn in with</u> you tonight." Notice that as a reflection of Rachel's dominant position in the bargaining over Jacob, she refers to him (in Tonga) as "my husband", an expression which only the favored wife employs. She, or any wife, would not mention his personal name (cf. GNB) in public, least of all to a fellow-wife -- unless she had reason for insulting him!

The narrator chooses to omit what might seem to be the climax of the entire conversation, namely, Leah's agreement finalizing the bargain. However, what is important from his perspective has already been said, and that is a verbalization, albeit socially restrained in euphemisms, of the bitter rivalry between Jacob's two wives. Leah's agreement, then, is simply presupposed in speech act (e). As in (d), mention of the sexual act must be kept appropriate to the setting. In the case of a wife addressing her husband, the language becomes more intimate. Both Chewa and Tonga have: "Today you must sleep at my place." An additional situa= tional factor in Tonga is the precise time: "in the evening".

The result is given before the reason in both languages (after the Hebrew), because this is the focal proposition -- the end, and not the means. In each case, however, the reason cannot be announced as boldly as in the original. That would be too crass and unbe= coming in this interpersonal setting. Thus the Tonga employs a rhetorical question to soften Leah's words: "Isn't it true that (implying: how can Jacob refuse?) I've hired you with the fruit of my son" (the latter being the same euphemism that was discussed under (d)). The Chewa avoids all overt reference to Jacob and simply states: "...because I have already paid for the medicine that my son found for me." A great deal is implicit here, as in the original, and we can only assume that Jacob was fully aware of what was going on. The literal translation of the old Chewa Bible twists the meaning to read: "...because I've paid for the medi= cine of my son on your behalf" -- as if Jacob himself needed it!

The result, or perlocution, of Leah's demand (not a request) is explicitly noted at the close of this minor narrative unit because the later outcome of this event is significant: Leah gets pregnant again and bears another son (v. 17). It is almost ironic that all of Rachel's dealings profit her nothing: Leah is the one who continues to have children -- as a blessing of God.

A translator (or any exegete for that matter) dare never allow the apparent simplicity of the narrative surface blind him to the many intricate sociolinguistic forces that are operating on a deeper level of communication to structure the ultimate form of the message being transmitted. The preceding analysis has also demonstrated the importance of the cultural component in producing a dynamic equivalent translation of direct speech acts. This is a subject that we will focus on at greater length in Chapter 6. We now begin a study of how these same situational factors may be applied to the external level of communication to assist in the establishment of a programme for transmitting the Word of God meaningfully in a new sociocultural and linguistic setting.

CHAPTER   4

Contexts of Literary Communication

Since it involves at least two distinct events of literary-crea=
tion, the context of communication as it relates to Bible transla=
tion is complex and can therefore be reduced to separate compo=
nents. This context has two primary settings: the original
(biblical) and the translation setting; each of these has at
least two levels: the external as distinct from the internal
level. These different aspects of context are described and
illustrated below.

The Original Setting

Any valid exegetical study of the Scriptures must begin with an
investigation of the original setting which contextualized the
production of the book under consideration. This setting may
itself be complex, as in cases where a single book consists of a
number of distinct literary creations (e.g. Psalms, Proverbs), or
where the message, or its various constituents, originated in oral
form and perhaps remained in an oral religious tradition for a
number of years before finally being compiled, perhaps edited, and
put into written form (e.g. Hosea, Joel, the gospels). But even
in instances where the communication event is relatively straight=
forward, as in a New Testament epistle, the analyst may still face
some significant difficulties in interpretation due to the fact
that so little is known about the situational context, both perso=
nal and impersonal, out of which the message arose (e.g. Gala=
tians, Hebrews, Jude). It is useful to distinguish as a minimum
two levels of setting.

a)   The Internal Level:

As was mentioned, the "original" setting of communication refers
to the context and circumstances surrounding the initial creative
event (or series of events) which gave rise to the books of Scrip=

ture. The "internal" level of the original setting then pertains
to the different factors that apply to the individual speech
events found in the Bible -- factors such as the nine sociolin=
guistic variables which were considered in the preceding chapter.
In the first instance, we are dealing with the inclusion of a
single participant's speech within that of the author. However,
within this first internal setting there may be additional levels
of embedding, as when one narrative participant, for example,
quotes another, e.g.

> "...And the rich man said, 'Then I beg you, father, to
> send Lazarus to my father's house, for I have five
> brothers, so that he may warn them, lest they also come
> into this place of torment'..." (Lk 16:27-28).

Here we have four strata (^{o}) of embedding:

1° -- Luke: NARRATES that...

$\quad$ 2° -- Christ: NARRATES that...

$\quad\quad$ 3° -- Rich Man: PLEADS that...

$\quad\quad\quad$ 4° -- Lazarus: WARNS that...

The inclusion of direct speech ends at level three. Level four is
reported as indirect discourse (possibly due to its hypothetical
nature), but it is not too difficult to posit what might have been
said in direct speech, e.g.

> "Repent (and care for the poor -- conjectural),
> lest you, too, go to the place of torment!"

The important thing to note in cases like this is that theoreti=
cally every such stratum upon the ladder of quote inclusion has
its own distinct complement of sociolinguistic properties which
may or may not coincide with those of another level. The goal of
the translator is to accurately reflect in his text those situa=
tional differences which have formal correlates in the RL. If
anywhere, there is likely to be a stylistic difference (e.g. in
the degree of colloquialism allowed) between the 1° level and the
rest, in particular, those secondary strata that are encoded in
the form of direct speech.

When the depth of quote inclusion becomes too great or involved,
the reader/listener may well experience difficulty in decoding the

message. In such cases it is necessary to uncomplicate things through the introduction of indirect discourse, which removes some of the levels. The following passage illustrates three strata of quotation (Jr 21:3-4):

Then Jeremiah said to them:
(a) "Thus you shall say to Zedekiah,
(b) 'Thus says the LORD, the God of Israel:
(c) "Behold, I will turn back the weapons of war..."'"

There are different ways of simplifying the embedding of this passage; here are two of the possibilities:

Then the LORD spoke to me and I told the men who had been sent to me to tell Zedekiah that the LORD, the God of Israel, had said,

"Zedekiah, I am going to defeat your army..." (GNB)

In this version, the top two levels of quotation have been merged and transformed into indirect speech. This procedure simplifies the quotation structure, but it results in a rather complex introductory sentence, i.e. several dependent clauses, pluperfect verbs, and alternating subject shifts. The second solution treats the embeddings less drastically (a Chewa back-translation):

Then Jeremiah said to those men,

"Go tell Zedekiah that this is what the LORD, the God of Israel, says to him,

'Listen, I am going to blunt the weapons of war...'

Observe that it is possible to remove any one of the different levels of quotation present (here (b) is absorbed into (a)). But normally in cases like this the translator will want to give pro= minence to the central words of Yahweh (i.e. the inner quote) by retaining them in direct discourse, especially when these comprise the bulk of the text recorded.

It is usual to find the speech of a biblical character inlcuded within that of the narrator/author. Occasionally, however, the reverse is true: the narrator will insert his words into those of one of the personages quoted, e.g.

> "If a prophet...says, 'Let us go after other gods, <u>which you have not known</u>, 'and let us serve them,' you shall not listen..."   (Dt 13:1-3)

The underlined portion is an aside, introduced by the speaker, Moses, into a hypothetical quotation which is part of his exhorta= tion, in this case, to the people of Israel. The insert is not as trivial as it may sound in English, for in Hebrew the verb 'to know' frequently means "to experience a personal relationship with", and that, with reference to Yahweh, is one of the central themes of Moses' long discourse (as it is set forth in Deutero= nomy). However, since a listener will most likely fail to dis= tinguish the two speakers as the text is read, many modern trans= lations transform the quote into indirect speech in order to pre= vent misunderstanding, e.g. GNB:

> "A prophet...may promise...in order to lead you to worship and serve gods that you have not worshipped before...do not pay attention to him..."

b)   The External Level

The external level of the original setting of biblical communica= tion pertains to those situational factors which relate to the original author(s) and his intended addressees via the text (the sum total of speech acts, whether oral or written) that he trans= mitted to them. This would include all of the distinct internal communication events that are embedded within it. As far as this SL setting is concerned, there is not often a great deal that can be said. The text itself (particularly) in the case of prophetic and epistolary literature) sometimes supplies a certain amount of background information pertaining to the general situation that gave rise to the message, who was being addressed and why. But specific details are usually hard to pin down, and that includes information regarding the source/author and the situation prevail= ing at the time of writing (speaking), viz. the total cultural environment as well as the dramatic circumstances in which he found himself when moved by Yahweh to write (or to speak).

Speech acts which constitute the internal level of communication are generally contextualized by the author himself since they are an integral part of his message. Furthermore, their perlocutio= nary effects are frequently specified as well, and these can serve as a check on any postulation of speaker intention. But all this information must be deduced with regard to the situational context of the message on the external level of communication. It is a task whose difficulty is compounded due to the lack of similar texts, contemporary with that of the original, which could have shed some light upon the personal and impersonal circumstances surrounding the initial composition of these documents (chroni= cles, songs, oracles, epistles, etc.).

The original situation is by no means beyond recovery, however. Traditional coupled with current studies in the fields of archeo= logy, linguistics, biblical history, comparative religion, and the classics continue to uncover new facts which help to delineate the context that enveloped and influenced the formation of Scripture, and these discoveries enable scholars to better understand the form, content and effect of its diverse array of messages. The following is but one example illustrating the application of these insights.

Hosea 6:1-3 has traditionally been interpreted as a model prayer of repentance on the part of Yahweh's errant people Israel:

> "Come, let us return to the LORD;
> for he has torn, that he may heal us;
> he has stricken, and he will bind us up.
>
> After two days he will revive us;
> on the third day he will raise us up,
> that we may live before him.
>
> Let us know, let us press on to know the LORD;
> his going forth is as sure as the dawn;
> he will come to us as the showers,
> as the spring rains that water the earth."

On the surface at least, these words certainly sound sincere and devout. And that is how most commentators have viewed them, i.e. as speaking about fallen Israel's imminent "revival, resurrection,

and restoration to the Divine favor and protection" (Pulpit Com=
mentary, vol. 13, Hosea, p.166). However, the larger discourse
structure of this book, which we cannot discuss here (see Wend=
land, 1982), as well as its situational setting provide strong
evidence for adopting the opposite position, viz. that this song
demonstrates "The People's Insincere Repentance" (GNB).

In the first place, that is the major theme of the entire message
of Hosea: the unfaithfulness of Israel as contrasted with the
longsuffering fidelity of Yahweh. Hosea's ministry constituted a
final call to repentance, but up until the time of delivering
these oracles (and beyond, as subsequent events showed), he had
met with little success. Israel's dramatic plea to "return" and
"know" the LORD was just so much pious propaganda, composed as a
matter of convenience in a shallow attempt to avert impending
disaster, which was now looming large on the Assyrian front.
Indeed, these were key religious terms in the oracles of God's
prophets, Amos in particular, but this rebellious people had
emptied them of all meaning. And this wasn't the first time that
such outrageous verbal hypocrisy had been uttered. In fact, it
characterized the superficial spiritual life of the people whom
Yahweh was continually condemming through his prophetic messengers
-- and now Hosea:

> They have broken my covenant, and transgressed my law.
> To me they cry, "My God, we Israel know thee."
> (Ho 8:1-2)

A closer look at the prayer in its sociocultural context reveals
the superficiality of Israel's current theological thinking. They
clearly acknowledge the fact of Yahweh's sovereignty and his right
to punish them, employing imagery that was typical of laments at
times of national crisis. Yahweh himself had pictured the rela=
tionship to his people in similar terms: "I kill and I make
alive; I wound and I heal" (Dt 32:39; cp. Ho 5:14, 13:7-8).
However, one vital element was missing, namely, the recognition of
guilt on the part of the people. There is no word of this, unless
it is to be taken as implicit in the exhortation to "return". But

this is not supported by the rest of the prayer. Even the Psalm=
ist who pleads for relief from those who maltreat him because of
his uprightness (Ps 38:19-20), first finds it necessary to confess
his own iniquity and unworthiness before Yahweh (Ps 38:18). By
way of contrast, in the prayer which acts as a counter to this one
(Ho 14:2-3), the confession of sin and expressions of repentance
are of central concern.

The reference to a resurrection and revival to come (6:2) do not
in this context give evidence of a valid hope -- of a genuine
spiritual attitude and a right relationship with Yahweh. Rather,
it manifests the presumptuous assumption that Yahweh is automati=
cally going to put things right again once the people go through
the appropriate rituals of worship. Thus, this passage does not
refer or even allude to a universal resurrection of the dead, as
some have proposed. It is simply a figurative expression that
points ahead to a material restoration of the nation to its former
position of wealth, power, and prestige. The words betray a
stimulus-response attitude toward religion: if we do this, God
must do that. Whether the idea of renovation is a corruption of
some genuine elements of Israel's religious faith or merely a
veiled allusion to contemporary Syrian myths describing a god's
resurrection is difficult to ascertain. In any case, it gives a
clear expression of Israel's insincere, unspiritual, and super=
ficial concept of their relationship to Yahweh. As such it again
contrasts with the prayer of chapter 14 where the people dedicate
themselves to a new attitude toward Yahweh and a way of life in
keeping with his will.

In their attempt to put themselves right with Yahweh, the people
intensify their efforts to experience ("know") him in some way
(v.3). The crass cause-effect concept is continued. But now it
is expressed in natural metaphors that reflect the worship of Baal
which prevailed in Israel's midst. As surely as the dawn breaks
each day and the rains return every year to enliven the land, so
Yahweh is bound to come to them again to provide material bles=
sings. The people don't pray for help, they simply assume it will
be there in answer to the performance of ritual. The historical

dimension of God's saving acts manifested among their fathers has been lost together with the spiritual meaning of his ancient cove= nant bond with Israel. Yahweh's sphere of activity has instead been reduced to something which differed little from that of the surrounding Canaanite deities who were concerned with nothing more than operating in nature to ensure the fertility of the land. The perlocutionary effect of this impious prayer is found in the words of Yahweh himself: "What shall I do with you?" (6:4). In the verses that follow (4-6), the LORD goes on to specify the reasons for his rejection of Israel.

Thus the interpretation of Hosea 6:1-3 depends to a great extent upon one's analysis of the situation that applied when the origi= nal event of communication occurred, that is, the setting, both textual and extratextual. The former cannot be properly under= stood without the latter -- which is true no matter which inter= pretation is preferred -- for the linguistic text derives its essential meaning, yes its very existence, from the extralinguis= tic context in which it was first realized.

The Translation Setting

Any translation is removed from the original communication event in at least three respects: in time, language, and culture (with all that the latter in its widest sense includes). This presents some serious barriers to the accurate transmission of the SL mes= sage. These may be overcome in part by a version which is based directly upon the original languages of Scripture (provided that the proper principles of translation are also followed). In many cases, however, translators have little if any competence in Hebrew and Greek, and this state of affairs necessitates a type of literary "embedding" where one translation must be derived from another. Most translations in Central Africa, for example, are based upon various English versions (the RSV and GNB in particu= lar), with occasional reference to the biblical languages effected through exegetical advisers and translation consultants. In such a situation, there is always the danger of serious sociocultural distortion if translators allow their decisions to be guided by

the situational (and even semantic) features which are associated
with the interposed (i.e. English, French, Spanish, Swahili, etc.)
language rather than those of the original. Observe the histori=
cal-cultural skewing that has already occurred in these passages
from the Living Bible:

> Now a <u>population explosion took place</u> upon the earth.
> (Gn 6:1)
>
> And the Lord said to me, "Write my answer <u>on a bill=
> board</u>, large and clear, so that everyone can read it at
> a glance..." (Hk 2:2)
>
> So he sent other servants to tell them, "Everything is
> ready and <u>the roast is in the oven</u>. Hurry!" (Mt 22:4)
>
> Someone may say, "I am a <u>Christian; I am on my way to
> heaven</u>..." (1 Jn 2:4)

These deviations may well be compounded through literalism if this
version is employed as a translation base text.

The diagram below portrays the various aspects of context that
must be taken into consideration during the process of transla=
tion:

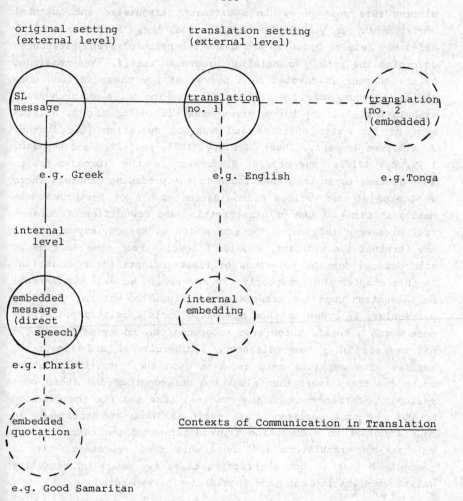

original setting
(external level)

translation setting
(external level)

SL
message

translation
no. 1

translation
no. 2
(embedded)

e.g. Greek

e.g. English

e.g.Tonga

internal
level

embedded
message
(direct
speech)

internal
embedding

e.g. Christ

embedded
quotation

Contexts of Communication in Translation

e.g. Good Samaritan

Situational Variables and the Contextual Setting of a Translation

The nine areas of sociolinguistic relevance described in the pre=
ceding chapter may be applied not only in analyzing the speech
events of Scripture, whether on the external or the internal
levels of communication, but as we have seen, they are also impor=
tant in determining the type of language to be used when trans=

mitting this message within a different linguistic and cultural
environment. In yet another application, these situational vari=
ables may help to organize and guide the principles and procedures
governing the actual translation programme itself. The remainder
of the chapter is devoted to a survey of how these various con=
textual factors may be utilized in drawing up a comprehensive
translation strategy for a given area, including the establish=
ment of its basis policies and mode of operation (for further
detail, see Wonderly, 1968; Smalley, 1975, pp.3-29; and Kopesec,
1979, pp. 42ff.) The present discussion is thus a broader treat=
ment of this topic than that found in the preceding chapter. There
we looked at the various communication events of Scripture pri=
marily in terms of the original setting and how different contex=
tual pressures influenced the production of speech, especially on
the internal (participant, embedded) level. From time to time we
also pointed out the relevance of these insights for translation.
In this chapter the perspective is reversed. We will concentrate
our attention upon the translation setting, the external level in
particular, in order to show how basic sociolinguistic principles
must guide a total, integrated programme for conveying the origi=
nal message in a very different socio-cultural and linguistic
matrix. The emphasis here is more upon the interrelationships
among the translators themselves and between them and their con=
stituency, rather than on the original text and its transmission
as was the case earlier. This shift is focus and treatment is
made in order to systematize a presentation of the concerns most
relevant to translators and those whom they represent. It is
recognized that in actual practice these two areas of sociolin=
guistic application can (and should) not be separated.

1. Spatial-Temporal: The time factor relates to both the type
of language used in a translation as well
as to the translation process itself. An obsolete or obsolescent
form of the language which may be spoken or understood only by the
elders as opposed to the dialect of the younger generation, is to
be avoided as a matter of policy. An exception might be where it
is necessary to distinguish biblical features of a specialized
nature, such as those pertaining to weights, measures, pottery-

making, animal husbandry, farming, and so on, by employing terms which the youth are no longer familiar with. The use of an out-of-date word (or set of words) in such cases, supplemented perhaps by a footnote, would generally be preferable to an importation, i.e. a transliteration of an English (or French, etc.) original (to be distinguished from a genuine loanword that is widely under= stood). Another instance where an older form of the RL code may be required involves the use of certain stereotyped genres and styles which may be marked by some ancient formulaic vocabulary (e.g. praise poetry, blessings, curses, proverbs, oaths).

On the other hand, modern colloquialisms, certain loanwords, and calques (loan translations) may be regarded as slang by the elder generation. Therefore, they should not be used in a translation either, for they may sound offensive, or at best incongruous, in the mouth of God or when uttered in his House. The matter of medium also needs to be considered in this connection since an acceptable written form of the language tends to be more tradi= tional and less innovative in structure and/or expression than the spoken word.

The temporal process of modernization affects not only vocabulary, but grammar as well. For example, according to the rules of con= cordial agreement (a prominent characteristic of Bantu languages), "Holy Spirit" (Mzimu Woyera) ought to manifest the properties of a Class 3 noun (along with rivers, trees, rocks and other natural phenomena), for that is where mzimu 'ancestral spirit', strictly speaking, belongs. In recent years, however, as a result of the flood of new words entering the language as borrowings from English, Portuguese, etc., the noun class/concordial system has tended to become more flexible, thus allowing a word like Mzimu Woyera to cross ancient morphological and syntactic boundaries and to enter an analogically more appropriate class, namely, that of personal beings (Class 1).

In many translation programmes, the decision-making process with respect to linguistic usage in the church is often under the control of the older clergy who tend to be rather conservative in such matters. This group may be old-fashioned regarding current speech conventions in the community, but since they are often in a position of casting the deciding vote on the language policy of a translation, their wishes, however arbitrary, will have to be respected. Therefore, an ideal general policy which states that "the use of language by persons twenty-five to thirty years of age has priority over the language of the older people or children" (Nida and Taber, 1969, p.32) may have to be modified in practice due to the exigencies of the local situation. However, whenever possible, translators and reviewers who represent the primary receptor age group for a modern common/popular version should be selected so that a contemporary form of the language might be favored. This temporal factor is often overlooked as positions on a translation team are filled by elderly retired pastors (to help supplement their pensions) or by experienced ecclesiastical poli= ticians, whose duty it is to defend and maintain time-honored denominational positions.

Time also affects the practical aspects of translation production. When this resource is insufficient or improperly utilized, the programme may suffer in a variety of ways, e.g. neglect of pre-project sociolinguistic surveys and the training of personnel; work of inferior quality (exegetically, stylistically, etc.); inadequate testing of the texts produced for feedback on accuracy, acceptability, and so forth. However, individual organizational factors vary so much in this regard that few, if any, useful guidelines of a general nature may be given.

Turning then to the spatial aspect of this dimension, we note that one of the first major decisions to be faced by a translation committee is the question of dialect: which of several (the number varies considerably according to the criteria observed) geographically-determined varieties of a given language ought to be chosen as the basis for a translation and the selection of a team of translators? Studies have shown that a mixed, or "union", version does not work out satisfactorily since the language so produced "belongs" to no one. Patchwork versions consisting of one book in dialect A, another book in dialect B, and so on (depending on who the translator happens to be) are rejected for the same reason. Formally, semantically and psychologically people just cannot identify completely with such Bibles. The choice of a principal dialect with which to reach the intended receptor group most effectively is rarely an easy task since so many often-competing factors have to be considered. The following is a listing of some of the more important ones:

a) topographical -- relative accessibility of the speech area, facility of internal transportation and communication;

b) positional -- centrality, the location of one dialect in rela= tion to another, to the cluster as a whole, and to the region's other major languages;

c) demographic -- current population distribution and movement patterns, in particular with respect to cer= tain key centres of growth;

d) economic -- the current rate of economic growth in the area along with accompanying infrastructures, services and the potential for further investment;

e) developmental -- degree of present and projected private and governmental investment for schools, clinics, extension services, etc.;

f) historical -- traditional cultural locus of prestige and in= fluence;

g) political -- amount of power exercised by a group in the circles of leadership on a regional or national level;

h) religious -- areas of the greatest ecclesiastical involvement from which the translators and reviewers are likely to come -- this may or may not coincide with the area of greatest potential for evangeli= zation;

i) attitudinal -- speakers' self-image and their respectability in the estimation of other speech communities that comprise the language;

j) formal -- the mutual intelligibility factor -- which dialect has the most linguistic features in common with the others in terms of grammar and lexis.

The cumulative result of the operation of these variables is the property of prestige -- which variety of the language do members of the total linguistic community either consciously or uncon= sciously desire to be able to speak (for whatever reason) and/or to read as their preferred form of literature (the two are not necessarily the same). A more basic question is this: which geo= graphical variety does the majority feel that God and his messen= gers would sound best speaking when communicating to them? Cer= tainly this would not be an issue to be resolved by drawing a name out of a hat.

2. External Setting: This factor as it relates to any transla= tion programme has two aspects: the per= sonal and the impersonal. The personal aspect pertains to the natural ability and supplementary training of the translation committee -- the translators in particular, but also to the various members of reviewing board. In the first place, if these individuals do not have the necessary competence and/or the proper attitude towards their own language or the activity of transla= tion, especially if a dynamic, functional equivalent is intended, then there is no way that the enterprise can succeed. Indeed, the quality of the product is very much dependent upon the capabili= ties of those who produce it and the efficiency of the method of production (i.e. the latter is one of the impersonal aspects of the total context). Natural aptitude is quickly dissipated, how=

ever, if it is not augmented and developed by thorough training in
the basic principles of meaningful and idiomatic translation -- in
both exegetical (SL focus) and also stylistic (RL focus) matters.
Such instruction needs to be given by experienced consultants,
ones who are at least acquainted with the original as well as the
receptor languages and cultures. The training is best carried out
as a short intensive course before the project begins, which
should then be supplemented at periodic intervals once the trans=
lation is underway. The literature of the Bible is so rich and
diverse, and the translation process so complex and demanding,
that without continual guidance and encouragement, the progress
may slow considerably or the quality of work may deteriorate once
initial enthusiasm wanes under the continual pressure of deadlines
and the magnitude of the task. Inevitably, its level of difficul=
ty, as perceived by the translators themselves, rises as they
become more experienced and better trained, for they then realize
more fully what the job entails. Thus self-correction, feedback
and revision become contextual factors of ever increasing impor=
tance.

The _impersonal_ aspect of the context includes a host of variables
which can affect the translation team for better or for worse
while they are carrying out their work, for example: the time
alloted for completing a project and the level of financial sup=
port it is granted; the relative freedom of translators to devote
themselves entirely to the project without outside interference
and interruptions; the physical circumstances under which the
translators work (whether they are together or separated, their
living conditions, and the adequacy of auxiliary facilities,
etc.); the quality of mechanical and technological equipment
(typewriter, duplicating/photocopy machines, a computer for word
processing, spelling/consistency checks, etc.); the number and
kind of scholarly helps available (translations, commentaries,
dictionaries, etc.); the encouragement, feedback and support
which translators receive from the Christian community with regard
to their work (this could also be considered a "personal" factor);
whether the current project is the first translation being prepar=
ed for a particular group or in a given language, or a second

(third, etc.) version; and so forth. It is possible for the pro=
gress of the entire translation programme to be hindered due to a
failure to take into consideration just one of these crucial
"limiting factors".

3. Interpersonal Setting: In addition to the appropriate tem=
poral and geographical varieties, or
dialects, a translation must also manifest the correct social
style for the constituency for which it is intended. As was
pointed out earlier, there is usually a number of distinct social
codes within a given speech community, which differ from one
another according to factors such as age, sex, and class. Social
class, in turn, may be differentiated along such lines as educa=
tion, economic standing, occupation, religion, mutual interest,
and so forth. To achieve acceptability with regard to this
situational variable requires translators (or reviewers) who are
at least familiar with, if not conversant in, the different socio=
logical codes that need representation in the RL text.

In a community with social dialects that are quite clearly defined
linguistically (e.g. in sentence length and complexity, lexical
choice, pronunciation, etc.), which usually correlates with a long
(written) literary tradition and a well-established system of for=
mal education, more than one translation is often necessary in
order to reach the diverse groups involved. Two types of transla=
tion are basic in this type of situation: a literary version,
which makes use of the full stylistic resources of the language,
and a "common-language" version, which is restricted more or less
to usage that is shared by both the so-called "upper" and "lower"
socio-educational/economic classes of the constituency.

In a speech setting where the social dialects are not as yet so
sharply defined, which frequently correlates with a relatively
short (written, as opposed to oral) literary history and period of
general formal education, one seeks to produce a "popular-lan=
guage version. This is a translation which is characterized by a
contemporary form of language that is shared by virtually all
speakers in the community, excluding both the jargon of specia=

lists (e.g. religious practitioners) and also the slang of the
teenage generation. Most current translation projects in Africa
are aiming to produce a popular-language version, but the situa=
tion is rapidly changing due to the steady rise in literacy and
under the influence of factors such as urbanization, ethnic
mixing, economic differentiation, and so forth. This will undoub=
tedly result in the need for several types of translation within a
given (major) language group in the near future.

Translations may also be undertaken with a focus upon special so=
cial segments within the speech community, such as new literates,
children, women, Muslims, etc. Such versions need to be modified
considerably in form in comparison with the standard translations.
Literacy versions, for example, are characterized by a graded
series of readings of increasing lexical and grammatical complexi=
ty; texts composed of selections consisting largely of narrative
portions, especially at the elementary levels; a style that is
natural, yet not always idiomatic to avoid rising above the
readers' ability to decode the material; and modifications in the
format (type size, layout, use of illustrations, etc.) to enhance
readability. The United Bible Societies are convinced that where
the sociolinguistic circumstances warrant, then one or more of
these linguistically more circumscribed types of translation are
required in order to ensure adequate comprehension of the message
within the particular target groups and, indeed, to achieve the
widest coverage in the speech community as a whole. This decision
has not gone unchallenged, however, and from time to time one
hears objections raised against such "special audience" transla=
tions, e.g. that they are "distortions" of the Word of God and
furthermore contribute to the fragmentation of the Christian com=
munity. Such opinions often stem from an overvaluation of the
form of the original text and a depreciation of the importance of
sociolinguistic factors in the process of communication.

The sociological dimension also becomes relevant when considering
the type of language to be used in an individual book of the
Bible, the New Testament in particular (since there exists a much
larger corpus of extrabiblical texts to use as a basis for stylis=

tic comparison). The NT books were written in various levels of Koine Greek -- under the influence of Semiticisms originating from both the Septuagint translation of the OT as well as the Aramaic spoken as a common language in Palestine. These stylistic levels range from the more literary types, such as Hebrews and 1 Peter, to the less polished compositions, e.g. Mark, 2 Peter, Revelation. To what extent can (or should) these divergences be duplicated formally in a translation? The answer to this question cannot be given with certainty until we are in a position to clarify the linguistic differences between authors according to function, as opposed to their being regarded as pure stylistic or idiolectal variation. The lexical and grammatical innovations may well be due to Semitic influence, but that does not necessarily account for their use in the text. It is likely that at least in some of the instances there is a functional motivation, whether linguistic (discourse structure) or extralinguistic (sociological, etc.), behind their appearance in a given context. Thus it is not simply a matter of reproducing the stylistic form of the original in a translation; more important from a communications perspective is to duplicate the principal function of those forms. And that would do no doubt demand a degree of literary sophistication and artistic, as well as exegetical, expertise which would be diffi= cult to find among members of the average Bible translation team.

The interpersonal dimension also involves the role relationships between speakers and the associated level of formality adopted, which in turn governs the type of language that they use when communicating with one another. It is the latter aspect which is of particular concern when considering the context of the transla= tion as a whole. A decision with regard to formality that is made on the external circuit of communication will naturally affect all of the speech events which are included within it on the internal level. Thus if a "formal" style has been decreed throughout a version in order to preserve the "dignified" nature of God's Word and the role relations implied thereby, i.e. a holy supreme being communicating with fallible and finite human beings, then it will be difficult, if not impossible, to achieve a natural style when transferring the direct discourse of Scripture into the RL. Many conversations, then, no matter how much casualness or familiarity is suggested by the situational setting and the role-relations of the speakers involved, will manifest a degree of formality that is foreign to the context of occurrence. Internal stylistic varia= tion and sociolinguistic fidelity to the interpersonal setting will have to be sacrificed in order to preserve an artificial, externally imposed principle that demands uniformity of register. Obviously, the subject matter of the discourse is also an impor= tant factor for consideration in this connection.

In cases where the degree of formality has not been arbitrarily pre-determined for the entire version, where faithfulness to the interpersonal dynamics of the ever-changing dramatic situation is desired, the translators will naturally face a far more difficult task. That will be to match registers between the SL and RL texts as part of the total transfer of "meaning". The original message will first have to be analyzed according to variations in the formality-informality scale of usage as influenced by shifts in the extralinguistic setting and the role-interaction of partici= pants, i.e. external level: author -- readers, internal level: speaker -- hearer(s). The appropriate linguistic markers for indicating these varied interpersonal associations must then be sought out in the RL -- in corresponding contexts if possible -- and finally utilized appropriately in the translation so as to preserve communicative equivalence. It will clearly enhance a project's chances for success in this endeavor if its translations personnel receive the intensive training necessary to enable them to recognize these distinctions and how to apply this knowledge to their task.

Both directly and indirectly, the interpersonal factor also effects the relations among the various members of the translation team, the translations consultant, the review committee, and even local Bible Society staff. A wide diversity of backgrounds are represented, ecclesiastical, and educational being probably the most pertinent, and this non-uniformity has the potential to adversely affect the role relationship which all have in common as brothers and sisters in the Lord (Mt 23:8). Where patterns of

dominance and denominational prejudice develop and surface any=
where along the line, progress on their joint project will cer=
tainly be curtailed if it does not cease entirely. But where a
genuine spirit of cooperation and mutual respect prevails, then
the resources of all can be pooled most efficiently and each can
perform his assigned role to achieve the common goal. Paul sums
this principle up in the clearest way possible in Romans 12:3-10.

4. <u>Language Medium</u>: The medium of message transmission is of
crucial importance in determining an
appropriate form for use in a translation. To a certain extent,
this will depend upon the particular literary tradition that has
developed in a language. Where this tradition is long and well-
established -- with rules, guidelines, standards, and so forth --
there is little problem in finding out what is the expected style
of writing and the appropriate level to use as a model. Primers
and even textbooks are probably available on the subject. How=
ever, for reasons mentioned earlier, this form of language may not
communicate effectively to the masses. A new, common-language
standard will have to be adopted -- provided that this is accept=
able to the constituency for whom the translation is intended.

If, on the other hand, the literary tradition is not extensive,
the problem lies rather in establishing an appropriate norm. This
will be based to a large extent upon the manner of speech employed
in effective oral communication, whether spontaneous or prepared
(including traditional models). But certain modifications will be
necessary due to the shift in medium (e.g. less redundancy pre=
ferred in print, but less ellipsis as well), the subject matter
and discourse type (e.g. fictional genres may be composed in a
different style than factive ones, such as history), the setting
of use as this affects the degree of formality (e.g. public read=
ing in church versus private devotions at home), and so on. Again
we see the effect of the mutual interaction of major sociolinguis=
tic factors in a given setting of communication. A translation
committee will have to try to predict the primary ways in which
they expect the translation to be received: whether via reading
the printed page or hearing the words spoken (including the medium

of records and cassettes where no speaker is physically present),
and whether accompanying helps will be used (depending on the
measure of literary competence on the part of the receptors), such
as cross references, footnotes, a glossary, section headings, in=
dividual book introductions, maps and illustrations (the last two
involve additional codes of communication distinct from the
verbal).

Once these matters have been agreed upon, the structure and style
of the translation can then be fixed accordingly. But this does
not guarantee the acceptability of the text, for audience prefe=
rence (e.g. for a distinct written form of the language) may con=
tradict the facts of message reception (i.e. primarily aurally
rather than visually). That is why much testing and trial publi=
cation needs to be carried out during the initial stages of a pro=
gramme -- to see whether some consistent patterns of preference
emerge.

The issue of which medium of transmission is most effective in
reaching the masses in Africa with the Scriptures has developed
into quite a debate. It is indeed a significant issue in that it
affects everyone -- source (ecclesiastical officialdom) and recep=
tor (laity) alike -- and upon the outcome depends the commitment
of vast sums of financial and human resources. The traditional
answer has supported the written medium and hence the initiation
of literacy training courses, building schools for the education
of an indigenous clergy, and the establishment of Christian pu=
blishing houses and literature programmes all over the continent.
This approach has been defended by Watkins in his book, Literacy,
Bible Reading, and Church Growth Through the Ages (1978). He con=
cludes:

> "We have seen that down through the centuries the church
> was strongest when the leadership was literate and when
> the church membership was also able to read God's word
> ...We believe that the power of the written Word is just
> as great or even greater than the spoken Word..." (pp.
> 159, 178)

The priority of literacy training and reading the Scriptures in

Christian communications strategy has in recent years come under attack by a number of writers. For example, in his book, _Oral Communication of the Scripture_, Herbert Klem argues:

> "Western education and literacy has generally threatened indigenous leadership structures inside and outside the church...It is (an African) view of the power of words about events to cause them to happen that brings strong aversion to even mentioning evil events. It is a magi= cal view of power in (spoken) words." (pp.39, 114)

Respective appeals to the communication setting in Bible times to support these two opposing positions are naturally based on con= flicting interpretations of what that situation actually was:

> "The Hebrews (i.e. Jews of Palestine at the time of Christ), with their life rooted in the Scriptures, were probably as literate as any people of the ancient world ...They were truly a 'people of the Book'...A large num= ber of people at the beginning of the Christian era were able to read and write." (Watkins, pp. 5, 11)

> ---

> "...at the time of Christ the combined efforts of all the educational institutions in Palestine had not succeeded in bringing more than five percent of the populace to the stage that we have defined as functional literacy in Hebrew...(a vast majority) of the population (was) not likely to be able to read or write a letter in any language." (Klem, pp. 67, 73)

The former position appears to be more accurate. To be sure, Hebrew was for the most part a language of the religious leaders and scholars. However, there is a considerable amount of evidence (e.g. from the papyri and indeed from the Bible itself, Acts 19:18-19) that during this period of history the literacy rate in Greek, if not Aramaic, was as high as it has ever been, although exact estimates are extremely hazardous to make due to the insuf= ficiency of reliable data.

As far as a literary strategy for the effective communication of the Scriptures is concerned, a combined approach is no doubt the safest solution, viz. oracy and oral/aural techniques being used as a _bridge_ to literacy and the printed word. Both authors cited above acknowledge this fact, though it is somewhat buried in their polemic. A great deal of first class sociolinguistic study is necessary, however, to evaluate each individual situation in order to determine what is <u>going</u> to work pragmatically speaking -- not simply what we would <u>like</u> to see work because of its theoretical advantages. A host of intricately interrelated factors are involved, and thus what might be the best plan from a communica= tions point of view may have to be rejected in view of the stark realities of what is actually possible. For example, comprehen= sion tests may show that information transmitted orally as opposed to the printed word is greater in both quantity (amount) and qua= lity (retention), but innovative oral communication programmes may contradict or counteract government-established literacy training schemes and official educational policies (whether such interfe= rence actually occurs or not is beside the point, it is government perception that matters). The oral presentation of texts may be well received, with more overt interest and enthusiasm than those in written form, but the needs in manpower, materials, and money required to establish an on-going oral-oriented approach may simply be beyond the available resources of most Christian agen= cies, even if they joined together in a cooperative venture.

This little excursus on the issue of oral versus written communi= cation of the Scriptures in Africa has been intended merely to highlight the need for an in-depth sociolinguistic profile of a speech community to be completed before the question of the medium and the mode (i.e. form as influenced by the medium) has been finalized.

5. <u>Subject Matter</u>:   The factor of subject matter, impinges upon the form of a translation as a whole in situations where the RL community deems it appropriate that content of a sacred or divine nature, the Holy Scripture to be specific (just as the oracles, rituals, prayers, etc. of traditio= nal religion), require a special dialect of the language in order for it to be communicated in an acceptable way. The preferred form of recording God's messages in the Old Testament, for ex= ample, was Hebrew poetry. Such a liturgical sub-dialect is fre= quently characterized by its opacity, that is, by linguistic items

which are no longer in common usage among the RL constituency at
large, for example, by archaic and highly technical terminology, a
restricted, often eccentric syntax, extreme elliptical patterns,
distinct poetic structures, and even rhythms.

Since an early "missionary" translation of the Bible normally
satisfies two of the principal criteria of such "sacred" language,
i.e. it speaks about God and it does so in a verbal form that is
esoteric at best, it becomes established as the standard by which
all subsequent translations are measured. In this case, its over=
all foreignness and low intelligibility turn out to be a point in
its favor, rather than undesirable features to be removed through
revision or retranslation. Thus, the old Chewa Bible, for exam=
ple, (like the KJV) continues to dominate the liturgical forms and
usage in church services despite the fact that speakers acknow=
ledge that it is much less understandable than the new "popular-
language" translation (its difficulty is due to a combination of
influences: it manifests an older form of the language, prepared
by non-mother tongue speakers, following a literal method of
translation). Outside the church building itself, however, the
new version is used almost exclusively whenever a choice is
available.

The relationship between divine topics and linguistic form does
not pertain only to versions which were prepared decades ago. For
many conservative Christians, the need for a translation whose
language reflects the supposed "other-wordliness" of the Scrip=
ture's subject matter is greater now than ever before in view of
the proliferation of Bibles on the market today, especially in
English. This development is often seen as an undesirable off=
shoot of the individualism of the age and the product of modern
consumer-oriented marketing techniques.

On the other hand, the criteria that would define the one
"reliable" version for all Christians are quite specific. Van
Bruggen cites seven characteristics which he hopes would counter=
act the "modernizing" and "adapting" tendencies of "dynamic equi=
valence" translations: "faithfulness to the form (of the origi=

nal), clarity, completeness, loyalty to the text, spirituality, authoritativeness, and ecclesiastical usage" (1978, p. 99). Seve= ral of these attributes will be considered later in the chapter on evaluating a translation (ch. 7). The final three relate in par= ticular to the topical dimension: "spirituality, authoritative= ness, and ecclesiastical usage". In short, what these are refer= ring to is the need for a distinctive terminology to convey con= cepts of a theological nature. It is not possible, so the think= ing goes, for a version to sound "spiritual, authoritative and/or ecclesiastical" if it is written in a "common" or "popular" language; there is then a contradiction between content (holy) and form (profane). It is sadly ironic that this genuine concern for preserving the content of God's Word through its original forms so often results in just the opposite, namely, ambiguity (where everyone is free to interpret as he wishes), obscurity (where the text becomes too difficult for the non-cleric to under= stand), and even complete unintelligibility in a translation. This consequence is inevitable whenever content is bound too closely to linguistic form, in total disregard of the context of meaningful communication.

It is essential to go beyond the basic search for RL equivalents to express the many diverse topics contained in the Scriptures. One must discover what uninitiated receptors really understand by the terms that they are reading/hearing. Which subjects make sense -- which do not, and why? Which RL terms do not transmit the intended content on account of conceptual as well as linguis= tic barriers? And what about non-designative, specifically conno= tative meaning: which topics (as distinct from the terms used to convey them) elicit positive reactions among receptors, which negative responses, and which have seemingly no emotive overtones? Do any unwanted cultural associations still cling to the vocabu= lary selected to convey key biblical ideas and values? When a fundamental concept like saving "grace" (charis, e.g. Ep 2:8) is transformed in the process of linguistic transfer from a benevo= lent attribute/activity of God to a charismatic quality in man, as has happened in Chewa (chisomo 'good fortune' or by metonymy the 'potion for producing luck'), then something is drastically wrong

-- the original message has been distorted, yes even denied. And no amount of teaching by the church is going to completely undo the damage that has been done as long as such terms continue to be used. A book could be written on this subject alone. Suffice it to say that a vital component of every translation programme is a comprehensive procedure for testing both the quantity and quality of comprehension (of topics as well as terms) on the part of those to whom we are attempting to communicate the Word of God.

6. Discourse Types & Genres: This formal dimension must be evaluated in the translation process just as any linguistic feature of the SL text, at whatever point in the structural hierarchy this may be. The same potential pitfalls and possibilities (depending on one's perspective) exist for this highest level of verbal organization as are found on the lowest level -- that of the individual proposition (clause). In other words, a given generic form in the SL may be present also in the RL having a similar function, including receptor associations, expectations, and assumptions with regard to the use of such a form. In the Bantu languages of Central Africa, for example, it is usually not too difficult to find an equivalent for historical narration since the ethnic groups concerned normally do preserve traditions about their origin, migrations, royal family, great events, etc. in narrative discourse. These may from a scientific or scholarly perspective appear to contain many internal incon= sistencies, illogicalities, as well as magical and even supernatu= ral elements. However un-historical these may seem to the out= sider, to a member of the in-group they (i.e. mbiri = 'historical tradition') are regarded as factive and hence a dependable and normative record of the past. On the other hand, the translator must take care not to apply in his rendering of biblical history literary forms which are characteristic of fictive types of narra= tion (e.g. formulaic introductions, character reference, tense usage, episode endings, vocabulary selection and collocation, etc.) In Chewa, for example, there are two types of non-histori= cal narrative that are distinguished from each other according to the presence (nthano) or absence (mwambi) of interposed choral songs.

Secondly, there may be generic types in the SL which are also pre=
sent in the RL context, but with a different function and/or
distribution (setting of use). Letters, for example, are as
common in Chewa literary communication as they must have been in
Koine Greek, but formally and functionally they do not match in
some significant respects. Sheer magnitude is one factor: a let=
ter the length of 1 Corinthians for instance, would be unheard of.
In addition, the purposes for which letters are written (and their
resultant formal and semantic properties) differ widely. A typi=
cal letter written in Chewa consists largely of phatic material,
especially at the beginning and ending, with the body consisting
of informative (telling about one's current life situation) and
affective statements (notably requests and replies to the same).
One would not expect to find the extensive didactic, hortatory,
and admonitory speech and associated style that we have in the
Pauline epistles. In such cases, the bounds of what is normal and
expected in the RL may have to be stretched to accommodate the
biblical record.

Thirdly, one may encounter situations where a SL discourse type
having a particular function (or functional complex) is represent=
ed in the RL by a different generic type, but one which has a
similar function. The heavily didactic wisdom literature of the
OT, such as Proverbs, would be classified as a type of poetry in
Hebrew. But it would not sound entirely natural if this were to
be rendered as poetry in Chewa, for the subject matter and themes
of the latter are largely of a lyric or descriptive nature. Even
Chewa proverbial forms would not work in most cases (except for
passages like Pr 27:7, 22) since they require a more enigmatic and
at the same time more rhetorical manner of presentation than the
Hebrew would support. A possible solution, one which remains to
be researched and tested, would be to pattern such didactic
material after the admonitory addresses (<u>malango</u>) recited at
initiation ceremonies. There would be a correspondence obviously
in purpose and to a certain extent also in general content, but
not in the formal characteristics of the discourse.

And finally, there are certain generic forms of the original which have absolutely no equivalent in the RL with regard to either form or function. Fortunately, this situation occurs only very rarely in the case of some rather specialized SL sub-genres, such as the acrostic poems.

The process of genre-matching does not present too many problems for the translator as long as two general guidelines are followed:

a) a thorough analytical description of both SL and RL text types and genres in their normal situational settings must precede the activity of searching for suitable equivalents; and

b) the criterion of equivalence must rest upon function (i.e. involving both the designative and the associative aspects of meaning), not on form -- which is the same translation prin= ciple that is observed on the basic clause level of composi= tion.

The subject of discourse types and genres concerns not only their respective linguistic forms and communication functions in both the SL and the RL, but also their representation on the printed page. What type of typographical format is preferred in the case of biblical poetry, for example? Does it make any difference, readability- and comprehension-wise, whether these portions of Scripture are written as ordinary prose or in some distinctive "poetic" arrangement (e.g. thought units, one thought/clause per line) -- even if the translation does not qualify as a genre of poetry in the RL? Getting reliable answers to questions such as these would call for rather sophisticated and extensive receptor-response testing techniques. Unfortunately, most project resour= ces do not stretch that far.

7. Psychological Setting: The psychological setting as it re= lates to the sociolinguistic con= text of a translation deals with the "mind set" of the receptors, which includes also the translators, assuming that they are of the same cultural group. This mind set encompasses their knowledge,

presuppositions, assumptions, value system, world view, attitudes, beliefs and emotions, particularly as these qualities pertain to the form and content of the Scriptures. To simplify the presenta= tion somewhat, we will include here under "psychological setting" two dimensions relating to mental processes and states which were treated separately in chapter 3, namely, "implicit information" and "frame of mind". This is because one's underlying presupposi= tions and assumptions have a great influence upon the formation and expression of one's attitudes and emotions. The mind set, or cognitive-emotive framework, of a certain group of receptors is affected by a number of important contextual factors, such as: their linguistic competence, mental and emotional stability, degree of literacy, level of general education, and degree (length + intensity) of Christian influence, including its theological and denominational orientation (e.g. "liberal" vs. "conservative", Western/expatriate dominated vs. national independent, etc.)

The average reader (or listener) thus approaches a text with cer= tain presuppositions and assumptions that are derived from the cultural setting as well as from his personal background and experience, and this knowledge governs the way in which he under= stands and interprets the text as it is being received. For example, if he has only a superficial acquaintance with the bibli= cal setting, he will normally have more difficulty in understand= ing what is going on in the text than someone who has received a thorough theological training. His standard of education in general as well as his level of linguistic and literary competence (the latter is important for interpreting the rhetorical modes of Scripture) will likewise determine his ability to decode the Bible's message. Deep-seated attitudes and emotions may be in= volved as well, for instance, in the case of someone who approaches the Christian Scriptures from a totally different religious perspective (e.g. Muslim, Hindu, or traditional Afri= can), or one who has a strong emotional attachment to the "old" Bible (perhaps it is closely associated with his conversion, at least psychologically, or it played a big part in his upbringing, or in meeting one of life's crises). A person's reason(s) for reading the Bible is more of an individual matter, and yet he may be part of a larger group which shares the same motivation, e.g. mere curiosity/pleasure in a great work of literature, to pass a school religion assignment or catechumen examination, to derive some personal or corporate physical or spiritual gain (healing, tongues-speaking, etc.), or a real desire to know more about God and his will. One's cultural orientation is another major consi= deration, for the individual's mind set will always be colored to a great extent by the customs, traditions, the value system, and way of life of his people. All of these factors interact with one another and upon a specific RL constituency to define the precise form of the translated text that will be needed to communicate effectively with them. And as Nida has pointed out: "...the nar= rower the segment of the code which can be employed for a particu= lar group of receptors, the greater the number of adjustments which must be introduced" (1981, p.32).

These adjustments entail decisions regarding matters such as the rate at which information is presented in the text (and correspon= dingly, the rate at which it needs to be processed by receptors), the ratio between old and new information being conveyed by the message and its status as either explicit or implicit, the amount of figurative versus non-figurative language that is present in a given pericope, the level of textual redundancy necessary to ensure adequate comprehension of the message, and the use of mar= ginal notes to clarify the nature of SL-specific presuppositions, etc., especially where these differ from those of the RL. One of the most important of these criteria is the so-called "horizon of difficulty", that is, the level of linguistic and literary com= plexity above which individuals typical of the receptor group experience significant difficulty in understanding the message being communicated to them, i.e. their decoding capacity has been surpassed. This difficulty may also be a result of the unpredict= ability of the content -- the reader's unfamiliarity with the con= cepts being conveyed. Some novelty and complexity is necessary to challenge him, to capture his attention and to maintain his inte= rest. But when his horizon of difficulty -- or "threshhold of frustration" -- is consistently exceeded, there is a real danger that he will simply give up his effort to understand, thus termi= nating the communication process.

To prevent such a communications "breakdown" from occurring, care=
ful testing must be conducted, not only to ascertain the degree of
comprehension, but also to pinpoint areas where other factors of a
sociolinguistic nature are acting to block or to skew message
transmission, in particular, those biases, beliefs, and assump=
tions arising from one's cultural background that one might not
even be aware of. At these points of special difficulty, where
either the receptor's insufficient knowledge, inadequate compe=
tence, or his culturally-specific presuppositions and frame of
reference interfere with the smooth flow of communication, the
text has to be formally restructured in order to introduce the
redundancy (reiteration or rearrangement of information/semantic
components) required to permit decoding to proceed at a reasonable
pace. For a description and illustration of some of the main
techniques whereby the information flow may be linguistically
regulated, see Nida and Taber, 1969 (ch. 7) and Wonderly, 1968
(ch. 7). It is necessary to add only that these restructuring
procedures concern mainly the cognitive side of the message and
the effort to achieve equivalence of content during interlingual
message transmission. But translators must never disregard the
psychological presuppositional, attitudinal, and emotive) com=
ponent of their translation, and this will necessitate an exami=
nation of the message in relation to the source, his receptors,
and the situational setting -- in short, the sociolinguistic
aspect of the communication process.

The matter of presupposition, assumption, and emotional bias
affects not only the receptors of the message, but also its
source, which in the case of Bible translation is a surrogate,
that is, serving only as the agent of message transmission, not
its author. Translators, too, bring to their task certain
beliefs, values, opinions, and so forth, the most important being
those of a theological and moral nature. So firmly fixed is this
conceptual framework that it can easily lead the translator to
"cheat" at his task -- to alter the facts of Scripture, ever so
slightly, so as to conform it to a particular doctrinal position
or to make it internally consistent (for example, to "harmonize"
divergent gospel accounts of the life of Christ). Naturally, the

most likely places for such alteration to be carried out concern
issues which have divided denominations throughout the ages, e.g.
the Sabbath Day, the Virgin Mary, the primacy of Peter, the mode
of Baptism, the essence of the Lord's Supper, the person of the
Holy Spirit, the nature of justification, and so on. However,
when a translation team/committee is denominationally well-balanc=
ed and when they work together in harmony, such problems rarely,
if ever, arise, for there are always ways of striking a mutually-
acceptable compromise either within (e.g. through the use of more
generic expressions) or without (e.g. footnotes) the text.

Other theological presuppositions and assumptions may motivate a
translator to engage in eisegesis rather than exegesis -- to read
meaning into the original text rather than extracting it from the
text. An example of this is the temptation to read some of the
New Testament into the Old at certain controversial passages, such
as Genesis 1.2:

> ...and the Holy Spirit of God was moving over the face of the
> waters.

The point is not that the Hebrew ruach cannot be a reference to
the third person of the Trinity, but that the addition of "Holy"
in the translation locks the text into that one interpretation and
explicitly excludes all other alternative readings (e.g. "power of
God", "wind from God", "mighty wind"). In cases like this where
several defensible readings are possible, a translator must learn
in the spirit of compromise to be content merely with "protecting"
his own particular theological position (if exegetically substan=
tiated in the first place) while at the same time allowing other
valid alternatives "access" to the text. Sometimes the solution
lies in an ambiguous rendering (i.e. two or more "meanings" are
simultaneously possible); a better method is to allow the most
widely supported interpretation to be reflected by the actual
text, while other attested readings are given in a footnote. Cer=
tainly one should not attempt to incorporate every exegetical
option into the translation as the LB has apparently tried to do
in this amplified rendering of Romans 3.22:

> Now God says he will accept and acquit us -- declare us
> "not guilty" -- if we trust Jesus Christ to take away

our sins. And we can all be saved in this same way, by coming to Christ, no matter who we are or what we have been like.

(Cp. RSV: ...the righteousness of God (has been mani= fested) through faith in Christ Jesus for all who believe. For there is no distinction.)

8. Communication Function: In the following discussion, the term "function" will be used to denote the combination of (illocutionary) intention and (perlocu= tionary) effect. The various functions of communication (e.g. in= formative, affective, aesthetic, etc.) are realized by the diffe= rent discourse types and genres to be found in a given language, more specifically, in a given literary tradition. But notice that whereas the functions are universal, some genres are widespread while others are highly language-specific. Furthermore, the same genre may have very different functions within the socio-literary context in which it is realized. A folktale, for example, may be told primarily to instruct, warn, entertain, validate social norms, etc., or any combination of these, depending upon who is telling it, to whom, and under what circumstances.

When translating, then, it is necessary that there be a matching of function in the process of message transmission. In order for this to be achieved, translators must first be trained in the functional analysis of texts. Often, however, such study gets no further than an introduction to the basic discourse types: narra= tion, description, argument, and dialogue, and translators simply assume that these generic forms are interchangeable between SL and RL. This is for the most part true in both Chewa and Tonga; that is to say, the larger forms of the original can usually be trans= ferred directly into both of these languages with at least an approximate functional correspondence.

But this does not work out so well in the case of poetic and highly rhetorical discourse. Here one has to use much more discrimination with regard to both function and form. This is best accomplished by first making a complete inventory of all literary genres in the RL, both oral and written, and noting what they are used for as vehicles of artistic communication. During this type of exercise, the potential for functional diversity in the use of a given genre must be fully investigated and documented if possible. To cite another example from a Bantu context: a pro= verb may be used on one occasion, to discipline a child, princi= pally as a teaching device (informative and affective functions); at another time the expressive element may predominate -- in the repartee of elders engaged in a judicial palaver; in yet another context the compositional aspect may be in focus, as at the con= clusion of an oral narrative performance; and the aesthetic function may complement any and all of these -- the use of an intricately structured form for verbal play, to heighten the sheer beauty of language in action.

Translators need to be actively involved in such a research project every step of the way, for they will learn best by doing -- from gathering a corpus of data to inverviewing various recep= tors for their personal reactions and opinions. Once they have become thoroughly familiar with the poetic resources of their language and literature, they can apply the results to Scripture -- not according to form (for by now "poetry" will be too general a category to be useful), but according to function, employing RL genres to convey the rhetorical intentions of the SL text (e.g. warning, praise, exultation, condemnation, complaint, etc.). If the translators are not able to compose in a particular poetic genre themselves (at least at first), they can take the lead in the search for artists who would be willing, and able, to help out.

The following are some notes on the initial stages of such research in the Chewa and Tonga projects: The use of poetic forms to carry out a serious affective (admonitory-minatory) purpose as we have in the OT prophets is not very natural in the Central Bantu languages. In Chewa, for example, there is only a remote correspondence in the extemporaneous songs (nyimbo) which a person may compose either to verbalize his feelings and current mood (expressive) or to air his grievance and complaints (affective). But these songs, including those of a "popular" variety, are quite limited in scope, normally being directed to or on behalf of an individual, unless they happen to have a political motivation. The latter are of two types according to their historical origin. Those composed before Independence all attacked the government, a "colonial" regime, through disguised pleas, complaints, accusa= tions, and warnings. All those composed after Independence, on the other hand, function to praise the government and its leader= ship, largely through an enumeration of their outstanding accom= plishments. If the transposition from a musical idiom to the printed page should prove to introduce too many problems, a possible alternative, especially in the case of the prophetic oracles, would be to take the most general and widespread type of written poetry in Chewa, namely, expressive lyric (ndakatulo) and to extend its range simply through usage and context to encompass more of the sub-functions and topics that occur in the OT prophe= tic books.

In the Tonga literary tradition, on the other hand, there is a specific (predominantly) male genre of poetry (i.e. ciyaabilo), which is employed to attack social injustice, whether on an in= dividual or community level. It may also include reference to future events, especially predictions about what a person intends to accomplish. The subject matter does not usually have to do with a man's relationship to God, i.e. they are not considered "religious". Nevertheless, the genre is quite flexible, being comprised in the main of subjective, personal compositions rather than a corpus of pieces that have been collectively established in the oral traditions of the people. However, ciyaabilo involves several serious sociocultural limiting factors which may well prevent the genre from being used to express prophetic oracles. Topically, it is often sung in a boasting manner to extol one's own virtues and accomplishments. Source-wise, it would be deemed inappropriate for God (Leza) to -yaabila when speaking to man (in any case, according to Tonga traditional religious belief, God does not communicate directly with man in words, let alone poetic verse). And situationally, a common setting for performing ciyaabilo is either a beer-drinking party or a funeral, and both of these social contexts arouse negative associations in the minds of the people which would militate against their being used for a religious purpose (for similar findings in a different cultural context, see Ansre, 1984). This brief study has suggested that in the effort to achieve communication equivalence, a consideration of form and function alone is not enough. This must be coupled with a careful examination of the content and setting in order to be sociolinguistically valid -- to be reliable enough to apply as a basis for achieving a meaningful and acceptable result in the RL text. Thus, the interaction of situational variables is high= lighted once again.

In the case of both the Chewa and the Tonga projects, plans have not yet reached the stage where sample poetic compositions can be prepared for testing audience reaction (see Klem, 1982). This has been due to restrictions in the time and financial resources available for the research and development of such literary-quali= ty materials, coupled with limitations in artistic ability, i.e. no poets have yet been found to contribute to the project). In the meantime, as is so often the case, the poetic lines of the Hebrew (or English RSV) are simply followed without attempting to create any indigenous rhythms, except to aim for a certain balance in strophic units and to incorporate as much natural figurative language as possible to compensate partially for what has been lost from the original. Yet even this is better than nothing -- than to simply arrange the material in prosaic blocks, as is typi= cally done in GNB. This is because the poetic format at least serves the function of highlighting the parallelism of ideas, which is such a dominant feature of Hebrew verse.

As the preceding discussion has suggested, our functional grid needs to be constructed with a finer mesh, particularly in the case of the affective function. The latter may be subdivided into its constituent intentional acts, e.g. rejoice, rebuke, appeal, accuse, ridicule, console, entice, insult, and so forth. Equiva= lence between the SL and RL texts should then be sought on this level of specificity. This would narrow the range of form-func= tional consideration to the different genres and subtypes of discourse that are manifested within a particular book. Here one would expect a greater degree of incongruence between the SL and RL. To give one example: a natural way of rendering the Queen of Sheba's words lauding the wisdom of Solomon, which is represented as prose in the original (1 Kg 10:8-9), would be as praise poetry in many Bantu languages. This genre would certainly fit the situ= ation, the topic and the addressee, but it may not correspond with the speaker, that is, a royal personage herself in place of a court poet. Whether the final, interpersonal factor would be enough to offset the others remain to be tested. This example and the others cited above call attention to the complexity of the problem and the difficulty of finding completely satisfactory solutions. The equivalence between texts in terms of form and function will rarely, if ever, be exact, but a sociolinguistic approach can help a great deal to narrow the intertextual gap in communicative value, and if nothing else, to explain the failures that inevitably do occur.

That completes our survey of the major sociolinguistic variables as they affect the wider context of communication during the pro= cess of translation. Clearly, these factors cannot be ignored in the organization and operation of any Bible translation programme. The specific applications may be summarized in the five guidelines below (cp. Kopesec, 1979, p.58):

1. An intensive sociolinguistically oriented language/literature survey is definitely a prerequisite for any Bible translation project. Such research would consider, as a minimum, the nine factors outlined above within a broad form-functional communication based model. It would also attempt to isolate the diverse forces working either for stability or for change with a view toward accurately predicting future trends within the speech community. Such forward planning is necessary in order to prevent the translation from becoming linguistically obsolete before a generation passes (i.e. the normal life-ex= pectancy of an idiomatic version).

2. The results of such a survey (repeated, if necessary, to focus on areas of special sociolinguistic concern) would form the basis for establishing a comprehensive language programme relating specifically to the translation itself, according to which all policy decisions would be made, whether on the external or the internal level of communication. These deci= sions would have to be reassessed, and perhaps revised, at periodic intervals through various testing procedures in= volving preliminary/draft translations.

3. The general language policy decided upon would, in turn, guide the selection of translation personnel, both drafters and reviewers, so that the dialect chosen as being central would have adequate representation on the several committees established to oversee and run the project. These people, laypersons and clergy alike, should all receive thorough in= struction in basic sociolinguistic principles (exemplified and perhaps even taught in their own language) as part of an overall translator-training programme.

4. A similar detailed sociolinguistic analysis of the SL texts must be undertaken (utilising whatever prepared helps are available) in order to pinpoint what forms of the original are used to realise which functions in the various interper= sonal and contextual settings to be found in the Scriptures. The results should later be published in a form that is accessible to the average (Bible-school trained) translator. These may then be explicitly compared during translator training sessions with the results obtained from the RL research, to demonstrate in particular how the diverse array of situationally determined functions may be realised by the linguistic resources of the RL. Again, this needs to be done on all of the different levels of discourse structure.

5. At periodic intervals during the course of a translation pro= ject (and not just at the end), a trained consultant should work together with the team to re-evaluate the sociolinguis= tic framework adopted at the beginning of work and modify

this as required. Part of such an exercise would involve
both spot and extended checking of actual text material to
see how these principles were applied in specific situations
of language use and in particular cultural settings. Notable
problem areas ought to be recorded for consideration at a
later date since it may take some time and testing before a
comprehensive and integrated pattern of sociolinguistic usage
will emerge, particularly if speakers from different spatial
and sociological dialect areas are contributing to the
effort.

From the preceding consideration of individual communication
events on both the micro- and macro-levels of discourse and how
sociolinguistic influences converge to affect the style, or form,
of both the SL and also the RL texts, we move on to a study of the
structure of speech events in combination, specifically in dialo=
gue. We shall observe how speech acts on the propositional level
interact both in combination (syntagmatically) and in patterns of
similarity and contrast (paradigmatically) to constitute and
define the organization of discrete segments of direct discourse
in the Bible.

CHAPTER 5

Sociolinguistics and Discourse Analysis

A Discourse Framework

As we have seen, sociolinguistic study is vitally interested in
the context of communication, and that includes the textual con=
text as well. In this chapter we will examine the contribution
that discourse analysis can make to a sociolinguistic approach
towards the description of speech events in the Scriptures.

The term "discourse structure" refers to the overal lexical,
grammatical, phonological, and rhetorical composition of a parti=
cular verbal text, i.e. a unified group of utterances which form
levels of linguistic organization higher than the sentence. This
textual framework is author-motivated, that is, it reflects the
intention of its author and is not simply a random collection of
sentences. It is the direct product of what has been termed the
"compositional", sometimes combined with the "aesthetic", function
of communication. Now, in addition to a more specific illocutio=
nary function, or functional complex, (e.g. to inform, exhort,
rebuke, warn, comfort, etc.) a well-formed discourse manifests
three other principal characteristics. These may be viewed as
general strategies whereby the functions of discourse are effect=
ed. They are briefly described according to their respective
operations below:

1. SEGMENTATION: focuses on diversity in discourse; it deals
                  with how the text is demarcated into interre=
lated units of various size and scope (each with definable bounda=
ries), which combine to form a hierarchical structure that encom=
passes the entire composition.

2. CONNECTIVITY: focuses on unity in discourse; it deals with
                  how the various discrete segments of the text,
from its most basic constituent, the proposition, right on up to

the composition as a whole, are unified through syntactic, lexical, thematic, and interactional (including conversational) linkages to give cohesion (of form) and coherence (of ideas) to the discourse.

3. <u>PROMINENCE</u>: focuses on impact in discourse; it deals with how specific units and/or relations of the text are either foregrounded or backgrounded by means of various rhetorical devices; a particular segment's high point of proposi= tional development is referred to as "peak", being distinct from its high point of interpersonal interaction, which is designated as "climax".

In addition to these three major features of discourse, it is necessary to draw attention to a prominent literary technique which is frequently employed in their realization:

<u>PATTERNING</u>: This technique does much to create appeal in dis= course. It refers to the various ways in which a text may be artistically heightened by superimposed poetic arrangements of a syntagmatic (associative, horizontal relations) and/or paradigmatic (analogical, vertical relations) nature to enhance the effectiveness of each of the three principal discourse properties. Patterning, which essentially involves the structured reiteration of similar and contrasting linguistic elements, serves to magnify a text's thematic as well as aesthetic value as a com= munication event, thereby giving it the quality of "literariness"

The interrelationships among these four aspects of discourse structure are schematized below.

UNITS	BOTH	RELATIONS
SEGMENTATION	PROMINENCE	CONNECTIVITY
P A T T E R N I N G		

A reading of this diagram is as follows: the discourse property of segmentation applies chiefly to the units, or segments, of a text; connectivity applies to the relations within as well as between units; prominence is applied selectively to either units or relations; and patterning is a device that is utilized to enhance the effect of any of the three preceding global features of a text.

There are many different methods of discourse analysis, ranging from those whose interests are more linguistic (with an emphasis upon the aspects of segmentation and connectivity) to those whose concern is primarily literary (with an emphasis upon the aspects of prominence and patterning). But one feature that most studies of this kind have in common is their virtual preoccupation with the so-called "propositional" mode of discourse organization. A text is segmented into its constituent semantic propositions, and these are in turn logically related to one another on various levels of structural generality: sentence - paragraph - episode - section, etc. Different classificatory schemes have been proposed to assist in the categorization and labelling of the interproposi=tional relations (e.g. Beekman and Callow, 1974, ch. 18; Longacre, 1972, ch. 3; Nida, 1975, ch. 3).

By and large it is possible to employ any one of these methodolo=
gies and come up with a reasonable exposition of the semantic con=
struction of a biblical text (or any other), be it narrative,
prophetic/apocalyptic, or epistolary in nature. However, when one
encounters texts that contain a large proportion of direct speech,
these designative-logically oriented systems diminish considerably
in their explanatory adequacy. Since their main emphasis is upon
denotative content (i.e. reference and predication), they tend to
overlook the sociolinguistic realities of the text -- the situa=
tional context in particular and how this determining factor
affects the actual composition of stretches of conversation. There
is evidence to support the position that a dialogue is structured
independently of its propositional development in the form of a
succession of speech acts. And these, considered together as a
unified piece of discourse, manifest the same characteristics of
organization as does a propositional chain (or tree): segmenta=
tion, connectivity, and prominence with patterning again operating
in all three. These features are effected in any coherent speech
to form what we might term the "interpersonal" constituent of
discourse composition. The two structures, propositional and
interpersonal, are of necessity closely related to one another in
their articulation and functioning, and yet they are disparate
enough to warrant separate investigation. To omit the interper=
sonal (or pragmatic) element in mixed texts (i.e. narrative, etc.
plus dialogue) renders an analysis partial at best and may well
produce misleading results.

A study of the text of John 4:7-26 will illustrate the point. The
aim is to demonstrate the way in which the discourse manifests the
above-mentioned properties, which interact to constitute a
distinct interpersonal component of structure. Our principal con=
cern is with the latter, but reference will also be made to the
propositional framework for the purposes of comparison. This
exposition, despite its preliminary nature, also shows that in the
case of a text consisting almost entirely of direct speech, a
pragmatic-sociolinguistic analysis is indispensible for arriving
at an adequate understanding of its communicative form and
function in the context in which it occurs.

The Textual Setting

The pericope of John 4:7-26, which will be analyzed in detail below, first needs to be examined in terms of its textual setting and the author's larger thematic purpose or it may not be under= stood completely, or even correctly. In its wider context, which encompasses the bulk of chapter 4 (until verse 43), we might view this account as a dramatization of two contrasting reactions to Christ's message and ministry of salvation. This theme is developed in the form of two narrative threads, clearly distinct and yet also closely interlocking. There are correspondingly two sets of participants: the disciples and the Samaritans, while Jesus is the personal, as well as the thematic, link, or mediator, between the two potentially antagonistic groups. Thus a section heading such as we find in GNB: "Jesus and the Samaritan Woman" is somewhat misleading and therefore probably ought to be revised so as to reflect more of the dynamics of this discourse, e.g. "Jesus and his Disciples Visit the Samaritans."

To help one visualize the intricate way in which this narrative is constructed, the following diagrammatic display is presented. This will be supplemented by some explanatory notes (keyed to the verse numbers on the diagram), which will call attention to focal points in the thematic progression. It will not be possible to discuss everything of exegetical importance or interest in this passage, and so consideration will be limited primarily to topics involving the interaction of participants, which serves as the vehicle for manifesting the story's central theme. (A) = the narrative event/ dialogue line involving Jesus and his disciples; (B) = the line involving Jesus and the Samaritans, of whom the woman is a select representative.

DIAGRAM of the narrative and thematic development of John 4:1-42

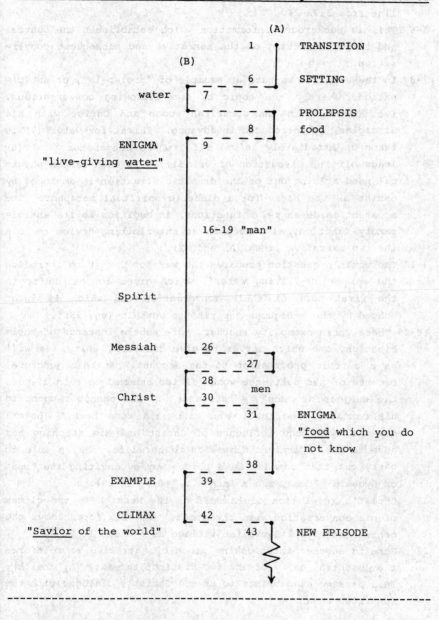

Verse	NOTES

1-2 This is a transitional piece which continues the narrative line from 3:22-24.

3-6 This is background information which establishes the spatial and temporal setting of the narrative and subsequent conver= sation.

7-8 In these verses we have an example of "prolepsis", or antici= pation, whereby the topic of two following conversations, i.e. Christ with the Samaritan woman and Christ with his disciples, is introduced in advance. Thirst for water (7) is taken up immediately in vs. 9ff., while hunger for food (8) leads off the discussion of vs. 31ff. In each case a physi= cal need arising out of the dramatic situation is employed by Christ as the basis for a didactic spiritual metaphor. The apparent aside in vs. 8 functions, in addition to its antici= patory function, also acts as an interlocking device to join the two narrative lines (A) and (B).

9-10 The woman's question prepares the way for Christ to introduce the enigma of "living water", which gives topical unity to the first part of their conversation and which is later echoed by the ambiguous "spirit" in worship (vs. 23ff.)

16-19 These verse exemplify another, more subtle instance of anti= cipation, one which serves to give cohesion, unity, as well as a certain progression to the account. At this juncture, because of her past, the woman is too ashamed to even discuss the subject of "men" (= "husbands"). She cannot respond to his command: "Go, call your man and come here." Later, however, when the influence of Christ and his teaching has added a new, spiritual dimension to her life, she is able to carry out that command in a unique way by inviting the "men" of Sychar: "Come, see a 'man' ..." (vs. 28-29).

26 Christ's revelation of himself as the Messiah is the climax of his conversation with the woman. It also foreshadows the confession of the Samaritan village as a whole in v. 42.

27 Here is another interlocking piece of narrative to reinforce the essential unity of the two distinct threads, (A) and (B). This passage also brings to an end Christ's dialogue with the Samaritan woman.

Verse	NOTES

28-30 The effect of their conversation was that the woman was transformed into an enthusiastic witness for Christ. Her energetic action contrasts markedly with the disciples' reaction: sullen silence and prejudice -- an attitude which constitutes the antitype of effective evangelism.

31-32 Corresponding to vs. 9-10, the disciples' request leads to Christ's second enigma, this one concerning "food...which you do not know." The spiritual metaphor of food and the harvest then becomes the vehicle for conveying the second half of his theme. The disciples' negative reaction to Christ's talking with the woman, coupled with the dramatic pause effected by his consequent speech to them, serve to focus upon the cli= mactic positive response of the Samaritans. There is thus a gradual build-up of suspense throughout the discourse. The tension so created is emotive, thematic, and narrative (plot- related) in nature. From a narrative perspective, Christ's lecture to his disciples also allows for the passage of time, during which the woman can go and carry out an unexpected evangelistic mission to her countrymen.

39-42 For all practical purposes, the two story lines merge at this point. The disciples, however, are conspicuous for their absence -- for not being an explicit part of this con= version scene. Here we have exemplified a positive practical result of the saving work of Christ, which is even more sig= nificant because of its occurrence among a "heathen" people.

42 This is the high point of the entire narrative, and in typi= cal fashion (for the Bible) it is encoded as direct speech: "This is indeed the Savior of the world." The process of self disclosure, which Christ initiated at the very beginning of his talk with the woman culminates here in their conclu= sion that the one whom she had introduced them to was truly the promised Messiah. His ultimate revelation has been pre= viewed at several key steps along the way (i.e. vs. 18, 25, 29, 39), a fact which also contributes to the thematic unity of the account as a whole.

43 A shift of time and space clearly marks the onset of a new narrative unit.

Generally speaking, narrative/theme line (B) emphasizes the <u>source</u> of the life-giving gospel, namely, the person and work of Christ, the Savior. Line (A) stresses the <u>receptors</u> of the gospel mes= sage: its scope must be <u>all</u> people, and the time for this pro= gramme to go into operation is <u>now</u>. The disciples misunderstood the mission of the Jews (cf. v. 22) and hence also that of the Messiah in their midst (cf. v. 26). Their less than enthusiastic response to Christ's extension of his ministry throws into relief both the need for reaching out to the non-Jews as well as the dra= matic success of this effort.

Literary devices found elsewhere in John's gospel (e.g. chs. 3 and 6) also appear here. In this text similar rhetorical techniques on the macro-, meso-, and micro-level of discourse, i.e. the use of double entendre, the unexpected, irony, and enigma, function within the narrative-conversation to provoke controversy and/or to raise religious questions in the minds of those with whom Christ has contact, including his own disciples. His purpose is to focus their thinking upon some crucial theological issue. Christ then (or sometimes also the author/writer, e.g. 3:31-36) employs this tension-filled situation to discourse upon the subject, either to resolve the controversy or, more often, to highlight the opposing positions over against it -- positions which ultimately involve each individual's spiritual relationship to him.

The Sociolinguistic Setting

The following summary of the situational and interpersonal setting of the dialogue recorded in John 4:7-26 is based upon the nine sociolinguistic variables discussed earlier. This type of back= ground study is necessary to contextualize the conversation in terms of those features which may have a bearing upon the content and style of the participants' speech in the RL. These operative factors will be indicated in parentheses as they arise in the discussion.

There is no evidence of any time-influenced irregularities in the speech of Jesus and the Samaritan woman. Both appear to use a

contemporary style (Temporal), especially since the topic of con=
versation deals largely with current issues. The historical allu=
sions found in the text are cited with reference to their present
application. The Aramaic language was probably used as the medium
of communication, with some differentiation likely between their
dialects because of their respective ethnic and geographic
origins, i.e. Jew vs. Samaritan, Judea vs. Samaria (Spatial). Any
dialectal differences, however, were obviously erased during the
transfer into Greek (at whatever stage this took place) and trans=
position from an oral to a written medium (Language Medium).

Initially, this conversation takes the form of a repartee, or
alternating exchange, with one point being raised in response to
the immediately preceding one by way of objection, interrogation,
and/or elaboration. But the type gradually changes into a didac=
tic exhortation as Jesus assumes a dominant role in the interac=
tion (Discourse Type). No other, more specific genres may be
linguistically demarcated in this pericope, though from a literary
perspective the discourse follows the thematic pattern of an
enigma, as is typical of John's gospel, i.e. (a) assertion
(Christ), (b) misunderstanding (addressee), (c) explanation
(Christ). The topic of discussion is of a serious nature since it
deals with a person's manner of life and worship as this reflects
his/her relationship to God (Subject Matter), and on a higher,
more abstract level it serves to reveal Christ as the promised
Messiah. The style thus tends to be formal, as revealed by the
elevated, theological language, especially in the mouth of Christ;
by the respectful terms of address (e.g. kurie 'sir' and gunai
'woman'): and by the grammatically complete and semantically
explicit manner of speaking (Interpersonal). The role-relation=
ship of the interlocutors reinforces this level of discourse,
namely, a rabbi/religious professor vs. a laywoman. Features of
code (Interpersonal), i.e. sex, age, class, race, etc., do not
seem to play a part in the discussion after the woman's initial
response to Jesus' request for a drink, which could be inter=
preted as simply an indication of her surprise, or, more tenta=
tively, as a somewhat hostile reaction that reflects her self-
assumed inferior status, viz. woman, Samaritan, low social
standing.

The physical and circumstantial environment (External Setting) has considerable influence on the dialogue in that it provides an immediate topic of conversation, i.e. Jesus' presumed need for a drink. The setting is later referred to on several conversation-extending occasions, i.e. Jacob's well and Mount Gerizim. In the latter instance, a deictic gesture may have accompanied the reference: "...on this mountain" (v. 21). The narrative situa= tion explains why these two participants came into verbal contact in the first place. Why was the woman alone? Normally women in Bible times (as in rural Africa even today) went to draw water twice a day, morning and evening, and in groups. The fact that this particular woman was very likely a social outcast due to her uninhibited life style caused her to come by herself to the well during the hottest part of the day, when other women in the village would not be there. From this situational cue alone, a cultural insider could surmise that something was wrong socially with this woman, even though her background is kept hidden from the reader until the dramatic disclosure of verse 18. Secondly, why were the disciples not there on the scene? This detail is carefully revealed in an aside (v. 8). Thus the stage is set, so to speak for a personal interaction which under normal circum= stances would probably not have taken place at all.

Attitudinal and emotional elements enter into the conversation during its initial stages when the woman is still ignorant of who Jesus is and perhaps suspicious of his motives in speaking to her (Frame of Mind). Her opening question, for example, conveys over= tones of both doubt and surprise, possibly accompanied by an annoyed, even sarcastic, gibe (i.e. we Samaritans, though regarded by you Jews as the scum of the earth, are nonetheless "good" enough to supply you with water to drink). These feelings take expression in the very form of her words -- through the rhetorical question, the opposed personal pronouns, and the specifying appositional phrases: (literally)

"How (is it that) you, a Jew

from me ask a drink, being a Samaritan woman?" (4:9)

The subsequent authorial aside is inserted to clarify the implica= tion of her words:

Jews will not use the same cups and bowls that Samaritans use. (GNB: Note that the situational context favors this interpretation.)

Factors of a suppositional and intentional nature (Implicit information and Communication Function) will form the basis for our discussion below, and therefore need not be illustrated here.

The Text Analyzed

The chart below indicates the progression of interpersonal verbal interaction by breaking up the discourse of John 4:7-26 into its constituent speech acts according to the basic utterances (roughly "kernel" clauses) whereby they are realized. Each utterance is classified by its generic form: I = imperative, S = statement, Q = question, as well as by its conversational function. The latter, which specifies only the main speaker intentions, consists of an ad hoc list of illocutionary labels applied to the various speech acts; most are of an informative and affective type. Often several functional labels are assigned to a single speech act. Sometimes these reflect different levels of generality in classi= fication, but more often they merely indicate the complex nature of the phenomena being analyzed and the need for a multi-dimen= sional grid with which to categorize them. The utterances not composed as direct speech, largely quote introducers, are indi= cated but not numbered. These clearly mark the sequence of turn-taking in the conversation. Authorial asides, too are not included in the analysis of speech acts, though their importance to the discourse as a whole is recognized.

One must also take note of the fact that all speech acts are evaluated on the internal (participant) level of communication for this exercise. They could also be classified on the external (writer's) level, but that would be much more speculative and would require an even broader discourse perspective than the one presented earlier.

One frequently finds that in the absence of clear formal signals, a given utterance may be construed attitudinally, emotively, and

functionally in several different ways. The loss of the phonolo=
gical and non-verbal aspects of the message make this ambiguity
inevitable. Where a literal translation cannot preserve this
equivocality (and it usually cannot), a text will have to be ren=
dered according to an exegetical decision made in favor of what
would be most probable in the sociolinguistic context. The fol=
lowing results, then, are quite tentative: they are offered both
to illustrate the methodology and also to suggest the potential of
such interactional analysis.

Verse	Speech Acts	Form	Function
7	Jesus said to her,		
a)	"Give me a drink."	(I)	request, conversation opener
8	(For his disciples had gone away into the city to buy food.)		
9	The Samaritan woman said to him,		
b)	"How is it that you, a Jew, ask a drink of me, a woman of Samaria?"	(Q)	objection, evaluation, challenge, sociological marker (status)
10	Jesus answered and said to her,		
c)	"If you knew the gift of God	(S)	correction, enigma$_A$
d)	and who it is that is saying to you,		
e)	'Give me a drink,'		
f)	you would have asked him		
g)	and he would have given you living water."		offer, enigma$_B$, evaluation
11	The woman said to him,		
h)	"Sir, you have nothing to draw with,	(S)	objection, observation
i)	and the well is deep;		
j)	where do you get that living water?"	(Q)	inquiry, probe
12			
k)	Are you greater than our father Jacob,	(Q)	evaluation, challenge
l)	who gave us the well,		description, evidence
m)	and drank from it himself, and his sons, and his cattle?"		

Verse	Speech Acts	From	Function
13	Jesus said to her,		
n)	"Everyone who drinks of this water will thirst again,	(S)	correction
14			
o)	but whoever drinks of the	(S)	offer, enigma$_B$ (cont.)
p)	water that I shall give him		
q)	will never thirst;		promise, evidence
r)	the water that I shall give him		
s)	will become in him a spring of water	(S)	description, prediction
t)	welling up to eternal life."		

15	The woman said to him,		
u)	"Sir, give me this water,	(I)	request, acceptance
v)	that I may not thirst,		explanation
w)	nor come here to draw."		

16	Jesus said to her,		
x)	"Go call your husband,	(I)	command, test
y)	and come here."		transition (shift topic)
17	The woman answered him,		
z)	"I have no husband."	(S)	denial
	Jesus said to her,		
a')	"You are right in saying,	(S)	evaluation, agreement
b')	'I have no husband;'		
18			
c')	for you have had five husbands,	(S)	description, accusation$_a$
d')	and he whom you now have is not your husband;		reproof, accusation$_b$ test failed
e')	this you said truly."	(S)	evaluation (irony)

19	The woman said to him,		
f')	"Sir, I perceive that you are a prophet.	(S)	admission (guilt) conclusion, evaluation
20			
g')	Our fathers worshipped on this mountain;	(S)	challenge, transition (shift topic)
h')	and you say that in Jerusalem is the place		contrast description
i')	where men ought to worship."		

Verse	Speech Acts	Form	Function
21	Jesus said to her,		
j')	"Woman, believe me,	(I)	appeal
k')	the hour is coming when neither on this mountain nor in Jerusalem	(S)	correction ─────┐
l')	you will worship the Father.		prediction$_a$ ─ ─ ─ ─ ─ ┐ │
22			
m')	You worship what you do not know:	(S)	evaluation, correc= ──┘ tion │
n')	we worship what we know	(S)	contrast │
o')	for salvation is of the Jews.		explanation ─ ─ ─ ─ ─ ┤
23			
p')	But the hour is coming, and now is,	(S)	pronouncement │
q')	when the true worshippers will worship the Father in spirit and truth,	(S)	offer (implicit) ────┘ prediction$_b$ ─ ─ ─ ─ ─ ┐ solution$_B$ │
r')	for such the Father seeks		explanation ─ ─ ─ ─ ─ ┘
24			
s')	God is spirit,	(S)	assertion, description
t')	and those who worship him must worship in spirit and truth.		prescription

----

Verse	Speech Acts	Form	Function
25	The woman said to him,		
u')	"I know that the Messiah is coming	(S)	testimony, transition
v')	(he who is called the Christ);	(S)	identification (aside)
w')	when he comes,	(S)	prediction
x')	he will show us all things."		
26	Jesus said to her,		
y')	"I...am he	(S)	emphatic assertion
z')	who speak to you."		revelation = solution$_A$

What, then, is the practical value of such an analytical break-
down? That will become more apparent when the larger discourse
properties of this pericope are discussed below, for the exposi=
tion there is based to a greater or lesser degree upon the above
speech act analysis. In fact, the former could not have been
carried out satisfactorily without the completion of the preceding
as an essential preliminary exercise. However, a few general
remarks are in order at this stage.

The analysis of speech _form_ is obviously not very useful. It merely confirms the fundamental problem that besets all form-oriented studies: the same form may manifest many different functions (e.g. S = challenge (g'), correction (k'), offer (q'), etc.), and conversely, the same function may be effected by seve= ral different forms (e.g. challenge = Q (k)', I (= test, x), and S (g' ff.)).

The factorization into speech _functions_, on the other hand, is quite revealing. First of all, we present the general plan which outlines the interpersonal dynamics of the conversation as a whole. The patterning of speech acts in a dialogue is clearly demonstrated in this text (see the connecting lines along the right-hand margin), in particular, the triad: challenge - correc= tion - offer. This may be just coincidental, but the fact that the set occurs three times, with the most complex instance last, would suggest that it is indeed an illustration of the generic rhetorical form which is characteristic of dramatic narration, in this case, an argument that is enclosed within a narrative account. In addition to its simultaneous cohesive as well as demarcating function in the discourse, this functional triad is also of thematic significance, for it shows how Christ gently moves the woman from an antagonistic position (theologically and otherwise) and points her in the direction of a new spiritual horizon through his offer to reveal himself and his unique message to her with no strings attached. The chiastic unfolding of the twofold enigma and its solution is also a key structuring device and thematic principle which spans the conversation:

$$\text{Enigma}_A(d) : \text{Enigma}_B(g) :: \text{Solution}_B(q') : \text{Solution}_A(y')$$
$$(A = \text{Who is Christ?} \quad B = \text{What does he have to offer?})$$

Other important formal and semantic correspondence as well as con= trasts will be pointed out in the separate analyses that follow, each of which focuses upon one of the four principal qualities of verbal discourse.

Segmentation

The conversation between Christ and the Samaritan woman may be divided into three major sections as follows:

A. Introduction -- preparation: a --- w (vs. 7-15)
B. Bridge -- transition : x --- e' (vs.16-18)
C. Argument -- presentation: f'--- z' (vs.19-26)

In part A, Jesus prepares the way for the burden of his argument, which occurs in C. B is a transitional piece that enables the discussion to proceed from A to C. The boundaries of these three units are quite clearly defined. The conversation obviously begins in v.7 when the woman comes onto the scene, and it ends at v.26 when the disciples arrive to interrupt their talk. The opening boundaries at 16x and 19f' are both marked by a sudden shift in topic. Section A concludes with a "request" which is the reversal of the one that initiated the unit:

(a) Jesus: "Give me a drink."

(u) woman: "...give me this water..."

This might be considered a type of _inclusio_, which is a rhetorical device that is typically employed to demarcate the extremities of a certain segment of discourse. Similarly, B ends with a minor inclusio, i.e. one that does not quite span the entire unit:

(a') Jesus: "You are right in saying..."

(e') Jesus: "This you said truly."

The latter statement (e') is emphatic, and thus it also serves to mark the close of the section.

Turning to the organization of the individual segments, we note that the internal structure of A and C is similar. This corres= pondence functions to call attention to the thematic interrela= tionships between these two segments. Each begins with an inter= change between Christ and the woman (i), which sets the stage for a unified piece of didactic discourse spoken by Christ (ii). This is then followed by a significant concluding portion (iii), which represents the conversational climax of the entire unit (to be distinguished from the thematic peak that occurs in (ii)). In dramatic operation, each of the three sections may be viewed as building up to a climactic point, which is immediately dissipated in the subsequent utterance. This interactional structure may be diagrammed as follows, with a rising arrow signifying an increase in tension as the area of climax nears:

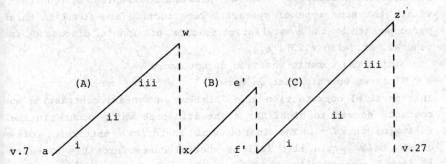

The respective internal segments (i-ii-iii) are these:

	(i)	(ii)	(iii)
A:	a --- m	n --- t	u --- w
C:	f'--- a'	j'--- t'	u'--- z'

Each of the middle segments (ii) is bounded by the speech of the woman, while it consists entirely of theological assertions made by Christ to challenge the faith of this foreign addressee.

There are additional features pertaining to the other discourse dimensions which also help to demarcate the dialogue into the three sections given above. It will be assumed that the relevant evidence will be applied as it occurs to the structural framework for segmentation which has just been proposed.

Connectivity

Four types of connectivity reinforce one another to give unity to the text as a whole as well as to its constituent sections: syn= tactic, lexical, thematic, and conversational.

Syntactic connectivity is effected by a repetition in grammatical construction. This often serves as an invariable frame (ground) to draw attention to the content which is contained therein (figure). When the content is the same or similar on each occa= sion, then we have an instance of overlapping involving formal and

semantic connectivity. Several prominent examples of contrast
within the same type of syntactic construction are found in this
pericope (this is a stylistic feature of John's discourse in
general, cf. also v.22), e.g.

(m') "You worship what you do not know;

(n') we worship what we know."

This parallel construction (i.e. similar in syntax, contrasting in
content) serves to highlight a thematic peak which occurs in the
following verse. The instances of rhetorical patterning dis=
cussed below would also fall as special cases into this category
of formal connectivity, which gives "cohesion" to a text.

Lexical connectivity is manifested on the microstructure of the
discourse. It is brought about largely by anaphoric reference
(e.g. "This water" (u) refers back to "the water which I will give
him" (r) as well as by the repetition and interrelation of key
lexical concepts. Frequently the latter will also have thematic
implications. The reiteration may be exact, synonymous, or
approximate, i.e. the lexical items are selected from the same
semantic field, e.g.

(A) drink - drink - drink - living water - draw - well -
living water - well - drank - drinks - water - thirst -
drinks - water - never thirst - water - springs of water -
welling up - this water - thirst - draw

This continuity of like concepts, which gives a text "coherence",
also serves to demarcate section A from the other two, as was
pointed out earlier.

Thematic connectivity refers to the macrostructure of the dis=
course and the expression of the larger semantic organization of a
text. This pericope reveals the following underlying plan:

FRAME:	(A)	(C)
	(a) Give me a drink	(f') you are a prophet
	(d) who it is that is saying to you	(u') Messiah is coming
	(e) Give me a drink	(y') I am he
	(g) he would have given you living water	
FOCUS:	drink -- living water	worship...in spirit

The "frame", corresponding essentially to sub-parts (i) and (iii) of the segments A and C, represents the main thrust of the central illocutionary progression of speech acts. It is concerned with the revelation of Christ to a heathen woman; it thus manifests WHO (object) we are to worship. Section A prepares for C in that it leads the woman to desire something that Christ has to offer, though initially at least her conception is limited to the worldly sphere of blessing. In the "focus" section, i.e. sub-part (ii) of each structure, Christ elaborates on the theological implications of what he is telling the woman. He endeavors to lift her from a purely materialistic idea of religion to a higher spiritual plane. The metaphorically-related themes: water (A) and spirit/Spirit (C) are prominent also in other of Christ's discourses recorded in John, e.g. 3:5 and 7:37-39 (this is an instance where "intertex= tuality" has a bearing on the interpretation of a text). The ma= terial in this "focus" portion of the discourse points to HOW (manner) we are to worship. The transitional segment (B) then gives the thematic antitype, i.e. an instance of hypocrisy (non-truth, non-Spirit), and in the process it also continues the illocutionary "frame", for it moves the woman to conclude that the person talking to her was a "prophet" (f'), whom Christ later reveals to be the Messiah whom she was waiting for (u'). Thus sections A and C are closely interrelated thematically, while B functions to make that relationship possible.

<u>Conversational</u> connectivity is particularly concerned with the ordered progression of speech acts and how one presupposes or builds upon another to encompass the entire discourse. The im= portance of the recurrent series: challenge - correction - offer, has already been pointed out. An analysis of a smaller portion of the text will further demonstrate the indispensability of conver= sational linkage for connectivity on the microlevel of discourse. Consider these four utterances from the conversation of John 4:

    (d') "...and he whom you now have is not your husband;

    (e') this you said truly."

    (f') "Sir, I perceive that you are a prophet.

    (g') Our fathers worshipped on this mountain..."

From the point of view of overt content, there is not much evi=

dence that would lead one to conclude that these sentences, if taken in isolation as a group, comprise a coherent segment of speech. Only the "this" of (e') establishes a linkage that depends upon some prior utterance in the set. And yet, the antecedent cannot be (d'), for that could not have been spoken by the "you" referred to in (e'). Except for the general references to religion in (f') and (g'), i.e. "prophet" and "worshipped", there is little semantic overlap, except for the repetition of "you" in (d') and (e'). Propositionally, then, this would seem to be an unrelated group of utterances.

When we read them in context, however, the four sentences did not present much of a problem. We took for granted that they were somehow connected with one another. This interpretation was based not so much on their respective semantic properties, for as we have seen, these are too few and tenuous to establish any meaning= ful relationships. Rather, our conclusion was based largely upon the situational features of the textual and extratextual context. In other words, where explicit content links are missing, the receptor looks for functional associations in the sequence of speech acts in order to forge a connective bond among the diverse elements. What are these associations?

The textual context, (c') in particular, suggests that (d') is likewise an accusation. It is a charge which both supports and contradicts the woman's claim that she has no husband (z). A "man" she had; a "husband" he was not (the Greek aner can mean both, and this no doubt intentional ambiguity betrays her desire to prevent Jesus for probing further into her personal history). Indeed, now she has no husband, but previously she had already lived with five of them. Jesus' assertion thus verifies the truth value of her claim, but at the same time it confounds her devious illocutionary intention in making it, namely, to deceive him. His next statement (e'), which is emphatic by virtue of its repetition (i.e. a'), is also ironic: Christ's assertion that the woman was telling the "truth" was not meant to be a compliment. It was rather a subtle rebuke, for by disclosing the facts of her marital background, the truth of her misleading statement was fully expos=

ed. The content of the woman's words was correct, but her moti=
vation was not, and the manner of Christ's reply reveals to her
that he fully understood the situation. Only a recognition of the
sociolinguistic factors that operate in a given situation can
enable one to detect the influence of irony.

The woman's reaction to Christ's supernatural insight (f') is not
only a profession of faith, it is more significantly an admission
of guilt -- an implicit response to his accusation. Her conclusion
here is also one further step in the gradual process of revelation
which forms the thematic-interactional backbone of this conversa=
tion. Her next observation (g') has very little semantic connec=
tion with what has gone before. Its appropriateness and inter=
pretation must therefore be established solely on pragmatic
grounds. In the context it may simply be an attempt to evade the
issue at hand, which has reached the stage where her immoral life
might be exposed before this Jewish prophet. From another per=
spective, however, these words constitute a challenge, one which
manifests an illocutionary force that she has tried to effect
twice before (i.e. b and k) in an effort to investigate the
genuineness and authority of the stranger she was speaking to. If
he truly were a seer, then he ought to be able to provide a satis=
factory answer resolving one of the major issues that divided the
Jews and the Samaritans in their religious beliefs. As in (k),
this challenge furnishes an occasion for a more lengthy didactic
statement by Christ (sub-section (ii) in the respective struc=
tures).

This short example has not only substantiated the existence of a
speaker-oriented intentional development which joins the various
segments of a dialogue together, but it has also demonstrated the
advantage of a situational perspective in interpreting the sig=
nificance as well as the sense of the individual speech acts
within the sequence. The sociolinguistic (including the illocu=
tionary connections) along with the linguistic setting must
therefore be taken into account when determining the communicative
value of any particular part of the whole.

Prominence

When searching for the point(s) of greatest emphasis in a text,
the analyst must utilize the formal signals which the author
introduced to indicate his major areas of concern. These formal
indicators would include devices as minute as shifts in the order
of clausal constituents and as broad as the shape of a text's
structural framework. One might also distinguish between two main
types of prominence:

> PEAK ---- the high point of thematic (propositional/logical)
> development in narrative (= plot), expository,
> hortatory and/or argumentative discourse -- in=
> volves primarily designative meaning;
>
> CLIMAX -- the high point of interactional (intentional/atti=
> tudinal/emotive) development in stretches of direct
> (or indirect) speech -- involves primarily associa=
> tive meaning.

It often happens that the two types of high point may coincide in
a given text, but that does not appear to be the case with the
dialogue recorded in John 4:7-26.

We will consider first of all the three climaxes of this
discourse. Each one occurs at the conclusion of a major section
of the text (cf. segmentation above). Each one also confronts the
reader/hearer with a case of situational irony, that is, a combi=
nation of circumstances that is the opposite, or at least signi=
ficantly different, from what is or might be expected or consider=
ed appropriate. The three situations may be briefly described as
follows:

v.15 (u-w): The situational reversal which this utterance rea=
lizes (cf. a) has already been noted. The roles of
giver and receiver have been exchanged. The woman's request is
tantamount to an acceptance of Christ's offer to her of living
water (cf. g). He has thus accomplished his first communicative
objective by winning her confidence -- by stimulating her interest
and a desire to know more about who he is and what he has to offer
her. But before he can proceed any further on the spiritual
plane, he must first raise her up to that level, for she has ob=

viously misunderstood the significance of the "living water" by construing it in a strictly literal sense, i.e. as fresh/running vis à vis life-giving water.

<u>v.18 (b'-d')</u>: Christ here exposes both the futility of the woman's attempt to deceive him with half-truths (cf. z) and the sinfulness of her life style. She has no "husband" because of her immoral ways. This dramatic revelation also firmly establishes Christ's credentials as a "prophet" (f'), namely, one who possesses superior spiritual insights. The woman is therefore compelled to continue her discussion with him on this level.

<u>v.26 (z')</u>: The peak of the illocutionary chain occurs at this point as the realization of the communicative pur= pose of the entire conversation. Christ's revelation is now com= plete (i.e. from d to f' to u' to z'), though some further sub= stantiation would be necessary later (v.42). He identifies him= self (in a syntactically focused construction) as the Messiah whom she had already laid claim to and thus obliges her to personally face the commitment that she has made for herself (unwittingly, i.e. u'-x'). The amazing perlocutionary effect of this conversa= tion (vs. 28ff.) is that a wanton woman is transformed into a witness for Christ.

There are also two peaks of thematic prominence in the discourse. Each is explicitly marked in the text by a variety of literary devices. One occurs in verse 14 just prior to the climax of section A (see above). Jesus makes a claim that the "water" which he dispenses is superior in both quality ("will never thirst for= ever" -- q) and quantity ("a spring of water welling up..."--s+t). Notice that the clause-final word duplicates the focal concept, viz. <u>aiona</u> and <u>aionion</u>, which serves to highlight the significance of these two phrases. Jesus thereby refutes the woman's corres= ponding claim concerning the water of Jacob's well, i.e. with respect to its quality ("(he) drank from it himself" -- m) and quantity ("and his sons and his cattle" -- m). Verse 14 is given additional emphasis through reiteration of the phrase: "that I

will give him" (with the stress upon "I"); by the dramatic meta=
phor: "a spring of water welling up to eternal life;" and by the
emphatic negative construction, i.e. a double negative plus the
future indicative: 'he shall never again become thirsty forever.'

The second peak is found similarly in sub-part (ii), this time in
section C, namely, vs.23-24. As was the case with the earlier
peak, so also this one centers upon Christ's prediction regarding
those who worship God aright: they have drunk of his life-giving
water and have received the divine Spirit. The thematic and situ=
ational correspondence between verses 14 and 23 supports the con=
clusion that they are focal in the discourse. The prominence of
v.23 is also shown by the initial emphatic <u>alla</u> 'but'
(= "indeed!"); by reiteration of the key terms "Father" and
"worship"; and by the syntactically foregrounded adjectives
"true" and "such". The verse also epitomizes the theme of this
section by drawing together several crucial expressions: looking
back first of all to "the hour is coming" (v.21/k'), which announ=
ces a significant eschatological statement, coupled with the
climactic addition here of "and now is" to forge an oxymoron; and
then also looking ahead to "must worship in spirit and truth"
(v.24/t' -- the arrangement of constituents in these corresponding
phrases is chiastic (see below)). As was the case with peak one
(A), so also peak two (C) appears just prior to the onset of
sub-part (iii) of the section.

Patterning

The various rhetorical patterns of literary discourse are utilized
to heighten selected aspects of the three constitutive discourse
properties: segmentation, connectivity, and prominence. Each
pattern involves some type of unique or novel configuration of
formal elements. Occasionally, these may encompass the entire
text, as the parallel series of speech acts, or the linear organi=
zation of structural constituents shown earlier, including the
devices of anticipation and thematic interweaving. The same in=
ventory of units found in the linear structure may also be viewed
chiastically on a interactional level as shown below (based on the

alternation of speakers: J = Jesus, W = Samaritan Woman):

J_W (x2) (Ai = 7-12) introduction: Christ begins the process of
self-revelation (who am I?)

J (Aii=13-14) thematic focus of A:

drink water→(-) thirst
(+) life eternal

W (Aiii=15) the woman acknowledges Christ's power

J_W (B=16-18) turning point: thematic/interactional bridge
J to link sections A and C

W (Ci=19-20) the woman acknowledges Christ's authority

J (Cii=21-24) thematic focus of C:

receive Spirit→ (-) ignorance
(+) salvation

J^W (Ciii=25-26) conclusion: Christ completes the process of
self-revelation (I am He!)

It is interesting to note that the center of this introversion
corresponds with the midpoint of the conversation (roughly 140
words of direct speech on either side), namely, at the woman's
statement of half-truth: "I have no man/husband (<u>aner</u>)" (v.17).
This utterance marked the low point, as it were, in her relation
to Christ -- she did not want to allow him into her life at all.
Later, however, after his climactic disclosure of who he was
(v.26), she realized that he was indeed the "man" (<u>anthropos</u>,
v.29) whom she needed to take possession of her life spiritually,
and she responded accordingly (vs.28ff.)

There are many other poetic patterns in this pericope that are
less broad in scope, but at the same time more clearly (i.e.
formally) marked. Some of these have already been pointed out,
such as the bounding inclusios of section A. Here are several
more noteworthy examples: When Christ broaches the subject of
"living water", which is to be the semantic focus of section A of
the discourse, he does so in the form of an introversion that
places the key terms in an emphatic position at the respective
extremities. This serves to identify "the gift of God" with
"living water". The chiastic structure thus aids also the exegete
in his interpretation of this verse:

```
A  gift:    "If you knew the gift_of_God - - - - - - - - -(c)
  B  giver:   and who it is that is saying to you - - - -(d)
    C  interpersonal link:  'Give me a drink,' - - - - -(e)
  B' giver:   you would have asked him - - - - - - - - -(f)
A' gift:    and he would have given you living_water- - -(g)
```

Notice that within the major introversion there is also a minor
one which highlights the participants in interaction, i.e.
who : you :: you : him. The interpersonal link (C) helps to tie
this particular utterance into the larger sequence of speech acts,
for it is the basis for both the woman's response (v.9) and also
Christ's counter-reply (v.10). It is important to see this con=
nection because the interchange is unified not only by its
respective intentions, i.e. woman: challenge---accusation,
Christ: correction---offer, but also by its underlying assump=
tions, i.e. woman: you should not be asking me for a drink,
Christ: you do not realize who I am. The latter is intended to
arouse the curiosity of the woman and to keep the conversation
moving along the course that Christ has charted.

In section B, a double introverted structure, interrupted by one
in parallel, throws the spotlight upon the present topic of dis=
cussion, i.e. "husband", and his (their) relationship to the
Samaritan woman'. By this rhetorical means, her flagrant sin is
also verbally foregrounded:

```
    (z)  I do not have .......... a husband
    (b')     a husband  ........  I do not have
    (c') five husbands  ........  you had
    (d') the one whom   ........  not your husband
         you have          .
```

A final example, this time from section C, again reveals the
programming power of artistic patterning. That is to say, infor=
mation that would otherwise be abstract, ambiguous, and/or un=
accented is given emphatic precision by the author's placement of
it into expected frames which presumably the original receptors
(as distinct from today's audience) could more readily decode and
appreciate:

A believers: "...the true worshippers will worship- - - (q')
           the Father in spirit and truth

   B Father: for such the Father seeks- - - - - - - - (r')

      C theme: to worship him.- - - - - - - - - - - - (r')

   B' Father: <u>God is spirit</u>.- - - - - - - - - - - - - - - (s')

A' believers: and those who worship him must- - - - - (t')
           worship in spirit and truth."

The problematic statement, "God is spirit" (RSV) is anomalous with
regard to both form and meaning. It fits the chiasm topically in
that it refers to the Father (God), but grammatically the utte=
rance is intransitive (copulative) in contrast to all the others
in the set. The expression, <u>pneuma</u> 'spirit' in particular, is
also ambiguous semantically and, from a larger perspective thema=
tically as well. In the immediate context <u>pneuma</u> refers to that
essence or principle, i.e. "spirituality", which distinguishes God
from everything that is not God, especially "evil". By association
(metonymy), this principle also characterizes those "true worship=
pers" of God. Worship, or religion, is not a matter of outward
formalism, like <u>where</u> the ritual is to be carried out as the woman
seemed to believe (vs. 20-21). Rather, emphasis must always be on
the <u>how</u> -- the quality of worship, i.e. "in spirit and truth".

In the wider context of John, <u>pneuma</u> also refers to that divine
person who makes genuine worship possible -- the Holy Spirit. In
keeping with the manifold meaning which typifies many of John's
key theological concepts (cf. 1 Jn 1:5, 4:8), the expression, "God
is spirit/Spirit" can also be viewed as a metaphor depicting God's
essential mode of operation, namely, as a life-giving power (cf.
v.14). God through his gift of the Spirit gives man new life (cf.
Jn 6:63, 14:16-17). The Holy Spirit is thus the motivating force
that makes "spiritual" worship possible. The association of the
Spirit with "truth" is another point of thematic relevance in John
(cf. 14:17). In fact, this quality characterizes the effect of
the influence of the Spirit upon a person's worship of the Father.
It is "true" in the sense of genuine or as a fulfilling of the
ideal. In characteristic Johannine style, the expression has

another possible meaning here, i.e. the Spirit that _reveals_ the truth -- about God, worship, true "life", etc. Furthermore, this vivifying work of the Spirit is likened to, or associated with, "water" by Christ elsewhere in John's gospel (e.g. 3:5ff., 7:38-39). It is likely then that the reference to living water (v.10) should be understood in a similar way. The fact that these two portions of the conversation correspond structurally (i.e. Aii---Cii, the former anticipating the latter) would support such an interpretation.

Thus we see again how an exposition of the structure of the dis= course in terms of both its conceptual organization as well as its participant interaction through speech acts can assist the exegete in his task of explicating the meaning of the original message, which must first be specified with respect to its situational and textual context.

Sociolinguistic Insights Arising from a Structural Description

A structural analysis of the type carried out above is useful for the understanding it gives of how the speaker/author has organized his thoughts in order to accomplish certain communicative objec= tives. In addition, it can also reveal something of the situatio= nal dynamics in force when two (or more) persons are engaged in conversation, particularly if there is a lot of interplay taking place on the implicit level of presupposition, assumption, and implication. Below several more examples from the text of John 4:7-26 will be discussed to illustrate this point and to demon= strate the relevance of such information to the Bible translator. These insights may be either directly or indirectly attributed to the preceding structural description. Indirect influence refers simply to the increased awareness of the sociolinguistic dimen= sions operating during dialogue that such an interactionally-oriented discourse analysis fosters.

Christ's initial utterance (a) accomplishes several functional objectives at once. Though expressed in the form of a command (in classical Greek, this would normally have been rendered by an op=

tative verb), it is in effect a polite request (cp. the sequence of petitions which constitute the Lord's Prayer, Mt 6:9-13). A translation ought to duplicate this important interpersonal factor, for if care is not taken, these words could turn out to sound like a rude order in the RL. In addition to initiating the conversation (which was no small accomplishment considering the social polarities separating the speakers), this request conveyed to the Samaritan woman the impression that no ordinary person was addressing her, for Christ thereby dropped himself in status by assuming the role of a dependent asking for a favor. This was a disarming approach, intended to overcome the layers of prejudice which under normal circumstances would have prevented the conver= sation from taking place at all. On the surface of it, his request expressed the desire for a drink. On a deeper level, however, it realized his decision to engage the woman in a dia= logue about spiritual water. In some Bantu languages, Tonga for example, one must be careful about asking a woman for a drink of water if she is alone, for under the right circumstances this could be interpreted as a desire to engage in sexual relations. Fortunately, the setting of our text, i.e. Christ at a well, after a journey, etc., precludes that possibility.

The woman's reply to Jesus' request (b) constitutes a challenge to his sincerity. Her words illustrate the effects of both presuppo= sition and implication upon the speech act. First of all, they presuppose the fact that Christ is behaving in a very un-Jewish like manner. They also imply that his motives are suspect. This implicit background explains why she responds as she does, with added emotive (surprise, irritation perhaps) and modal (doubt, possibly sarcasm) overtones. Observe also that in this instance there is a skewing between speech form and speech function, which often happens in direct speech. The interrogative form typically conveys a request for information, at least that is how people generally interpret it. In this case, however, as with all rheto= rical questions (which far outnumber the real questions in NT Greek), there is a transmission of information, largely of a situ= ational, interpersonal nature as was noted above. In Chewa and Tonga, rhetorical questions, provided they are accurately marked,

can convey almost the same diversity of function as that found in
the original.

Verse 10, as was pointed out earlier, is a very complicated utte=
rance -- formally, semantically, and functionally. It is a com=
plex sentence in which a direct quote is embedded. Propositio=
nally, its constituents are linked by a double condition-conse=
quence relation, including the referentially-similar nominalized
expressions "gift of God" (= God gives something) and "living
water" (= water gives/cause life). Of greater significance, how=
ever, is the intentional meaning, which is manifested on both the
generic and the specific levels. Generally speaking, then, we
have an "evaluation" (i.e. Christ assesses the woman's preceding
statement as to its correctness, reliability, appropriateness,
etc.) coupled with an "assertion" -- one that introduces a
non-literal (metaphorical) element. More specifically, this utte=
rance acts as a counter to the implications of her rhetorical
question (discussed above), namely, that he was not being serious
with her, or had ulterior motives for addressing her. Christ
offers a two-fold correction by implication in the contrary-to-
fact conditional form: (a) you do not really know me, and (b) you
should have asked me for something. Complementing these notions
are the assumptions of his reply: (a) I am someone you ought to
know, and (b) I have something important to give you. Thus his
speech act implicitly conveys the force of an offer, viz. she
should find out who he is, and this will lead her to desire (and
obtain) what he is referring to as "living water". Thematically,
then, the process of Christ's self-revelation begins here, albeit
in the guise of a partial enigma which the woman must solve
(through his guidance) before she can arrive at the "truth" that
he refers to later on. The translator's task is to ensure that
the underlying force of Christ's words is conveyed in the RL with
equal clarity and precision.

"Sir", the woman replies (h): what he had to say to her engenders
an attitude of cautious respect at least, if not credence. Accom=
panying the apparent shift in register, there is also a willing=
ness to hear the Jewish teacher out. She seizes upon the second

implication of his preceding statement and builds this up to the challenge of (k): if he cannot prove that his "water" is somehow greater than Jacob's, she need pursue the question of his identity no further. Again, this is conveyed by implication instead of direct assertion. The challenge facing translators is to repro= duce her words in the RL in such a way that there exists, at the minimum, the possibility that the average receptor will derive this implication from his reading of the text. Christ takes up her challenge (n-t), but his seeming success (u) is undone by her failure to look beyond the literal meaning of his words and to see their spiritual import. Nevertheless, her acceptance of his offer did present him with the opportunity of pursuing the discourse from a different perspective.

Christ's sudden shift in subject is, therefore, not an unmotivated break in the line of thought; rather it is an integral part of his argumentation. Indeed, the topic is new, and there is no logical continuity in the sequence of propositions, leading one commentator to conclude: "Jesus' request that she go and fetch her husband has no apparent connection with what precedes" (New International Commentary). The illocutionary development conti= nues, however, and thus the discourse exhibits the necessary con= nectivity in the sense of conversational congruence. As he did at the onset of their talk (this is a structural device known as "anaphora"), so here (x) Christ confronts the woman with an impe= rative that she would have a hard time fulfilling. Thus the un= derlying intention in both instances has the nature of a "test" in dramatic terms -- one which was intended to expose the spiritual "lack" in her life which only he could satisfy.

The curtness of her reply (z) contrasts markedly with the wordi= ness of her former utterances and suggests that she is hiding something. Certainly she does not seem very willing to pursue the subject. With piercing irony Christ uncovers what she was reluc= tant to confess; his indictment climaxes with the accusation in (d'). This charge presents the translator with another subtle problem of implication. In many Bantu languages the word for "man" and "husband" is the same (as it is also in the Greek:

aner). Now what exactly was the nature of her sin: was it one of quality (i.e. she was not <u>properly</u> married to those six men, the last in particular, according to social custom), or one of quantity (i.e. she was married <u>more</u> than once), or both (i.e. she could not remain <u>faithful</u> to any of them)? Apparently this is not a problem for the English reader since no commentary discusses this issue. In any case, the original seems to allow for all of these possibilities. But the context alone will not permit this in Chewa or Tonga, and to try to include them all would require a rather long, disruptive aside. A translator must therefore go with one interpretation or the other. A literal rendering (RSV) involves further difficulties. This was reproduced in the old Chewa Bible, and the implication conveyed is that the woman was not now living with a man-husband, but with someone else, e.g. father, uncle, son, brother, etc.! The new version interprets the original to read: "...and the man-husband whom you now have is not yours," i.e. she was living with the husband of another woman -- so he, too, was involved in her guilt. The Tonga rendering is somewhat more specific to eliminate a different implication, namely, that the woman's present marriage was not sanctioned by traditional custom: "...and the one whom you are married to now is not your husband at all." With these words Christ lumps all of her men together and implicitly condemns the morality of a rela= tionship that Tonga custom allows, i.e. divorce and remarriage. This discussion clearly indicates the need for integrating any sociolinguistic analysis of the original text with a careful study of the cultural context in which it is going to be realized.

The perlocutionary effect of Christ's accusation upon the woman was her acknowledgement that he did posses special prophetic powers (f'). She thereby admits, though not overtly, that his charge of immoral living was correct. On a more generic level, Christ's ultimate purpose in initiating this conversation was clearly succeeding. The woman was gradually beginning to recog= nize <u>who</u> he was, thus also confronting the key implication that he raised at (d) -- an issue which at that time she avoided. The illocutionary aspects of her reply (g'-i') have already been con= sidered. The important thing to note from an interactional per=

spective is that her words here constitute still another challenge to Jesus to reveal some more about himself, and this he proceeds to do.

The solemn, prophetic quality of Christ's subsequent statement (j') is conveyed by the vocative, "woman", and by the exhortatory asseverative, "believe me" (i.e. zoonadi '(it's) true indeed' in Chewa). The former is a polite term of address, which unfortu= nately does not turn out that way if rendered literally in a Bantu language, e.g. in Tonga, "You woman" would be an insult; the equivalent is "Baama..." 'Mothers'. Christ's mention of the "Father" (l') stands in significant contrast to the "fathers" referred to by the woman (g'); both words are structurally pro= minent at the extreme (beginning --- ending) positions of their respective utterances. Christ's assertion also triggers an aside (m'-o') in which this contrast is elaborated upon. Furthermore, the digression serves to focus her attention upon the personal object of worship rather than its external, physical setting, for that is the primary goal of this conversation as it is in many other conversion experiences. A repetition (p') is necessary then after the aside to return the discussion to the main line of Christ's argument, which as we have seen, centers upon the ap= propriate manner of worshipping the Father (q'-t').

The perplexing portion of this thematic peak for Bantu (and many other) receptors lies in the predication of "spirit" to God (s'). Whether this expression is construed in an attributive (i.e. spi= rit-like) or an active sense (i.e. life-/Spirit-giving, cf. discussion above), the unavoidable implication is that God has died and like any of the departed ancestors is continuing to manifest his presence and influence among the living. Such an idea represents an interesting twist to the ancient myth of the "withdrawal" of God, which is found in the oral tradition of many African peoples. This is related to the various difficulties one encounters in translating the term "Holy Spirit", e.g. Chewa: Mzimu Woyera 'white ancestral spirit'. Attempts to recreate and personalize pneuma by using a descriptive phrase in the RL (usually based upon some aspect of the etymology of the original) are not much more successful in conveying the concept, e.g. Tonga: Muuya Uusalala 'clean/red breath'. Transliterations are probably even less satisfactory, e.g. Luvale: Shipilitu Wajila 'clean shipilitu'. In view of the realities of the extratextual situa= tion, however, such expressions, hallowed as they are by long usage and to varying degrees clarified by the teaching ministry of the churches, are perhaps the best that can be done.

The woman's final statement (u'-x') may be understood in several ways: as yet another attempt to change the subject, this time away from Christ's emphasis on the need for genuine, "spiritual" worship, which she for obvious reasons felt herself unfit for; or simply as a means of keeping the conversation going with any bit of religious knowledge that she could summon up; or even as a last try (test) to find some way of putting Christ down in defense of the religion of her people (i.e. her assumption in this case being that he was not the Messiah). In any case, her sincere, if misguided, expression of hope does function proleptically to fore= ground Christ's reply -- the climax of the conversation.

It is not clear from the context whether or not the ego eimi 'I am' struck a responsive chord in the Samaritan woman as an allusion to the OT divine name whereby God revealed himself to Moses (Ex 3:14). For John's readers, on the other hand, the term probably did carry a good deal of semantic resonance, accruing from other OT passages (e.g. Is 43:25; 51:12) as well as from the gospel itself (e.g. 8:24, 28; 13:5-8, 19). Whether or not a single expression can be used naturally in all of these contexts in the RL, it is important that Christ's words here receive the necessary prominence. In Tonga this was effected by means of a rhetorical question of certainty: "Isn't it true that I who am speaking now, I myself am the one you are saying (i.e. referring to)." Christ's declaration is phrased thus on the assumption that the receptor will give an affirmative response. Within the inter= personal development of the discourse as a whole, this question therefore presupposes that by this time the woman is in a position to concur with this revelation of the Christ. Perhaps this is a bit premature, but that is how the translators felt it should be

said as they tried to relive the original situation for them=
selves.

And so, on several levels of communication and from various
literary and linguistic points of view, this examination of John
4:7-26 has demonstrated the indispensability of a thorough dis=
course analysis of the conversational structure in order to more
effectively interpret the dynamics of interpersonal interaction
via dialogue in a given situational and cultural context. Indeed,
the meaning (functional as well as propositional) of the whole is
greater than the sum of its parts. But without an intensive study
of the interrelationship of those parts to one another as compo=
nents of a total communicative strategy, a considerable portion of
the sociolinguistic significance of the speech event will be lost
-- and with that a good measure of the impact of the message as
well.

CHAPTER 6

Dialogue and the Cultural Component

Communication always takes place within a particular cultural environment. That cultural background will inevitably exert its influence on the specific realization of the nine contextual variables discussed earlier, thereby affecting the formal, seman= tic, and situational properties of any text produced. A transla= tor who does not take this cultural factor seriously, particularly with respect to his own language, will never be able to render an idiomatic version, and worse, he will often unwittingly distort of even contradict the meaningful intent of the original by trans= ferring the SL message literally -- as if it were to be manifested in a sociocultural vacuum. It is essential to give this point the attention it deserves. It is not simply a natural style in the RL that is at stake, but meaning -- meaning not so much with respect to designative content, though that, too, is involved, but espe= cially meaning as it concerns the functional (intentional, attitu= dinal, emotional, interpersonal, etc.) aspects of the message.

The influence of the RL culture upon the translation process has been pointed out on a number of occasions in the previous chap= ters. However, the importance of this subject is such that we will devote this entire chapter to it. The passages cited below are a sample of some of the ways in which the cultural component may impinge upon the translation of direct speech in the Scrip= tures. To be sure, a number of the cases discussed are similar in nature to those that occur elsewhere in the Bible, narrative in particular. And yet, the fact that these problems arise in quoted speech focuses one's attention upon them on account of the natural prominence which dialogue has in any type of discourse. Further= more, direct speech demands a greater degree of naturalness since it by its very essence claims to represent a certain reality, namely, utterances as they are spoken in actual conversation in true-to-life situations. Therefore, more care has to be afforded the rendering of speech acts in the translation process if one wishes to achieve dynamic equivalence in message transfer.

The transmission and reception of messages - communication of any sort -- is always to one degree or another culturally biased. For example, when a person hears or reads a text in his language, he generally assumes that its message is based upon the same values and reflects the same expectations, viewpoints, beliefs, etc. which he has, though this naturally depends upon the degree of homogeneity in the culture involved. In cases, then, where a contradiction or skewing occurs in these fundamental cultural pre= suppositions, there is always the danger that the average reader will misunderstand the communicative significance (i.e. content plus the other, non-referential aspects of meaning) of the message. If such difficulties, aggravated by an unnatural and inappropriate style, persist, he may be forced to conclude that the entire message is either irrelevant, invalid, or imcomprehen= siblé as far as he is concerned. Obviously, there will always be certain features of a translated text which sound strange and foreign to the reader/listener since the original message was for= mulated in a different language, at a different period of history, and under different sociocultural circumstances. And a transla= tor, one who is concerned about fidelity at any rate, does have the responsibility for keeping cultural distortion (away from the SL setting) and transposition (toward the RL setting) to a mini= mum. Nevertheless, there are often ways of handling cultural clashes so that the disparities are not accented in the RL text (see further discussion in the next chapter). A more basic pro= blem facing translators involves the matter of explicit versus implicit information: what the SL text specifies must sometimes be left unspecified in the RL translation, and conversely, what the SL does not specify, or specifies optionally, must sometimes be made explicit in the RL due to cultural as well as linguistic constraints. This principle concerns the associative and also the designative aspects of meaning, as exemplified in the passages cited below (taken largely from the book of Numbers). They will illustrate some of the diverse possibilities that relate to the expression of culturally-bound information, etc. in dialogue along with some solutions which were arrived at in the context of the Tonga (Central Africa) experience.

Attention has already been drawn to the need for communicative equivalence with respect to the emotive and attitudinal overtones that color the propositional content of utterances. These conno= tative vibrations are the product of a host of situational and sociological variables. It is important for the translator to keep in mind that just as there is no one-to-one correspondence between message content and the forms which languages employ to express it, so also these non-designative features of meaning are often manifested differently in different languages. The problem becomes especially acute in cases where the SL text offers no overt cues to alert the translator that such overtones are present in the original. Whether any explicit marking is detectable or not, the sociolinguistic characteristics of the biblical situation should always be mentally recreated in terms of the receptor cul= ture so that the two settings may be carefully compared for similarities and differences with respect to form and/or function. Such a contrastive comparison of situational contexts should suggest the appropriate manner of expression in the RL. For ex= ample, the voicing of Israel's discontent over their wilderness diet sounds in most English versions more like a pious wish or a longing desire than a rebellious complaint directed against Yahweh, as the context would suggest:

"O that we had meat to eat!" (Nu 11:4)

In Tonga, the translators tried to empathize with the speakers (some from personal experience) and came up with the following bitter lament -- one that expresses the people's resignation to the impossibility of ever being satisfied. In their opinion it is a hopeless situation:

"Please! if only there were meat!"

(In subsequent examples, the RSV will be quoted first for the sake of comparison, and that will be followed, as here, by a relatively literal back-translation of the Tonga; exceptions to this format will be indicated.)

The above suggests that someone is responsible for their lack, namely, God. Tonga also adds to the people's final note of despair (Nu 11:6) an overtone of disgust, directed at the divine= ly-provided staple, mana:

"There is nothing at all but this mana to look at."

(A literal translation would imply that the mana is fine as a food, but simply not sufficient in quantity.)

"All we eat (more literally: 'we've gone too far in eating') is mana -- it makes us sick!"

A similar set of circumstances to that of the preceding reference occurs later on in the book of Numbers (21:5), only this time, in response to the extra-textual situation, the translators chose to convey anger and resentment as the primary emotion, coupled with an attitude of scorn and derision for the hated mana:

"Why have you brought us up out of Egypt to die in the wilderness?"

"So this is why you brought us out of Egypt -- (you wanted) us to come and die here in the desert!"

(A literal transfer of the RSV, as was done in the old Bible, is regularly understood as a real question, one that awaits an explanation from Moses.)

"For there is no food and no water, and we loathe this worthless food."

"Isn't it true -- there's no food or water. And these little bits of food (prejorative reference) are not like they are (idiom, i.e. they are of no value at all) -- it gets stuck in our throats!"

(Depreciatory concordial alliteration plus two collo= quial idioms convey the sense here in a way that only a Mutonga could say it.)

The quest for naturalness in the RL often requires the use of forms that are quite different from those found in the original. The next example features the extra emotive force of a double negative in combination with an ideophone to foreground Moses' frustration and hence to substantiate his bitter conclusion:

"I am not able to carry all this people alone, the burden is too heavy for me." (Nu 11:5)

"I am no longer able to lift up this heap DDWI of people alone, not at all -- I'm tired (of it)!"

In the next verse (11:15), the words had to be carefully selected so as to correctly convey the irony involved:

> "If thou will deal thus with me, kill me at once, <u>if I</u>
> <u>find favor in thy sight</u>, that I might not see my
> wretchedness."

> "Now if this is how it's going to be (idiom, i.e. sets
> the tone for the rhetorical question to follow), then
> why don't you kill me right here on the spot (the ex=
> plicitness marks Moses' impatience). Yes indeed (empha=
> sizer), <u>if you want to be merciful to me</u> (irony), kill
> me so that I don't have to suffer any longer!"

A reproduction of the original form produces a contradiction in
Tonga. This can be avoided only through the use of the approp=
riate lexical indicators in the text, such as "Yes indeed" just in
front of the ironic words.

The question of connotation simply cannot be ignored. A literal
translation frequently communicates emotive nuances which deny
those that are present in the biblical account. Following the RSV
at Numbers 14:13-14, for example, transforms Moses' reply to the
LORD's offer to bless his descendants into an impolite, even
impudent, rebuttal:

> "Then the Egyptians will hear of it, for thou didst
> bring up this people in thy might from among them, and
> they will tell the inhabitants of the land."

Tonga restructures this passage through the use of rhetorical
questions and mollifying particles so that Moses' objections are
not put so forthrightly and absolutely -- after all, he is con=
versing with God! The order of the first two utterances is also
reversed, with the historical reference placed in initial posi=
tion, in order to effect a smoother transition to the climactic
line:

> "Now isn't it true that you were the one who brought
>   them out of Egypt with your power?
> So when the Egyptians hear (about this plan), what will
>   they say?
> Won't they tell the people (living) here about these
>   matters?"

The sociological factor of who is speaking to whom is very impor=

tant in all Bantu languages, for it directly affects the register that is chosen, whether formal or informal, honorific or familiar. For example, it is generally considered impolite to mention someone's personal name, either when addressing him (her) or when speaking about him in his presence, especially if the speaker is a social inferior. This rule of verbal etiquette necessitates a change such as the following in segments of conversation:

> And Joshua...said, "My lord Moses, forbid them." (Nu 11:28)

> Now Joshua told Moses saying, "My master, stop them!"

On the other hand, often a vocative of a phatic nature must be added to properly introduce a quotation, e.g.

> ...he said to his brothers, "My money has been put back." (Gn 42:28)

> ...he said, "Comrades (Basa), as for me, my money is right here in the sack."

> (Notice also the need for specifying the external setting more precisely in the Tonga quote. Furthermore, the broken underlining indicates the device of topicali= zation: the speaker thus sets himself apart, or so he thinks, from his brothers.)

The dramatic situation may complicate these matters. When the people of Israel speak with Moses, their leader, they do not employ an honorific register; in particular, second person singu= lar pronouns instead of plural are used, just as a Tonga chief would be addressed, e.g.

> "Why have you brought the LORD's people into this wilderness?" (Nu 20:4)

But when Israel's emissaries present a request to a stranger, the king of Edom, they shift to plurals of respect since singular forms would sound either insulting or overly familiar:

> "You know all about the difficulties we have been experiencing." (Nu 20:14)

In this case, the form and content contradict that of the origi= nal, where a singular is found. But the interactional meaning, namely, the expedient way of addressing a foreign potentate, remains the same, and that is of primary concern so that what they say is not contradicted by how they say it.

The quality of naturalness affects all levels of a text's lin= guistic organization, from the individual word right up to the largest segments of the discourse. Influence from a particular culture, whether material or conceptual, manifests itself in manifold ways. Take the seemingly straightforward statement:

> "...and if we drink of your water, I and my cattle, then
> I will pay for it..." (Nu 20:19)

Except for problems of reference occasioned by the pronominal usage in the entire speech event of which this utterance is a part, these words could slip rather easily into Tonga via a direct transfer of elements. The meaning would come through clearly, but not naturally, for these people, whose culture is strongly cattle-oriented, have their own unique way of expressing this:

> "If we drink water or give our wealth to drink, we will
> pay."

For the Tonga herdsman, toiling on the hot, dry plains of Central Africa, cattle do not simply "drink", they must be "caused (i.e. brought) to drink" -- that is part of his job. Furthermore, when publically referring to the animals which constitute his liveli= hood and make life in all of its physical, social and sacred aspects possible, he would never utter the common term (there is no generic word in any case), but would select one of a host of praise names, such as lubono 'wealth'.

What is true for individual words applies also to phrases and even clauses/sentences. Thus "natural death" (Nu 16:29 -- GNB; RSV-- "the common death of all men") becomes lufu-ng'anda lit. 'death-house', i.e. death at one's home, for this is where a person is expected to die, surrounded by friends and family (and distinguished from an accidental and/or unexpected death out in the bush). Such idiomaticity must sometimes be extended to entire utterances. In the case of Numbers 11:29, for instance, a ren=

dering based on the RSV would be completely misleading due to the sexual connotations which are always associated with "jealousy" in Tonga (and Chewa as well):

"Are you jealous for my sake?"

Using GNB as a model, on the other hand, would result in little improvement, for the question would be interpreted as a real one -- and in this context the expected answer would be "yes". Tonga, then, must reconstruct these words in the light of its own cultu= ral and conceptual setting:

"Say, how did it enter (you) and not me?"

Strong emotions and significant ideas, just like a 'spirit of possession' (masyabe), are viewed as entering into a person, especially his (her) heart, from outside influences, both personal and impersonal. Moses is here reproving Joshua for interfering in his affairs. The answer to this rhetorical question is: it couldn't, yes shouldn't, have happened at all -- Joshua ought to mind his own business. The idiom brings out this implication more clearly in the Tonga.

On the larger discourse level, we have already noted the shifts between direct and indirect speech as well as the reordering of propositions that is often necessary in order to coincide with the interpretive process of RL speakers. The conjunctive links between clauses, sentences, paragraphs, etc. are also crucial in this regard. Where these are overlooked or ignored, the thought patterns of the discourse become fragmented and unreliable as guides to thematic and logical relationships, e.g.

"...who led you through the great and terrible wilder= ness, with its fiery serpents and scorpions and thirsty ground where there was no water, who brought you water out of the flinty rock..." (Dt 8:15)

Where contrast exists in a text, the Tonga reader likes to have it explicitly marked and highlighted so that there is no mistaking the issues (points) involved. So this is how the above passage was rendered:

"...He led you in the big terrifying barren land, in
which there was only dryness, no water at all, <u>there
were only</u> snakes and scorpions. <u>Even though it was like
that</u>, he gave you water from a hard rock..."

A rearrangement of elements together with overt adversative
expressions (underlined) foreground the double contrast present in
this verse: between what was not in the land (water) and what was
(snakes and scorpions), and between these adversities and the
LORD's miraculous blessing (water), Numbers 14:25 is a somewhat
more complex example:

"Now since the Amelekites and the Canaanites dwell in
the valleys, turn tomorrow and set out for the wilder=
ness..."

The problem here is that the initial clause is not linked to the
second by the relation of reason/result, as the conjunction
"since" would suggest. It should rather be construed as either an
authorial digression, a situational aside noting the time of com=
position, or more probably as a simple adverbial clause of loca=
tion qualifying "land" of v.24 (the Hebrew connector is the
ambiguous <u>waw</u> 'and...'). In the context of the larger discourse,
the Tonga translators viewed the final clause as being joined most
closely in content and function (i.e. an announcement of judgment)
to v.23. Therefore, in order to signal more clearly the referen=
tial shift back to this point -- after the contrast introduced in
v.24 and the locative description of v.25a -- they employed a
combination of disjunctive function words:

"<u>But</u> (Pele) <u>now then</u> (<u>lino</u>, here in a logical sense,
i.e. new information) tomorrow you must return (since
they had already been there) to the wilderness, to the
area of the Red Sea."

The cultural component is often overlooked, too, in its relation
to the matter of presupposition and implicature in discourse.
This is easy to do since the information concerned is totally
implicit. But this does not mean that it is not as relevant or
important to the communication process, as the following examples
from two chapters of Numbers illustrate:

In the prohibitions against illicit sexual relations recorded in Numbers 5, particularly verse 12-13 and 29-30, the fact that in the case of the woman involved, she is always referred to as a "wife" suggests to the average Tonga receptor that it is perfectly legal for a man to have an affair with an unmarried woman -- just avoid the married ones! This misunderstanding stems from a clash in basic social presuppositions with respect to sexual relations. In the Hebrew community, sex by a woman before marriage was the exception rather than the rule. Thus the morality of young women before marriage could generally be taken for granted; the assump= tion was that she would keep herself sexually pure. Just the opposite is (or was traditionally) true in the Tonga cultural setting. Here sex before marriage was the rule rather than the exception. The practice was referred to as "playing" and had a social function in that it revealed which women could bear child= ren and thereby perpetuate the clan, the clan spirits (mizimo) in particular.

Verses 29-31 present a related problem of implicature. In this case the underlying Tonga sociocultural presupposition is similar to that of the Hebrews, namely, that a husband is expected to be jealous of his wife, and that if accusations concerning a breech of fidelity are made, the woman stands guilty until proven inno= cent. This results in a common misinterpretation of v.31:

> "The man shall be free from iniquity,
> but the woman shall bear her iniquity."

The context, however, indicates that the wife may, in fact, be innocent in the matter, although this has to be established. Therefore, in order to prevent the Tonga reader from jumping to a wrong conclusion, the propositions are reversed and the verse reworded so that it states explicitly what is present implicitly in the original:

> "If it be true that she has done it (i.e. adultery), she will have to be punished as befits her evil deed, but (her) husband has no case to answer (i.e. he is not guilty)."

Turning to chapter 20 of Numbers, we read in verses 4-5 about more of Israel's murmuring against the LORD:

"Would that we had died when our brothers died before the LORD!"

The verb "die" (-fwa) in Tonga has a component of (- volition), and so the conclusion is that the "brethren" referred to simply dropped dead by accident or misfortune. In this case, since the charge is being uttered by malcontents, it is possible to remove this misleading presupposition by switching to the verb "kill" (-jaya):

> "It would have been good if we had died at that time when our friends were killed by the Lord God."

Normally to predicate "kill" of God (Leza) entails a contradiction because the verb implies moral reprehensibility and guilt. In this passage there is no problem because it comes from the mouth of the impious. The complainers continue with an accusation stated in the form of a rhetorical question:

"Why have you brought (us to)...die here, both we and our cattle?"

Here again the implication of liability must be stated overtly in the translation, or the question may be understood as a real one. In Tonga this is effected by adding the appropriate rhetorical particle initially to correctly connotate the utterance:

> "Wasn't it because (Eeno) you wanted us to die and our cattle as well!"

In this case a praise name for "cattle" is not necessary since the point of the dissidents was that they were being treated no better than dumb animals.

Jumping to verse 24, the first barrier to overcome is one of ordering:

> "Aaron shall be gathered to his people; for he shall not enter the land...because you rebelled...at the waters of Meribah."

In this context, for God to lead off with a pronouncement of death upon Aaron (it is inappropriate for God, the giver and taker of life, to employ a euphemism as in the Hebrew) sounds too abrupt in Tonga. The secondary result has to be put first:

"Aaron, he too will not enter the land..."

The addition of "he too" (awalo) is necessary to avoid the impli= cation that he was the only Israelite to be punished in this way. Later, at the end of the verse, the reference to "waters" had to be removed, for that presupposes that water was present already at Meribah when the incident in question took place. But it was not, and that was the cause of all the misfortune to follow. Restruc= turing the final phrase does not help in this case because of the linguistic implications conveyed by the alternatives, for example: "...when water was obtained at Meribah" suggests that the LORD had nothing to do with this miraculous event, while "...when I gave you water at Meribah" transforms the event into the cause for the people's rebellion!

Moses is then instructed to take Aaron and Eleazar to the top of Mount Hor (v.25) and upon arrival to "strip Aaron of his garments" (v.26). A literal transfer of the latter phrase would certainly shock the Tonga reader, for he would have to conclude that Aaron was left completely naked there on the mountain before he died. Over and above the distortion of content which this entails, such an interpretation would represent a grave violation of Tonga custom whereby a person's clothes are removed only after he/she has died as part of the preparations for burial. The text was thus adjusted to read:

> "There remove (not 'strip', which would be understood as an act of punishment) from Aaron the priestly robe..."

The final aspect of cultural influence that we want to consider is that of concepts in general. There are certain matters pertaining to a people's values, beliefs, world view, religious experience, etc. which condition them into interpreting the text in a way that corresponds with their traditional perspective on life. Often these harmonize with the corresponding biblical outlook, especial= ly if the receptors represent a predominantly pastoral/agricultu=

ral pre-technological society. But even here, some serious
clashes in point of view may occur, and these obviously affect the
meaning that is communicated by the original message. We find one
such example in the closing words of v.26:

"and Aaron shall be gathered to his people."

This is, of course, a euphemism, one whose form transfers quite
readily into Tonga -- unfortunately, however, with a somewhat
different meaning. In the traditional Tonga world-view, there are
also occasions when a person is said to have been "gathered/car=
ried to the ancestors", viz. the ancestral spirits which inhabit
the "unseen world" on earth. This happens especially in situa=
tions where the person has been experiencing physical suffering or
for some other reason has lost his purpose for living. That would
seem to fit the context of v.26, and hence the passage would prob=
ably be understood that way by a significant proportion of readers
if the expression were rendered literally. In this case, however,
one is able to circumvent that possibility by replacing the poten=
tially misleading expression with a simple statement of its
meaning, as was done in the new translation:

"Aaron will die at that very place."

In contrast to figurative language as illustrated in the passage
cited above, it is not so easy to deal with conceptual incongrui=
ties which arise with a reference that is a literal, historical-
cultural fact. In Numbers 16:34, for example, the people of
Israel are quoted as they flee in terror from the judgment that
befell Korah and company:

"Lest the earth swallow us up!"

In Tonga this cry is made more explicit to mark the dramatic situ=
ation more precisely:

"Let's run away -- perhaps the earth is going to swallow
us up as well!"

Furthermore, the extra detail is necessary in order to eliminate
any likelihood that the words of the original might be construed
as a joyful shout of expectation. According to traditional
belief, such a supernatural event would normally be regarded as a
special blessing from God, for those who are "swallowed up" in

this way (and it is not considered to be a rare experience) are thought to enter a new, semi-divine existence underground. The fact that Korah disappeared with his whole family and all his friends and goods would support the belief that he was especially fortunate since he did not have to depart alone or leave any of his possessions to survivors. The spot at which such a miraculous vanishing act occurred would be revered as a holy place and would most likely function in the future as a rain-making shrine (maleende). Would the average Tonga reader today really view Korah's experience as being a blessing instead of a curse? Prob= ably not, for the context quite clearly indicates that such was not the case. But that is why the quotation was made very expli= cit and could even be strengthened by replacing the "swallow us up" with "destroy us" in order to fully convey the function of this awful event in the people's minds.

In the preceding passage, the (adjusted) verbal and non-verbal context acts in concert to specify the intended meaning. But nothing can apparently be done to block a transculturation of the words and actions of Numbers 5:11-28 to the realm of traditional religious-mystical practice. The "water of bitterness that brings the curse," though somewhat different in intent, is similar enough to the witch-finder's "ordeal medicine" to make such an identifi= cation almost unescapable for the average reader. The purpose of the Tonga ordeal may be different, but the process corresponds very closely in form to that which is reported in the Hebrew. Likewise, the words of the curse pronounced in v.22 sound very much like the typical spell of a sorcerer who is supplying this "medicine" to a jealous husband who has reason to believe that his wife is guilty of infidelity and wants to get even:

> "...may this water that brings the curse pass into your bowels and make your body swell and your thighs fall away."

Every circumstantial detail strengthens the correspondence, such as the way in which the punishment is designed to fit the crime as well as the response of the woman herself (in Tonga):

> "Alright, may that happen to me."

Everything corresponds except for the agents of the action, name=
ly, the priest of Israel (secondary) and Yahweh himself (primary).
As far as the words of this curse are concerned, the Tonga may be
rendered quite literally except at two critical points: the water
is described as "able to bring a curse" since it did not invari=
ably do so (cf. v.28), and the result is that the offending wo=
man's "thighs rot" (i.e. "her genital organs will shrink" -- GNB).
It is difficult to find a satisfactory euphemism for the sexual
parts, male or female, since even an oblique reference would be
regarded as "sacreligious" on the external level of communication,
while adopting a rendering such as GNB's would be considered
obscene! In situations like this where there is a danger of a
sociocultural factor misrepresenting the meaning of the original
for today's constituency, and where possible solutions such as the
use of a more generic expression or transforming certain informa=
tion from an explicit to an implicit status do not work out satis=
factorily, then the only alternative may be to employ a footnote
which succinctly conveys the sense of the SL text vis à vis the RL
cultural context. In the case of the passage referred to above,
if the role of the priest is recorded without comment, it would be
natural for the Tonga reader to conclude that he is either a
sorcerer or the agent of one, thus introducing an apparent paradox
into the text: the servant of the LORD is clearly practicing
"black magic"!

Thus far we have examined instances where the meaning of the SL
message is skewed in the process of recontextualizing it in a new
sociolinguistic environment. The particular nature of these
problems and where they occur is a culturally-specific matter.
Not all of those mentioned above for Tonga would arise in Chewa, a
related language of Central Africa, while the Chewa translators
experience their own difficulties in message transfer, ones pecu=
liar to their own language and culture. On the other hand, there
are issues of a cultural nature which present no problems at all
for Bantu receptors, whereas for Western readers, the biblical
scholars in particular, they provoke great exegetical and theolo=
gical controversies. Perhaps one of the best known examples from
the book of Numbers is the incident involving the speech of

Balaam's donkey. While most Western commentators may dismiss this story as simply incorporating fanciful folkloristic elements from an ancient oral tradition, for the average Tonga or Chewa reader this event is intensely real. It is not at all viewed as the Hebrew equivalent of the Sulwe (Hare) trickster tale (and the linguistic markers of that genre ought not be used here). Rather, it is readily understood as an actual historical event, for in their experience (and nearly every villager is acquainted with at least one) it happens all the time. An animal is temporarily given the power of speech to convey a special message from the ancestors. And woe to the individual who disregards or disobeys such an extraordinary communication! Thus, if the question ever arises as to what "dialect" to use when translating the donkey's words (e.g. Nu 22:28), the answer is simple: render its utte= rances as idiomatically human as possible. What register, code and so forth? -- let this correspond to that of Balaam its master!

CHAPTER 7

Sociolinguistics and the Evaluation of Translation Quality

Examples from the previous chapters have shown that sociolinguis=
tic variables can (or should) have a great influence on the way in
which the SL text is realized in the RL, that is, if the goal of
the translation is "dynamic equivalence". In short, the original
forms must frequently be changed in response to both linguistic
and extralinguistic pressures in order to communicate the closest
natural equivalent of the original message in the language of the
translation. However, once the possibility of "change" is intro=
duced into the translation process, questions rightfully begin to
be raised: change -- what, where, when, how, and why? And what
is going to guide or control the changes that are made so that the
Scripture is not distorted during message transfer? These ques=
tions are legitimate, and they imply that some sort of evaluation
of the translation has to be made with regard to its quality -- is
it good, bad, or mediocre and according to what criteria can such
a decision be arrived at? In this chapter we will take a look at
some of these criteria in order to assess their validity and im=
portance. During this exercise, we shall find that all of the
sociolinguistic principles which apply in the composition of a
text (whether this be the original or a derived/translation event)
must also be applied in its critical evaluation in order to pro=
duce satisfactory results. Moreover, these factors need to be
considered with respect to all of the constituents of a transla=
tion, from its textual base to its extra-textual footnotes.

We begin by considering four key aspects of the notion of "quali=
ty" as it pertains to Bible translation. A critical assessment
with regard to the quality of a text relates to both the form and
the meaning of the message that is being transmitted. Secondly,
in the case of translation, there may be an orientation toward
either the source language or the receptor language. With the
focus upon SL meaning, one is concerned about "fidelity": a trans=
lation should accurately transmit what the original author in=

tended to communicate to his readers/hearers. This includes the function as well as the content of the message. A consideration of the RL aspect of meaning requires "intelligibility": the ori= ginal message must be conveyed in such a way that it is compre= hensible to the average receptor for whom it is prepared. He/she ought to be able to arrive, fairly independently, at a correct understanding of the text (generally speaking, of course; there will always be certain information of a technical or culturally-specific nature that he will be unfamiliar with). Turning to the form of the message in the RL, we come to the matter of "natural= ness": a translation should manifest an idiomatic manner of expression -- one that reads as easily, yet also as forcefully, as if it had been originally composed in the RL. The text, on the whole, should not betray the fact that it is a translation, at least not as far as its language is concerned. But change merely for the sake of change is not valid. References to forms charac= teristic of the original cultural setting ought to be reflected in the translation whenever this is possible, i.e. when the function of these forms can also be preserved in the RL text (if they are in focus in the SL text). Furthermore, even a natural functional equivalent in the RL may have to be rejected in a context where it would clearly contradict the historical circumstances as recorded in the Scriptures. This criterion of "closeness" puts the damper on the amount of cultural transposition allowed in a translation, that is to say, unwarranted additions, deletions, and other alte= rations to the shape and structure of the original message in favor of the receptor language and culture -- variations which derive from ignorance about the true SL setting, pure personal preference, or experimentation for the sake of creating some sort of special effect.

The relationship among these four parameters of dynamic equiva= lence translation are shown on the figure below. The arrows indi= cate the direction of one possible priority sequence moving from the most to the least important factor in the communication pro= cess, i.e. (1) fidelity (2) intelligibility (3) naturalness (4) closeness. A different priority listing could be established, of course, depending on the larger context of the translation pro=

gramme and the particular receptor group envisioned as the primary
audience. No single factor may be considered in isolation, how=
ever, and whenever a shift in the ranking is being contemplated,
the translation committee must first anticipate the general effect
of this decision on the version as a whole as well as the possible
ramifications with regard to the response of the intended con=
stituency.

Focus	Meaning		Form
SL	FIDELITY 1	4	CLOSENESS
RL	INTELLIGIBILITY 2	→ 3	NATURALNESS

It is important to emphasize the fact that these generic dimen=
sions of "quality" do not constitute isolated attributes of a
translation. Though distinct in their respective areas of focus
and not mutually predictable (e.g. a version that is "faithful"
will not necessarily be "natural", and vice versa), they are all
relevant at any given stage of the transfer process, and one con=
cept cannot be applied in practice apart from the others. One
characteristic may, depending on the circumstances, have to be
emphasized more than another at any given point in the flow of
discourse, but as the linguistic and extralinguistic context
changes, so do the situational factors that need to be considered
in order to best communicate the message to the intended audience.

The conflicting tensions that exist among these four aspects of
quality control will be explored more fully in subsequent para=
graphs, especially as they pertain to the sociolinguistic in=
fluence which may be brought to bear in a translation. The frame=
work for this discussion will be a series of seven paired sets of

form-meaning relationships which interact with the four evaluatory features when applied either to the discourse as a whole or to any particular segment or aspect of it. Then, from this more ab= stract, generic perspective, we will narrow the focus of attention to another specific passage in order to see once more how such theoretical ideals work out in the actual practice of interlingual communication. The following presentation, which reviews some of the main points of this book, is not exhaustive by any means, but is merely suggestive of some of the crucial issues that transla= tors must keep in mind as they seek to recreate the biblical text in a different cultural and situational context.

1.   Optional -- Obligatory Adjustments

This polarity involves a basic decision that has to be made at every step of the translation process. When a change in form (not meaning!) away from that found in the SL text is proposed in the translation, for what reason is it being done: is it a matter of constraint, i.e. that is simply the way in which the original con= cept must be expressed in the RL -- or is there the possibility of choice in the use of the forms available to convey a certain idea? Obligatory modifications are also necessary in cases where the SL makes semantic distinctions that are not present in the RL, e.g. the different types of sacrifice distinguished in the Hebrew wor= ship system, which require descriptive equivalents in the transla= tion. In such a situation the matter is relatively straightfor= ward, though even here some variation in form is often possible, e.g. how the burnt offering _olah_ is to be most economically described in the RL.

That brings up the issue of explicit versus implicit information in a text. In the instance referred to above (i.e. SL specifi= city), there is generally a _loss_ of overt meaning in the transla= tion, whether of a designative or associative nature. What is thus lost will have to be conveyed implicitly in the text, or by means of a footnote, a glossary entry, etc. The opposite is true when the RL makes distinctions not found in the SL. Here there will normally be a _gain_ of explicit information in the translation when the obligatory adjustments are carried out on the text, e.g. as we have seen, in the indication of status -- honorifics, etc. -- in the personal references of direct speech.

Other alterations in the forms of the original are required by a meaning-oriented translation. Stated negatively, we might put it this way: change is needed to avoid a wrong meaning, no meaning, ambiguous meaning, an overly complex meaning, or poor grammar and a substandard style in the RL. Phrasing it positively, one might say that modifications in the linguistic form of the message are necessary in order to convey its meaning correctly and in an appropriate style in the RL. As was observed above, this would include making explicit in the translation information that is linguistically implicit or speech intentions that are contextually implicit in the biblical text. From both perspectives then -- to determine the interrelationships between form and meaning and their communicative ramifications in the SL as well as the RL -- an adequate sociolinguistic framework for textual analysis, description, and evaluation is of the essence.

Seemingly optional adjustments, such as those involving the com= munication of attitudes and emotions, are more difficult to deal with since it is not always so easy to decide which of a number of RL possibilities is the nearest natural equivalent of the SL concept/expression under consideration. In fact, if the socio= linguistic variables described earlier are ever refined to the point where they may be employed in drawing up a stylistic profile of a given term, it will probably turn out that there is no really "optional" set of expressions (in the sense of being mutually substitutable everywhere) in a given language. In other words, every difference in linguistic form probably corresponds to some specifiable difference in meaning, whether this be defined in terms of semantic components, distributional range, collocational restrictions, or functional appropriateness as determined by the interpersonal or situational context.

2. Meaningful Equivalence -- Formal Correspondence

Whenever a message is transferred from one linguistic and socio=
cultural setting to another, it often happens that either the form
or the meaning of the original must be left behind, or "lost", in
the process. Dynamic equivalence translation puts the priority on
meaning, as has been illustrated by numerous examples -- "meaning"
in all of its diversity: designative as well as associative, i.e.
emotive, attitudinal, collocational, textual (including the mean=
ingful features of the discourse structure, etc.) -- both explicit
and implicit (including presuppositions, assumptions, and implica=
tions). This meaning, molded into a message by the linguistic
forms of the SL, must be "repackaged" in the RL with as little
deletion, addition, or distortion as possible. This repackaging
process is what translation is all about. The RL product, then,
ought to possess the same ingredients (content) and taste the
same, i.e. effect the same results (function), as the original.

It is relatively easy to ascertain the degree of formal correspon=
dence that a translation exhibits in comparison with its original.
All one needs is a simple descriptive linguistic model and a basic
statistical method and it will not take too long before the amount
of correspondence stated in terms of relative percentages may be
given. However, it is a different matter should one attempt to
compute the amount of semantic equivalence between two texts, par=
ticularly if they reflect widely divergent sociocultural perspec=
tives. Furthermore, it is not only designative (cognitive) equi=
valence that many modern versions are striving to attain, but
"dynamic" equivalence, which is based not upon content alone, but
upon function (intention/effect) and the various associative
meanings referred to above. Clearly a purely referential model,
as most linguistic theories propound, will not be adequate for the
job of evaluating the extent to which equivalence in all of its
dimensions has been achieved due to its almost total disregard of
the sociolinguistic factor in communication. It may well be that
no descriptive and analytical method by itself would be equal to
the task, though Halliday's approach probably comes the closest
(e.g. 1973).

In any case, it is important that translators, as well as their constituency, fully realize the implications of the step they are taking when they propose that their goal is a dynamic equivalent rendering of the original. What do they understand by "equiva= lence" in the first place? If the scope of equivalence is limited to meaning in a purely referential sense then the translation will almost certainly fail to be dynamic. This property may be evalu= ated only within the framework of a sociolinguistic model that takes into serious consideration the interaction of speakers within a specific situational setting. A prominent component of such a model, then, would have to be an analytical grid comprised of something similar to the nine contextual variables discussed earlier. Only with the degree of precision which such a scheme permits (crude as it may be) will it be possible even to begin to describe the complexity of <u>communicative</u> (functional) equivalence between two (or more) literary documents.

Recently some objections have been raised against the idea of dynamic equivalence translation from a semantic and situational perspective. "Is it good translation to be <u>more</u> clear and mean= ingful than the original?" (Naden, 1982, p.335, emphasis mine). Does idiomatic translation pay too much attention to intelligi= bility and effect at the expense of proximity to the style of the various books of the Bible? "Did the average speaker of <u>koine</u> Greek find no difficulty in 2 Peter 2:4-9 or Romans 2:14-21?" (op cit, p.333). Van Bruggen adds: "Does not the process of restruc= turing in translation in fact mean an attempt to improve the work of the original author?" (1978, p.157). It is undoubtedly true that the techniques applied in restructuring the message (e.g. passive to active constructions, shorter and less complex sentence structures, fewer abstract nouns and technical terms, unpacked genitives, etc.) do tend to make the RL text clearer linguisti= cally -- formally as well as semantically. But that does not necessarily mean that today's readers automatically understand the message of Scripture more easily than did the original receptors, who had the advantage of a language and culture in common with those of the author, plus referential access to the context -- both personal and impersonal, verbal and non-verbal -- in which

that message was first composed. This contextual background often
included face-to-face contact with the writer on other occasions
and perhaps additional written materials as well (e.g. the "lost"
letter to the Corinthians). The question of who would understand
the message more readily and why is admittedly hard to prove for
certain one way or the other. But sociolinguistic evidence such
as that mentioned above would seem to indicate that the original
receptors would have (had) an easier time of it no matter how much
restructuring were built into a translation (with the content
being held constant, of course). Therefore, it may be argued that
a linguistic simplification of the text for a contemporary
audience/readership is justified in view of the fact that this
operation serves to compensate for the additional complexity in=
troduced due to the partial to total loss of the situational
setting of the original. It may be that these two factors to a
greater or lesser degree balance each other out so that the
cumulative communicative potential remains roughly the same in
both SL and RL. Indeed, the Bible was not meant to be read as a
"tract" or "today's newspaper" (Naden, op cit., pp.333-4), but
there are a significant number of sociolinguistic factors (text-
as well as context-related) which would tend to prevent that from
happening and which would counteract the alleged simplification or
"popularization" of form.

To what extent the distinct styles of the biblical authors can be
reproduced in translation is a matter requiring much more
research. But it would seem that the _formal_ aspects of an indi=
vidual style would be difficult if not impossible to duplicate
naturally in a language which is unrelated to that of the original
document(s). However, there should be a way of approximating the
different _functions_ (particularly the effects) of these diverse
styles -- from the literary elegance of Hebrews to the linguistic
roughness of Revelation -- once they have been correctly deter=
mined and described with regard to the SL text and the appropriate
formal equivalents discovered in the RL.

3. Closeness -- Naturalness

The translator encounters a major problem in his attempt to harmonize these two aspects of translation "quality" since they appear to be at the opposite ends of a formal continuum. In other words, when the SL and RL are unrelated (as is usually the case), it often happens that the "closer" the linguistic forms of a translation are with respect to the original, the less "natural" they turn out to be in the RL. And conversely, the utilization of forms that are more "natural" in the translation will result in a version that exhibits less "closeness" to the forms which are employed in the SL message. It is by no means a rigid either-or situation in practice, however; some variation, within limits, may well be possible without occasioning a stylistic violation of some sort. In certain instances, the verbal forms used in the SL text may just happen to be the most natural way of conveying the mean= ing of the biblical message in a particular RL (Wendland, 1984).

The evaluative criterion of "closeness", then, is neither gra= tuitous nor an impossible goal. First of all, when dealing with references to culturally specific items in the SL text (e.g. flora, fauna, technical religious terms, weights and measures, etc.), the translator should try to select RL expressions which reflect the formal as well as the functional properties of the original terms (e.g. "wild dog" instead of "leopard" for the "wolf" of Jn 10:12). Frequently he will find that he is unable to achieve this, but at least it is an ideal to strive for. This principle is especially important when translating passages of a historical nature, or when notable verbal symbols (e.g. lamb, fig tree, cross, salt, yeast, etc.) or key terms (e.g. "day of the LORD" in the prophets and "kingdom of God/heaven" in the gospels), or when there is a particular focus upon external form in the context (e.g. the "stairway" to heaven of Gn 28:12; the "ephod" of Ex 28:5ff.; "a large sheet being lowered by its four corners to earth" in Ac 10:11; or the numbers of measurement in Rv 20:16-17). With regard to linguistic forms in general, the quality of "closeness" will usually have to give place to that of

"naturalness", as was suggested earlier. But there will be occa=
sions when the translator has several semantically equivalent RL
expressions to chose from in rendering a given SL term. The
sociolinguistic, or stylistic, meaning of these different options
may in fact not be the same, but where such functional divergence
cannot be specified with certainty, they may be treated as syno=
nyms. In this case the lexical or grammatical form which most
closely approximates that of the original ought to be preferred --
if it is regarded as a natural expression in the RL (e.g. rheto=
rical question vs. a emphatic statement, exact vs. synonymous
repetition in a poetic couplet, direct vs. indirect speech in an
extended quotation). Such correspondent forms would thus remain
in the RL text pending more detailed comparative analyses of their
possible further designative or associative significance, which,
if established, could then be incorporated into future editions of
the translation. If, on the other hand, these forms were simply
deleted from the text arbitrarily, for no functional reason, one
would lose their potential signalling value (i.e. form has mean=
ing!), whether or not this is later shown to agree with or diverge
from that of the original SL form.

In similar instances of uncertainty, alternatives, and ambiguity
on the macrolevel of discourse, the characteristic of closeness
may also be useful as a guiding principle to help the translator
to arrive at a consistent decision (i.e. to favor the SL form),
for example, in texts incorporating a flashback when the need for
reordering verses in the RL text cannot be established with cer=
tainty; where to indicate paragraph and larger sectional breaks
in the text (dependent on a discourse analysis of the original);
or whether to use a poetic typographical format and parallel
phrasing (if naturally expressed) instead of simple prose to
render Hebrew poetry. Such a policy would be especially important
from a discourse perspective in cases of repetition in the origi=
nal text (which is often one of the first items to be cut out of a
translation for being "meaningless" or "boring"). Numerous studies
have shown that in addition to a cohesive function (connectivity)
and for emphasis (prominence), the reiteration of elements,
whether synonymous or exact, is frequently employed to demarcate

the larger literary units of a discourse (segmentation). Now it may well be that repetition does not have the same functions in the RL. But in situations where the precise function of a parti= cular recursion cannot be pinpointed with assurance, it would be wise to retain the form if possible (cf. the limitations mentioned above) so that it remains in the translation as an index of a potential larger rhetorical purpose yet to be discovered.

The quality of closeness also has a more pragmatic function in the assessment of a translation, especially in situations where recep= tors already have a Bible (a literal version) that they are used to, either in their own language or another. People become ac= customed, even attached, to the forms of tradition which have become hallowed by time and liturgical usage. Therefore, in cases of ambiguity, where no specific difference in meaning between alternative RL renderings can be discerned, it would be prudent to preserve the shape of the SL text, thereby retaining the positive associative values that may be linked to verbal forms which recep= tors are already familiar with.

As was pointed out in the preceding section, it is not really difficult to ascertain the relative degree of proximity between SL and RL forms. This is essentially an objective decision, limited only by the descriptive power of the linguistic model that is used. "Naturalness", on the other hand, is a somewhat different matter, for it is generally regarded as being a more subjective and variable concept. There are always a number of standards according to which the level of idiomacity may be measured, depending on the overall purpose of the text, who is making the evaluation, for whom the communication is intended, and the situa= tional context in which it is intended to be realized. Further= more, naturalness is a complex concept which must be judged not only with respect to linguistic form, but also in view of usage, that is, the frequency of occurrence of a given item, its distri= bution or range within a text (or corpus of texts), and its appearance in the appropriate linguistic and socio-linguistic con= text. The last criterion is especially critical, for as we have seen in many of the examples, it is the interpersonal and situa=

tional circumstances that determine which of several referentially equivalent expressions ought to be used on a given occasion. What this means for the translator is that he must learn to utilize the contextual cues of the SL text to construct in his mind an analo= gous situation within the framework of his culture. This exercise in turn will help guide the selection of forms in his language that will fit naturally in that setting.

"Natural" does not necessarily imply casual, informal speech. Rather, the term characterizes a style which fits the sociolin= guistic context of use -- one that harmonizes with all of the other factors operating during the process of communication. And the key here is consistency: the naturalness of a text's language is a feature that must be maintained on an even keel throughout the discourse, avoiding both the "lows" of colloquialism and slang as well as the "highs" of strict liturgical usage and overly-sop= histicated literary devices.

4.   Accuracy -- Acceptability

This pairing opposes the top and bottom halves of the diagram of quality components given earlier. It establishes what we might consider to be the minimum standards according to which a transla= tion may be judged. With regard to the SL, then, it should be "accurate". The communicative value of the original message needs to be reproduced in the text of the translation so that the cor= respondence is as close as possible, particularly with respect to the meaning, but when circumstances permit also with respect to form. A translation that is inaccurate in terms of its content (as determined exegetically) and/or intent (as determined by a functional analysis) is invalid and not fit to print, no matter how "acceptable" it may be otherwise. But any evaluation as to accuracy cannot be left to the exegetical "experts" alone; it must also be based on thorough comprehension tests administered to a sufficient sample of representatives from the RL constituency.

With the focus upon the RL, a translation must be "acceptable". Acceptability, as opposed to accuracy, applies primarily to the

style of a text, but there are also cases of certain diagnostic
passages of concern to individual denominations, where the accept=
ability of doctrinal content to their constituency, the theolo=
gians in particular, becomes even more important than exegetical
accuracy. The message should, of course, be intelligible to those
for whom it is intended. That is to say, with respect to both
form and content, the text must not rise consistently above their
"level of frustration" so that they either give up trying to com=
prehend the message or they misinterpret what has been written.
It is in the area of "naturalness" where a translation usually
sacrifices the most in order to be acceptable to its constituency.
It is always easier to concede the point to the literalist than to
convince him that the Bible really ought to speak his language
with meaning, yes, with even an idiomatic sounding style. Thus,
an acceptable translation is often the product of a series of
compromises whereby the translators seek to strike a balance
between literalness and literariness. Which side should they
favor? That depends very much upon the sociolinguistic environ=
ment in which they are working. They must be guided by the will
of the people as much as by their needs. And the people's prefe=
rence will derive from the presuppositions, opinions, and expec=
tations that they have about what a translation should be like. A
"liberal" translation (if it is perceived as such, for whatever
reason) is an anomaly among a conservative constituency, no matter
how "accurate" it may be. People may simply be used to an older,
literal translation, and familiarity often carries with it a host
of connotative associations that have nothing at all to do with
the text. So they may react with suspicion and even outright
rejection against a newer version which aims to convey the message
meaningfully by changing the verbal forms which they have become
accustomed to and derive a certain sense of religious "security"
from.

How, then, is one to ascertain receptor preference? Primarily
through extensive and meaningful contact with them, e.g. church
meetings, seminars, worship services, school lectures as well as
in secular settings: government educational agencies, literacy
organizations, institutions of mass media, etc. Such informatio=

nal talks would be directed primarily at non-translation people, church leaders in particular, including all persons who will somehow be connected with the evaluation and promotion of the translation. The purpose of such instruction would be to explain and illustrate in simple terms some of the basic principles not only of dynamic equivalence translation, but also of communication and sociolinguistics, showing how these factors interact to in= fluence both oral and written message transmission in their language as well as in the language of Scripture. Once the pur= pose of an idiomatic translation is fully understood -- that it is not being prepared to "compete" with the existing version(s) in use among the group, but simply to meet a different need -- it is likely that any opposition to the project will soon decrease if not disappear entirely. Only where there is an awareness of and an appreciation for the overall operation, including the goals of the new translation and the means for carrying them out, will there be a hope of gaining widespread acceptance among the consti= tuency. While the preceding comments apply particularly to a community that is already familiar with the Bible, the need for adequately preparing people to receive the Word of God in their own language (i.e. public relations) exists also in primary situa= tions where the translation is the first to be produced. Receptor group wishes and requirements can also be gauged through an on-going systematic testing of the translation as it is being finalized, by means of formal (e.g. comprehension tests, reaction questionnaires, etc.) as well as informal procedures (e.g. reli= gious dramatizations of the text, school quizzes, radio question-and-answer broadcasts, etc.) Once a version has been published in its entirely, it is too late. What constitutes "acceptability" will have had to be determined long before them!

5. Designative -- Associative Meaning

A sociolinguistic approach to communication takes for granted the principle that meaning is manifold. Just as there are different types of linguistic "form" (phonological, lexical, grammatical, etc.), so also there are various types of meaning, one being distinguished from another according to the primary function that

it (ideally) is intended to and/or succeeds in carrying out during
the communications process (informative, affective, expressive,
etc.). Though most of the attention in biblical studies, in=
cluding translation, still centers upon the designative (denota=
tive) component of the message, the non-designative (associative)
aspects are no longer simply ignored as in the past. Indeed,
analysts now recognize that in many passages, especially those of
a poetic/rhetorical quality, such interpersonal properties as
motivation, modality, and mood constitute the burden of the mes=
sage. This fact has been borne out by many of the examples cited
above. Furthermore, we have seen that functional varieties like
connective and situational meaning also interact with the content
to affect the form of utterances, particularly in direct speech,
e.g. with the use of vocatives, honorifics, and other devices that
are indicative of status, formality, solidarity, power, and so on.

Biblical research still needs to give us a clearer picture, how=
ever, of the extent to which such associative features of meaning
permeate the Hebrew and Greek texts as well as the degree to which
they act to modify its message. The form of the SL message has a
great deal to say to the translator today -- more so than in the
past when "meaning" was restricted to largely denotative content.
It has reached the point now where under the influence of dis=
course structure and sociolinguistic studies, one must conclude
that no change in form within a language is totally meaning-less.
The referential inventory may be preserved, but matters of focus,
emphasis, emotion, attitude, and so on, as modified by the context
of use, are very sensitive to any type of formal adjustment. So
we must press on in the effort to understand the full communica=
tive value of the original message so that we might come ever
closer to the ideal of conveying it completely to a contemporary
constituency.

It is the responsibility of the translator, then, to transmit both
the content (in terms of propositions, presuppositions, implica=
tions, etc.) as well as the intent (in terms of the illocutionary,
modal, and emotive force) of the original in his language. But
what is to be done in cases of conflict -- where it is simply not

possible to convey <u>both</u> the designative and the associative fea=
tures of meaning in the RL at once? Where should the priority
lie? Generally speaking, this remains with the denotative content
of the message, i.e. fidelity over naturalness. Even in cases
where the point of a passage is not primarily to transmit informa=
tion, but to carry out some other function instead, the translator
must beware of radically distorting the historical and cultural
context of the original in his attempt to duplicate the interac=
tional intent of the message. What constitutes a "radical" dis=
tortion? That can be decided only with reference to the linguis=
tic and extralinguistic context (see below), and it is not easy to
investigate this matter with the thoroughness that it requires.
One needs to be sympathetic to the impact of Scripture, to the
extent of "compensating" for aesthetic and connotative elements
lost at one point by reproducing the same effect at a different
place within the context. But, on the other hand, one must always
beware of the danger of over-emotivizing a translation in the
interests of idiomacity. The principle of no overall loss or gain
in communicative significance applies to associative meaning just
as it does to designative content. What is needed is to refine
our present tools and methods of sociolinguistic analysis so that
the translator is able to determine with greater certainty both
when an imbalance has occurred and how to remedy it.

6. Figurative -- Non Figurative Texts

Possible exceptions to the principle that designative meaning
takes precedence over associative meaning during translation arise
in the case of Scripture passages which are of a figurative as
opposed to a non-figurative, or historical nature. Figurative
texts are those which are characterized by a high proportion of
non-literal language, usually accompanied by associated poetic
techniques such as condensation, repetition, rhythm, syntactic
shifts, phonological patterning, and so forth. Here the emphasis
is upon feeling and effect (i.e. expressive and affective func=
tions) rather than upon the transmission of factive information.
In literature of this type, terms and expressions which are
oriented more to the RL culture and the everyday experience of its

people may be necessary in order to preserve the communicative significance of the original text. Where the designative intent is minimal to begin with, as in the case of lyric (expressive) poetry, to deprive a passage of its connotative force through literalism or generalization (i.e. the language level is raised to a more generic plane in order to prevent semantic clashes of a culturally-specific kind), would rob it almost of its raison d'etre. Thus in prophetic or epistolary texts, and especially in dialogue, where there is a danger of the emotive, rhetorical, or aesthetic impact being dissipated by a rendering that is consider= ed to be referentially "pure", the translator may be obliged to seek a RL adaptation that would duplicate the literary power and communicative value of the original, e.g. by introducing a figure of speech that incorporates a set of semantic components peculiar to the receptor situational evironment (i.e. a "cultural equiva= lent"). However, this procedure would be restricted to instances where the focus is not upon the form of the SL expression (i.e. physical and related attributes), but upon its function in the immediate context as well as the intended effect of the passage as a whole. Even in such cases, the translator will try to keep the degree of temporal/cultural skewing (anachronism) to a minimum by employing RL functional equivalents which are as similar in form as possible to the corresponding SL referents.

But if such a translation policy is adopted, it is obvious that a great deal of preliminary and on-going research into the figura= tive resources of the RL is required. In the case of a given figure of speech or idiom, for example, one would want to determine whether this is the only way to convey the particular concept, or are other figurative/non-figurative expressions available in the language. If an expression, however non-literal it may sound in a back-translation, is the normal, expected way of saying something (e.g. dziko la mwana alirenji 'land of what can the child cry for' = bountiful, productive country, for the original "land flowing with milk and honey" of Ex 3:8, 15:5, etc.), then it is probably true to say that the phrase has become conventionalized, or even solidified semantically, with only a minimal   emphasis,   if   any,   on

the formal aspects of its individual referents. In such instan=
ces, i.e. dead metaphors and some idioms, the expression is under=
stood and interpreted as a whole -- a unit concept -- and there=
fore any references to particular aspects of the RL cultural
setting are not really semantically active in the minds of either
speakers or hearers. However, one would still have to investigate
further to see whether there are any undesirable connotative or
stylistic associations attached to such expressions, thus render=
ing them unsuitable for use in a translation of the Word of God.
This would be the case, for example, with ideophones in many Afri=
can languages, which, if injudiciously used, can easily deflect
receptor attention to themselves rather than contribute to the
meaning of the passage as a whole.

The task of maintaining a proper balance between faithfulness and
forcefulness -- between fidelity to content and fidelity to func=
tion when translating the highly rhetorical and/or dramatic texts
of the Bible is indeed a difficult one. Often a final decision
can be reached only after an extensive testing of alternative
renderings among the receptor constituency and a careful study of
the entire sociolinguistic setting that surrounds a translation
project. The latter research would be necessary in order to
reveal where the bounds of acceptability lie at present and in
which direction they will most probably move in the future under
the influence of education, urbanization, Christianization, the
mass media, interlingual contact, indigenous literature, govern=
ment campaigns for cultural "authenticity", and so on.

7. Text -- Context

The mutual influence and interrelation between the text of Scrip=
ture and its context of realization or utilization have been the
center of attention in this book. It is the object of sociolin=
guistics to explore all of the relevant aspects of this dichotomy,
and as we have seen, such studies have much to contribute to our
understanding of the original text (exegesis), which is the basis
for a dynamic equivalent translation into another language and
human setting. Context, of course, comprises both the linguistic

as well as the extralinguistic environment in which a message is realized, but our particular focus has been upon the latter. That is to say, we have explored the various ways in which factors extrinsic to the message (i.e. source, receptor, channel, and setting) engage with the intrinsic factors (i.e. content, macro-structure, micro-structure, and code) to determine its ultimate verbal shape as a vehicle of communication. Nine sociolinguistic variables were proposed as an etic framework within which one might conduct an investigation of the situational context of the Scriptures, both in its original occurrence and when transformed to operate in another linguistic and cultural setting.

The fundamental sociolinguistic question that needs to be answered before a translation project can properly begin is: FOR WHOM is this version intended? Once the receptor group has been clearly delineated, with specific individuals actually in mind, it is possible to answer a host of related questions pertaining to the form of a translation, such as, the general nature of the trans= lation, i.e. whether it is intended as an ecclesiastical version (primarily for the "initiated" in terms of vocabulary, grammatical complexity, style, etc.), a literary version (one that employs the full resources of the RL for the enjoyment of those who are able to appreciate them), a common-language version (which uses lin= guistic forms characteristic of the area of overlap between lite= rary and colloquial styles), or a version aimed at some special group of receptors (e.g. new literates, children, Jews, Muslims, etc.). Well-intentioned, but misinformed pleas about the "need to return to the use of one reliable translation in all the churches" (van Bruggen, p.143) simply ignore the complex sociolinguistic realities of our times. Such a policy, if strictly observed, would in effect place the dynamic, living Word into a formal straitjacket and give the advantage in communication strategy to those who are already in the most privileged position, namely, long-standing church members who are familiar with ecclesiastical and theological jargon. A situation-functional perspective, on the other hand, recognizes that for any given society nowadays two or more distinct translations may be necessary, not only to reach separate socio-educational groups, but also to fulfill different purposes, e.g. a liturgical version for use in church (high-level style and diction) vis à vis a devotional version for private use in the home (familiar style and popular diction). Factors such as these affect in addition to the type of language found in a trans= lation also its physical format and the inclusion of supplementary aids (e.g. maps, illustrations, footnotes, introductions, glossa= ries, parallel references, and so forth).

Another important contextual variable is the situational milieu out of which a translation arises (e.g. strength of oral tradi= tion, quantity and quality of literature available in the RL, degrees of ecclesiastical homogeneity and interconfessional coope= ration, presence of an older, literal "missionary" version of the Bible, etc.) and into which it is cast (e.g. proportion of lite= rates in the constituency, government language and educational policy, amount of influence from area lingua franca and "world" languages, competence of translation personnel, availability of advisory resources such as consultants, exegetes, stylists, biblical study aids, etc.). These and other factors converge to influence receptor presuppositions and expectations about Bible translation, and therefore determine what is <u>possible</u> (in contrast to the "ideal") with respect to the objectives and procedures of the translation programme. The latter need to be formalized in a policy statement before the project gets underway and then revised as necessary in the light of future changes in the sociolinguistic setting or in the interpretation of previously analyzed factors (e.g. more resistance than anticipated to hearing God speak an idiomatic form of the language).

Text and context: both are distinct components of any communica= tion event, and yet each is indissolubly connected with the other at the moment of literary creation -- or re-creation. One cannot be analyzed without the other either to explain or to evaluate the process of interlingual message transfer.

This overview has touched upon some of the main issues that need to be kept in mind if one wishes to produce a high-quality trans= lation. There are many factors which contribute to this overall effect, and none must be overlooked, even those that seem to be the least related to the meaning of the message. The translators, for example, might feel that matters pertaining capitalization, punctuation, spelling consistency, headings and subheadings, format -- in short, the total appearance of the text on the printed page -- are not worth their time. For many readers, how= ever, this is a crucial item, one in fact which first catches their eye. An evaluation of quality, then, no matter how quali= fied the judges, can never be made in isolation from public opi= nion -- from those for whom the translation is intended (we keep coming back to this central consideration). The importance of this attribute is well summarized by Nida who points out that "the acceptance and influence of a translation over a period of years is directly proportional to its quality" (1982, p.332). And qua= lity, as we have seen, can be achieved only if due attention is given to the sociolinguistic aspects of the text in its diverse situational context.

An Example of Sociolinguistic Complexity -- Amos 4:1

A final example illustrates how a number of the factors discussed above interact to influence the form and the meaning (in the sense of what receptors understand) of the RL text:

> "Hear this word, you cows of Bashan,
>   who are in the mountain of Samaria,
>   who oppress the poor, who crush the needy,
>   who say to their husbands,
>
>   'Bring, that we may drink!'" (Am 4:1)

It is not the intention here to present a complete exegesis of this passage, or to survey all of the translational problems which it entails. Rather, the aim is merely to call attention to some of the main areas where a sociolinguistic approach can help one to interpret its meaning with respect to the original setting of com=

munication and also in its transferred context in a Bantu socio=
cultural environment.

The formulaic introductory summons to "Hear this word..." acts as
a discourse marker announcing that a new section of the prophetic
oracle is beginning. As such it is emphatic, and the same effect
needs to be reproduced in the RL using a form that would
naturally appear in a similar setting of discourse, e.g. Tonga:
"Amundiswiilile...." "Listen to me..." But first of all, the
translator must determine exactly who is speaking these words, for
there are several possibilities. The immediate (v. 2) as well as
the removed (5:1-3) context indicate that it is the prophet
himself who is calling for attention. This has to be explicitly
marked in both Chewa and Tonga (i.e. Amos said....) since this
verse is sandwiched in between judgments pronounced by the LORD
(3:15, 4:2). Amos' opening utterance acts as an official accusa=
tion or indictment concerning the wickedness of the addressees,
which is followed in turn by Yahweh's verdict in verses 2-3.

There is some controversy over who are the intended recipients of
these words of rebuke. Most commentators take the vocative "cows
of Bashan" as a reference to ladies (as the gender suggests) of
high social standing in the courtly community. The genitive "of
Bashan" extends the metaphor by implicating the ground of compari=
son, namely, well-fed cattle, which would be typical of the
fertile valley here named. This expression therefore designates
the high-living, well-to-do women of Israel's capital, Samaria
("mountain of Samaria" = a metonym of place representing the city
that was built there). That is what the original means in its
sociocultural context.

However, that is not what a literal rendering conveys in many RLs.
To publically address a woman specifically as a 'milk cow'
(mpwizi) in Tonga, for example, could carry along unwanted sexual
connotations, i.e. as referring to a woman of loose morals. Now
maybe that was true in the original instance, but that is not what
the SL figure implies. The Tonga term might also be used to
designate a divorced woman who had been sent back to her parents'

home; she is like a "cow" in that she bears children who do not belong to her (the Tonga are a matrilineal, but patrilocal society). To characterize these women, on the other hand, more generically as 'bovines' (ng'ombe) would not be acceptable for the opposite reason. "Cattle", as was noted earlier, have a good connotation in the culture of this people, and thus certain meta= phoric references can function as terms of endearment. They do have a particular word, however, that would fit the context quite closely, and that is gombe (morphologically, the augmentative/ pejorative form of ng'ombe), i.e. a big fat cow which grows to abnormal size due to its habit of breaking out of the corral at night to go and forage in people's fields or vegetable gardens. The associations of greed and unruliness would convey the desired depreciatory implications of the original:

> "Listen to me, you women of Samaria,
> who are like fat-cows (magombe) that..."

The Chewa, who are not cattle-oriented like the Tonga, do not maintain this distinction, and so for them the designation "cows" is rather meaningless, with the result that the whole accusation is opaque. In Chewa oral traditions, the epitome of rapaciousness and greed is the hyena (fisi), but this figure normally has a male referent, and besides, the associated formal characteristics of this animal are quite far removed from those of the original "cows" (thus violating the quality criterion of "closeness" men= tioned earlier). But there is in the language another fairly close equivalent of the ground of comparison, namely, the verbal adjective -nona, which can be applied either to animals (= fat, healthy-looking) or to humans (= wealthy, lacking nothing in life). This word was then employed as a figurative substitute to denote the women of Samaria, while the reference to "cows" was deleted.

The next decision that has to be made is the degree of negative feeling, if any, carried by the vocative, for this may determine the word chosen to translate "women". The textual and extratex= tual context would suggest some measure of scorn or antipathy here (e.g. LB: "fat cows"), and so a mildly pejorative (though not slangy) expression would be in order, such as the Chewa <u>madona</u>, i.e. a term which was used to designate European ladies in colonial times, but which now encompasses all women of high social standing, in particular those who exercise domestic authority. It can thus have a sarcastic ring when uttered by social inferiors. In Tonga this overtone is adequately conveyed by the simile of 'big/fat cows', and so the normal word for 'woman/wives' can stand.

How the subsequent information attributive to women/cows ought to be handled depends on several contextual variables, both linguis= tic and extralinguistic. If a poetic form of discourse is desired, then the language of the translation may have to remain more compact and concise (even literal!), with a greater concen= tration of figurative speech. On the other hand, if the amount of biblical background knowledge of the target group is low, then it may be necessary to supply more information explicitly in order to facilitate understanding, such as through the use of attributive "classifiers", e.g. "<u>fertile valleys</u> of Bashan", "<u>capital city</u> of Samaria". The need for this sort of adjustment, in particular the retention of a literal reference to Bashan, would depend, of course, on how the extended metaphor as a whole is dealt with. This decision for or against a greater degree of poeticality, with an emphasis upon rhetorical impact and aesthetic appeal, as opposed to a more prosaic stress on the ease of conceptual trans= mission, will also have to be guided by the general policies adopted by the translation committee, especially with regard to the level of language/style employed and the possibility of introducing supplemental aids like footnotes for passages such as this for a constituency having a higher literary sophistication.

The latter considerations also affect how one would translate the next three active relative clauses (based on the RSV, in the Hebrew they are all participles): "who oppress...who crush...who say." These utterances not only characterize the referents, they also constitute Amos' indictment against them before the LORD. Thus a greater measure of verbal intensity may be called for (than what would be conveyed by relative clauses) in order to bring out the emotive force in the prophet's words. In Chewa, for example, this may be done by prefixing each accusation with a combined relative-vocative construction: <u>ndinu amene</u>... 'you are the ones who...' -- to create a solemn, pounding effect upon the listener. This solution also has the advantage of harmonizing the pronominal references of this verse, which in the original shift from second to third person. It is not at all difficult to find terms with the necessary negative connotations to render "oppress" and "crush". The expressions once applied to colonialists now work equally well for the local power lords who have replaced them as exploiters of the masses.

The final clause, comprising the embedded quotation, raises quite a few interesting sociolinguistic questions. The first concerns whether these words should be rendered as direct or indirect speech. Both Chewa and Tonga, influenced perhaps by their oral narrative traditions, have a definite preference for the former, especially when, as in this instance, the quotation is being employed as a means of vivid characterization, i.e. highlighting the independence and authority coupled with the moral degeneration of the women of Samaria. Next, the addresses, "their husbands", may have to be specified more precisely than in the English versions. The original literally means "lords/masters" and it, too, envinces a bit of sarcasm since it is levelled by the prophet at husbands who were supposed to be the heads of their homes, but who had relinquished their position of authority to their grasping and domineering wives. In Chewa, the appropriate term of reference to convey this attitude would be <u>mabwana</u>, the masculine correspondent to the earlier <u>madona</u> (both words being loans from Swahili, the language of the slave traders). In keeping with these women's overpowering domestic relationship to their husbands, the inten= tional force of the Hebrew general quote introducer "say" needs to be sharpened to "command".

The quotation itself must be put into the right register -- un= doubtedly informal despite the reversal of roles. In Chewa as well as Tonga culture, for a woman to address her husband in this manner, even in private, would be almost unheard of, unless they both happened to be drunken already or perhaps living in an urban setting where social degeneration typically accompanies the all-too-often moral decay. So extraordinary would this utterance be that it would require a special introduction in Tonga: "That is why you say...", i.e. this type of talk would be viewed as a con= sequence of these women's unconventional, self-seeking behavior which was described in the preceding clauses. An idiomatic ren= dering of the request, or order, is nearly a photocopy of the Hebrew: "Ndiletele, ndinywe!" = "Bring (it) on (and) let me drink!" The context as well as the form of the expression would indicate clearly enough that some intoxicating beverage is meant.

In Chewa, the sociocultural problems are slightly different. A woman and her husband in a traditional setting would never drink (just as they never eat) together. The quotation must therefore be altered to: "Let's go to beer" -- which takes for granted that they will travel their separate ways to the place where beer is being drunk. The substitution of beer (mowa) for wine (vinyo) as implied by the original represents a cultural translation. One or the other must be specified, for to omit the object of "drink" would presuppose that ordinary water is being referred to. It is a case where the translators must decide which is primary: the conversational intent or the semantic content. The use of "beer" (perhaps disguised by a praise name) makes an immediate impact and impression upon the reader/listener. The incongruity of the si= tuation and the moral break-down which this implies, or at least the over-assertiveness of the woman in relation to her husband, would become apparent at once. If "wine" were used, on the other hand, the situation being depicted would become rather confusing for the reader. According to popular belief, the only people who drink wine are Europeans (only they can afford it) plus those Christians who happen to receive wine in the Sacrament. It might be possible to try to clarify things in a footnote, but there is no guarantee that the average reader would perservere that far, and even if he did, much of the punch of the passage will have been lost in the process. In the latter case, both the form and the content (in a strictly designative sense) of the message is preserved, but the function is not. And who can argue that this is not the greater loss? But then perhaps only someone with a sociolinguistic insight would be able to appreciate the difference!

Neither translation nor the evaluation of a translation is an easy task. Time and time again the translator finds that what seems to be the simplest of passages in reality presents serious exegetical and stylistic difficulties beneath the surface of the text. For anyone concerned about translation "quality" (fidelity, intelligi= bility, naturalness, and closeness) as it relates to the goal of dynamic-functional equivalence, a sociolinguistic approach is an essential aspect of the four-step process of interlingual communi= cation: analysis - transfer - restructuring - comparison. With such an orientation, even the apparent failures are much more meaningful for those who have taken up its challenge.

CHAPTER 8

The Apostle Paul and Sociolinguistics

This study concludes with a selection of quotations taken from one of the most effective cross-cultural communicators that Christia= nity has ever known. The Apostle Paul, especially in his letters to the Corinthians, enunciates and exemplifies in intensely perso= nal terms some of the chief sociolinguistic principles that we have been examining in this book.

It is indeed significant that Paul does have so much to say about this topic in his epistles. The manner of communicating the Good News about Jesus Christ -- over and above its content -- was obviously very important to him. He was therefore fully prepared to make all the adjustments possible within a given set of circum= stances -- yet without comprising the content -- in order to ensure the most efficient and effective transmission of the mes= sage. As these passages indicate, Paul was accutely aware of the various problems posed by inter- as well as intra-lingual communi= cation, and he responded with the appropriate situational-inter= personal oriented strategy. That strategy, briefly put, was based on context, both textual and extratextual: context gives rise to the need to transmit meaning in the first place; it influences the process of encoding as well as decoding that meaning; and it also guides and governs our current attempts to determine and apply the meaning of a sacred text that is far removed from us in space, time, and culture. Can the translation teams of today, living in an age that is undoubtedly even more complex communica= tionally than the one in which Paul worked, fail to respond to his inspired words of advice? (All quotations are from the GNB.)

On the priority of content over form:

(Christ) sent me to tell the Good News, and to tell it without using the language of human wisdom, in order to make sure that Christ's death on the cross is not robbed of its power (1 Co 1:17)

When I came to you, my brothers, to preach God's secret truth, I did not use big words and great learning. (1 Co 2:1) And my teaching and message were not delivered with skillful words of human wisdom, but with convincing proof of the power of God's Spirit. (1 Co 2:4 -- this passage also points to the crucial difference between divine and human messages.)

On the need to adapt the form to fit the channel capacity of the receptors:

I could not talk to you as I talk to people who have the Spirit; I had to talk to you as though you belonged to this world, as children in the Christian faith. I had to feed you milk, not solid food, because you were not ready for it. (1 Co 3:1-2)

On the need for fidelity to the original message:

For I received from the Lord the teaching that I passed on to you. (1 Co 11:23) We do not act with deceit, nor do we falsify the word of God. (2 Co 4:2) For it is not ourselves that we preach; we preach Jesus Christ as Lord. (2 Co 4:5)

On the need for presenting the message meaningfully to receptors:

I would rather speak five words that can be understood, in order to teach others, than speak thousands of words in strange tongues. (1 Co 14:19) We write to you only what you can read and under= stand. (2 Co 1:13)

On the need for an unequivocal, unambiguous message:

When I make my plans, do I make them from selfish motives, ready to say "Yes, yes" and "No, no" at the same time? As surely as God speaks the truth, my promise to you was not a "Yes" and a "No". (2 Co 1:17-18)

On the need for sociocultural adaptation of communication methods:

While working with the Jews, I live (the original 'became' is more precise here, i.e. communication in the fullest sense: thought, word and deed!) like a Jew in order to win them.....In the same way, when working with Gentiles, I live like a Gentile, outside the Jewish Law, in order to win Gentiles,....Among the weak in faith I became weak like one of them, in order to win them. So I became all things to all men, that I may serve some of them by whatever means possible. (1 Co 9:20-22)

On the need for faithful non-verbal as well as verbal communica= tion:

You yourselves are the letter we have, written on our hearts for everyone to know and read. It is clear that Christ himself wrote this letter and sent it by us. It is written not with ink, but with the Spirit of the Living God, and not on stone tablets, but on human hearts. (2 Co 3:2-3)

On the importance of interpersonal (expressive, affective) aspects of communication:

I wrote with a greatly troubled and distressed in heart and with many tears; my purpose was not to make you sad, but to make you realize how much I love you all.....Now, however, you should for= give him and encourage him, in order to keep him from becoming so sad as to give up completely. (2 Co 2:4, 7) Dear friends in Corinth! We have spoken frankly to you; we have opened our hearts wide.....show us the same feelings that we have for you. Open your hearts wide! (2 Co 6:11, 13) For even if that letter of mine made you sad, I am not sorry I wrote it. I could have been sorry when I saw that it made you sad for a while. But now I am happy -- not because I made you sad, but because your sadness made you change your ways.....For the sadness that is caused by God brings a change of heart that leads to salvation -- and there is no regret in that! (2 Co 7:8-10)

On the importance of understanding the role relationships between source and receptors:

After all, who is Apollos? And who is Paul? We are simply God's servants, by whom you were led to believe.....For we are partners working together for God, and you are God's field. You are also God's building. (1 Co 3:5, 9) You should think of us as Christ's servants, who have been put in charge of God's secret truths..... I write this to you, not because I want to make you feel ashamed, but to instruct you as my own dear children. For even if you have ten thousand guardians in your Christian life, you have only one father. For in your life in union with Christ Jesus I have become your father by bringing the Good News to you. I beg you, then, to follow my example. (1 Co 4:1, 14-16) Even if others do not accept me as an apostle, surely you do! Because of your life in union with the Lord you yourselves are proof of the fact that I am an apostle. (1 Co 9:2) Here we are, then speaking for Christ, as though God himself were making his appeal through us. We plead on Christ's behalf: let God change you from enemies into his friends! (2 Co 5:20)

On the importance of recognizing distinctions in illocutionary force:

To the others I say (I, myself, not the Lord).....Now, concerning what you wrote about unmarried people: I do not have a command from the Lord, but I give my opinion as one who by the Lord's mercy is worthy of trust. (1 Co 7:12, 25) If anyone supposes he is God's messenger or has a spiritual gift, he must realize that what I am writing to you is the Lord's command. (1 Co 14:37) We know what it means to fear the Lord, and so we try to persuade others.....We are not trying again to recommend ourselves to you; rather, we are trying to give you a good reason to be proud of us.....(2 Co 5:11-12) I am not laying down any rules. But by showing how eager others are to help, I am trying to find out how real your own love is. (2 Co 8:18)

On the importance of the channel and setting of communication:

With my own hand I write this: Greetings from Paul. (1 Co 16:21)
I, Paul, make a personal appeal to you -- I who am said to be meek
and mild when I am with you, but harsh with you when I am away....
I do not want to appear that I am trying to frighten you with my
letters. Someone will say, Paul's letters are severe and strong,
but when he is with us in person, he is' weak and his words are
nothing! Such a person must understand that there is no diffe=
rence between what we write in our letters when we are away and
what we will do when we are there with you. (2 Co 10:1, 9-11)
Perhaps I am an amateur in speaking, but certainly not in know=
ledge; we have made this clear to you at all times and in all
conditions. (2 Co 11:6) That is why I write this while I am away
from you; it is so that when I arrive I will not have to deal
harshly with you in using the authority that the Lord has given
me... (2 Co 13:10)

On the danger to communication of false presuppositions and
values:

Their (Israel's) minds, indeed, were closed; and to this very day
their minds are covered with the same veil as they read the books
of the old covenant. The veil is removed only when a person is
joined to Christ. (2 Co 3:14) For if the gospel we preach is
hidden, it is hidden only from those who are being lost. They do
not believe, because their minds have been kept in the dark by the
evil god of this world. He keeps them from seeing the light
shining on them, the light that comes from the Good News about the
glory of Christ. (2 Co 4:3-4)

On the proper motivation for all communication:

The Scripture says, "I spoke because I believed." In the same
spirit of faith we also speak because we believe. (2 Co 4:13) I
may be able to speak the languages of men and even of angels, but
if I have no love, my speech is no more than a noisy gong or a

clanging bell.   (1 Co 13:1)

Without this principle as a basis, guideline, and priority for our
communication in life -- and with our lives -- all the sociolin=
guistic education and expertise that we may possess will be of no
personal benefit to us at all.   Rather, as with the Apostle Paul,
so may it be true of us: we communicate the Good News of God's
deliverance for all because "we are ruled by the love of Christ."
(2 Co 5:14)

R E F E R E N C E S

Alter, Robert. (1981)   The Art of Biblical Narrative. New York:
    Basic Books.

Ansre, Gilbert.   (1984)   "Disaster Genre in West Africa and the
    Book of Job." Paper presented to the UBS Translation Work=
    shop, Stuttgart, West Germany.

Archer, Gleason L.   (1974) A Survey of Old Testament Introduc=
    tion. Chicago: Moody Press.

Austin, L.L. (1962) How To Do Things With Words. Cambridge,
    Mass.: Harvard University Press (U.P.)

Barr, James. (1961) The Semantics of Biblical Language. London:
    Oxford U.P.

Beekman, John and John Callow. (1974)   Translating the Word of
    God. Grand Rapids: Zondervan.

Black, Matthew.   (1967)   An Aramaic Approach to the Gospels and
    Acts. Oxford: Oxford U.P.

Bowman, T. (1961) Hebrew Thought Compared With Greek. Phila=
    delphia: Westminster Press.

Bultmann, Rudolf. (1968)   The History of the Synoptic Tradition.
    Oxford: Blackwell.

Burke, Kenneth. (1961) The Rhetoric of Religion.

Calloud, Jean. (1976) Structural Analysis of Narrative. Missou=
    la: Scholars Press.

Catchpole, David R.   (1977)   "Tradition History," in I. Howard
    Marshall, ed., New Testament Interpretation. Grand Rapids:
    Eerdmans. Ch.10.

Cooper, David E. (1974) Presupposition. Paris: Mouton.

Criper, C. and H.G. Widdowson. (1975)   "Sociolinguistics and
    Language Teaching," in J.P.B. Allen and S. Pit Corder,
    eds., Papers in Applied Linguistics (vol. 2). London: U.P.
    pp. 155-217.

Cross, Frank and David Freedman.   (1950)   Studies in Ancient Yah=
    wistic Poetry. Baltimore.

Dewey, Joanna. (1980) Markan Public Debate. (Society of Bibli=
    cal Literature Dissertation Series 48) Chico, CA: Scholars
    Press.

Dibelius, M. (1971) From Tradition to Gospel. Cambridge: James
    Clarke.

Eissfeldt, Otto. (1965) The Old Testament: An Introduction. New York: Harper & Row

Farb, Peter. (1974) Word Play: What Happens When People Talk. New York: Bantam Books.

Fowler, Roger. (1974) Understanding Language: An Introduction to Linguistics. London: Routledge & Kegan Paul.

Frye, Northrup. (1957) Anatomy of Criticism. Princeton: Princeton U.P.

Geller, Stephen A. (1979) Parallelism in Early Biblical Poetry. Missoula: Scholars Press.

Halliday, M.A.K. (1973) Explorations in the Functions of Language. London: Edward Arnold.

_____ and Ruqaiya Hasan. (1980) Text and Context: Aspects of Language in a Social-Semiotic Perspective. Tokyo: Sophia University.

Hymes, Del. (1974) Foundations in Sociolinguistics. Philadelphia: University of Pennsylvania Press.

Jackson, Jared J. and Martin Kessler, eds. (1974) Rhetoric and Criticism: Essays in Honor of James Muilenburg. Pittsburg: Pickwick Press.

Jacobsen, Roman. (1960) "Concluding Statement: Linguistics and Poetics," in T.A. Sebeok, ed., Style in Language. Cambridge, Mass.: M.I.T. Press.

Joos, Martin. (1962) "The Five Clocks." International Journal of American Linguistics 28:2. pp.9-62.

Kautzsch, E., ed. (1909) Gesenius' Hebrew Grammar. Oxford: Clarendon Press.

Kempson, Ruth M. (1975) Presupposition and the Delimitation of Semantics. Cambridge: Cambridge U.P.

Klem, Herbert V. (1982) Oral Communication of the Scripture: Insights From African Oral Art. Pasadena: William Carey Library.

Knight, G.A.F. (1953) A Biblical Approach to the Doctrine of the Trinity. Edinburgh.

Koch, K. (1969) The Growth of Biblical Tradition. New York: Charles Scribner's Sons.

Kopesec, Michael F. (1979) "Sociolinguistics and Translation," in Pragmatics and Theme Identification. Dallas: Summer Institute of Linguistics. pp. 42-61.

Kugel, James L. (1981) The Idea of Biblical Poetry. New Haven: Yale U.P.

Labov, W. (1970) "The Study of Language in Its Social Context." Studium Generale 23. pp.30-87.

Leech, Edmund R. (1969) Genesis as Myth and Other Essays. London.

Longacre, Robert E. (1968) Philippine Languages: Discourse, Pa= ragraph and Sentence Structure. Santa Ana: Summer Institute of Linguistics.

_____. (1972) Hierarchy and Universality of Discourse Consti= tuents in New Guinea Languages: Discussion. Washington: Georgetown U.P.

_____. (1979) "The Discourse Structure of the Flood Narra= tive," JAAR 47.1 (Supplement). pp. 89-133.

Loos, Victor. (1978) Semantics II. Dallas: Summer Institute of Linguistics.

Louw, J.P. (1982) Semantics of New Testament Greek. Philadel= phia: Fortress Press.

Lyons, John. (1977) Semantics. London: Cambridge U.P.

Marshal, I Howard, ed. (1977) New Testament Interpretation: Essays on Principles and Methods. Grand Rapids: Eerdmans.

Mbiti, John S. (1971) New Testament Eschatology in an African Background. London: Oxford U.P.

McKnight, E.V. (1969) What is Form Criticism? Philadelphia: Fortress Press.

Morris, Charles W. (1946) Signs, Language and Behavior. Engle= wood Cliffs, N.J.: Prentice Hall.

Naden, Tony. (1982) "Understandest Thou What Thou Readest?" The Bible Translator 33:3. pp.333-335.

Nida, Eugene A. (1975) Exploring Semantic Structures. München: Wilhelm Fink Verlag.

_____. (1979) "Translating Means Communicating: A Socio= linguistic Theory of Translation" (I). The Bible Translator 30:1. pp. 101-107.

_____. (1981) "A Sociosemiotic Theory of Translation." (draft) pp. 1-66.

_____. (1982) "Quality in Translation." The Bible Trans= lator 33:3. pp. 329-332.

_____ and Charles R. Taber. (1969) The Theory and Practice of Translation. Leiden: E.J. Brill.

_____, J.P. Louw, A.H. Snyman, and J.V.W. Cronje. (1983) _Style and Discourse_. Cape Town: Bible Society of South Africa.

Pickering, Wilbur. (1980) _A Framework for Discourse Analysis_. Arlington: Summer Institute of Linguistics.

Polzin, Robert M. (1977) _Biblical Structuralism_. Missoula: Scholars Press.

Robertson, A.T. (1934) _A Grammar of the Greek New Testament_. Nashville: Broadman Press.

Schökel, L.A. (1967) _The Inspired Word_.

Searle, John R. (1969) _Speech Acts_. Cambridge: Cambridge U.P.

Smalley, Stephens S. (1977) "Redaction Criticism," in Marshall, ed., (q.v.) pp. 181-195.

Smalley, Wm. A. (1975) "Toward an Etic Taxonomy of Language in Discourse." Draft prepared for the United Bible Societies Staff Workshop, Rüschlikon, Switzerland.

Smith, Alfred G. (1967) _Communication and Culture_. New York: Holt, Rinehart and Winston.

Tannehill, Robert C., ed. (1981) "Pronouncement Stories" (= _Semeia_ 20).

Tannehill, Robert C. (1975) _The Sword of His Mouth_. Philadelphia: Fortress Press.

Turner, Nigel. (1976) _A Grammar of New Testament Greek_ (Vol. 4: Style). Edinburg: Clarke.

_____. (1981) _Christian Words_. Nashville: Thomas Nelson.

van Bruggen, Jacob. (1978) _The Future of the Bible_. New York: Nelsons.

von Rad, Gerhard. (1966) _The Problem of the Hexateuch and Other Essays_. New York: McGraw-Hill.

Watkins, Morris. (1978) _Literacy, Bible Reading and Church Growth Through the Ages_. South Pasadena: Wm. Carey Library.

Wendland, Ernst R. (1979) "Stylistic Form and Communicative Function in the Nyanja Radio Narratives of Julius Chongo." Ph.B. Dissertation: University of Wisconsin (Madison).

_____. (1982) "Demarcating the Larger Units of Prophetic Discourse." Nairobi: AFRETCON Workshop Paper.

_____. (1984) "Analyzing the Structure and Style of a Biblical Hebrew Narrative." _Notes on Translation_ 98. Dallas: Summer Institute of Linguistics.

_____. (1984) "When Literalness Is Idiomatic: Some Signi=
ficant Correspondences in Grammatical Form Between Biblical
Source Language and a Bantu Receptor Language." Notes on
Translation 101. Dallas: Summer Institute of Linguistics.

White, Hugh C. (1975) "French Structuralism and Old Testament
Narrative Analysis: Roland Barthes." Semeia 3. pp. 99-127.

Widdowson, H.G. (1978) Teaching Language as Communication. Ox=
ford: Oxford U.P.

_____. (1979) Explorations in Applied Linguistics. Oxford:
Oxford U.P.

Wonderly, Wm. L. (1968) Bible Translations for Popular Use. New
York: United Bible Societies.

INDEX OF OLD AND NEW TESTAMENT PASSAGES

lm